WAR AT SEA

USS *Yorktown*

During the Battle of Midway, the USS *Yorktown* was left bombed and burning.

WAR AT SEA
Pearl Harbor to Midway

Jack Greene

GALLERY BOOKS
An Imprint of W. H. Smith Publishers Inc.
112 Madison Avenue
New York City 10016

Note that the Japanese referred to various pieces of equipment, including planes, tanks, artillery, and even rifles by the last two digits of the year it was adopted into service. For example, the Zero fighter (00) was adopted in the year 2600 in the Japanese calendar (AD 1941). The Type 96 Nell bomber was named for the last two digits of 2596, according to the Japanese calendar, or AD 1936. The term Nell was applied by the Allies to this plane; fighters were masculine (thus the Zero was called the Zeke), and other air units were given feminine names.

Ship displacements are based on normal loads, not full, whenever possible. Plane ranges are normal and not extended.

★★★

Prepared by Combined Books
26 Summit Grove, Suite #207
Bryn Mawr, PA 19010

Project Director: Robert L. Pigeon
Project Coordinator: Antoinette Bauer

Produced by Wieser and Wieser, Inc.
118 East 25th Street, New York, NY 10010.

This 1988 edition published by Gallery Books,
an imprint of W.H. Smith, Publishers, Inc.,
112 Madison Avenue, New York, NY 10016.

Library of Congress Cataloging-in-Publication Data

Greene, Jack.
  War at sea.
  Bibliography
  1. World War, 1939–1945—Campaigns—Pacific Area.
I. Title
D767.9.G76   1988   940.54′26   88-5066
ISBN 0-8317-1257-0

CONTENTS

Introduction 7

PRELUDE TO PEARL HARBOR 9
The Japanese Situation 10
The American Situation 19
The Commonwealth Situation 25

THE WAR IN THE PACIFIC 29
Air Raid Pearl Harbor 30
The Fall of the Philippines 60
The Malayan Campaign 79
The Fall of Guam, Rabaul and Wake 97
The Fall of the Indies 100
Burma and the Indian Ocean Raid 115
The Early Carrier Raids 119
The Battle of the Coral Sea 123
Midway, the Turning Point 154

Bibliography 184

The USS *Arizona* was hit during the attack on Pearl Harbor, December 7, 1942. One eyewitness described the scene shortly after the *Arizona* blew up: "The cage-like foremast of the *Arizona* poked through the smoke at a crazy, drunken angle."

War at Sea is *dedicated to the Earthmoving Industry of San Luis Obispo County, predominantly an honest and hard working bunch of guys and gals, truly representative of what is good about America today; and to Buena Engineers, a most tolerant employer!*

Flagship USS *Pennsylvania* shows light damage, while the USS *Downes* (left foreground) and USS *Cassin* are ready for salvage.

Introduction

The Mediterranean is the ocean of the past, the Atlantic, the ocean of the present, and the Pacific, the ocean of the future.
— John Hay, Secretary of State

The war in the Pacific during World War II was one of the most fascinating struggles in the history of the world. The distances involved were immense. The Indian Ocean and both Atlantic Oceans could fit into the Pacific Ocean. The distance from Singapore to Manila is 1345 miles, and from Darwin, Australia, to Singapore, 1900 miles. In comparison, the basic limits of Hitler's Germany, from Amsterdam to Moscow, is only 1575 miles.

Many of the weapons used were virtually unique to the Pacific Theater of war, as well as relatively new. Air power came of age there. Five of the great powers were deeply involved in the war before it ended. America used fully one-third of her mobilized economic strength against the fifth strongest great power, and suffered one-third of her dead in the Pacific Theater. Japan was brought to her knees by strategic air power coupled with the garrote of American submarine power. Finally, the war ended dramatically with the ushering in of the Atomic Age.

Many Americans born after the war have been fascinated by the massive aircraft carrier operations, midget submarines, gung ho Marines, as well as knowing that if the invasion of Japan had taken place, the men in their families would have been going ashore against people whose motto in the closing days was "Let 100 million die."

In contrast to the war in Europe, the war in the Pacific was fought between different races. With racist sentiments rampant on both sides, it was not uncommon to hear Americans refer to the Japanese as "monkey-men" and apes, the Japanese refer to Americans as beasts and demons. Atrocities were committed by both sides, including the Bataan Death March and the Rape of Nanking. Fully one-third of the Australian prisoners captured with the Australian 8th Division at Singapore did not survive the war. Two American airmen shot down at Midway, Frank O'Flaherty and Bruno Gaido, the latter a hero during the raid on the Marshalls in January of 1942, were picked up by the Japanese destroyer *Makigumo*. After a week of interrogation they had weights attached to their legs and were dropped overboard.

Can American fire bombing of civilian populations at Tokyo and Osaka, and the atomic bombing of Hiroshima be considered less than high tech atrocities? Nor did the Allies treat all prisoners by the Geneva Accords. One former Marine and a buddy captured a Japanese soldier in the late morning, exchanged photographs of families, and after lunch shot and killed the prisoner. Such acts reinforce the words of Civil War General William Tecumseh Sherman: "War is Hell."

In many ways, the war in the Pacific is less well known than the one fought against Germany. A problem for the Western historian is the language barrier—the Japanese language is much less familiar than either German or Italian (or, for that matter, even Russian). Only three modern historians have made extensive use of Japanese source materials: Arthur Marder, Paul S. Dull, and Alvin Coox. The first two are no longer alive and Professor Coox has focused his studies on the Kwangtung army and its primary enemy, the Soviets, in trying to hold Manchuria.

The *Senshi Sosho*, the Japanese official history of the war, numering a massive 102 volumes, for Americans and Europeans remains virtually an untouched source of material. The volumes, filled with informative maps and reflecting years of work, were published in the 1970s and 1980s. As late as 1980, books published in English on the operation against Wake Island have been partly based on false information, which the relevant volume in the *Senshi Sosho* could clarify.

The goal of *War at Sea* is to give the reader an overview of some of the events of the opening days of the war in the Pacific. It is not meant to be a definitive work, but it does intend to give the reader the most up-to-date information on the war and to correct some of the many myths about the war.

This aerial view of Pearl Harbor was one of the last peacetime photos taken of the base. It was taken on October 30, 1941—five weeks before the "day of infamy."

PRELUDE TO PEARL HARBOR

December 7, 1941, a day of infamy. . . . World War II raged in Europe on this date. Nazi troops had just pulled back from their attempt to take Moscow before winter closed in. Operation Crusader was moving ahead in North Africa and General Rommel was about to begin his first withdrawal after the long siege of Tobruk. The Atlantic submarine war was in a calm as German U-boats were being transferred into the Mediterranean. The Free French had just recovered the island of Reunion in the Indian Ocean from the Vichy French after a short engagement.

Why did Japan attack Pearl Harbor on December 7, 1941? What were the motivations? There is no denying that in the 1930s Japan was building an empire, primarily from Chinese territory. Japan gained total control of Manchuria (recently renamed Manchukuo) in 1931–32, and won control of the most economically valuable sections of China in 1937. Fueled by the need to secure access to raw material and markets, Japan's imperialism was promoted by a fanatically nationalistic officer corps in both the army and navy.

In 1941 Japan's economic position was stretched. An Allied embargo was in place after Japan's seizure of French Indochina in July. Although Japan was the fifth most powerful economy in the world, only 10% of her oil needs were met by home resources. The 4,500,000 tons of stockpiled oil were not sufficient.

Japan needed 10,000,000 tons of shipping to meet her needs in 1940 and yet had only 5,900,000 tons under her flag (*only* 49 ships were oil tankers). Small and inefficient maintenance yards could not keep the merchant fleet operating. (As the war went on, more and more ships spent long periods in port awaiting vital repairs.) Japan's problems were not limited to economics.

Japan's military officers, especially her middle echelon officers, were involved to a large degree in Japanese national politics. It was expected that the Ministers of War and Navy would be serving generals or admirals. Thus the influence of the military was unusually strong. At the start of the war, General Hideki Tojo was Prime Minister, as well as Minister of War.

Several assassinations, attempted coups, and the unrest, which racked Japan in the 1930s, grew out of the nationalistic fanaticism and a form of Japanese Fascism that had its largest influence within the middle ranks of the military, primarily the army. One such officer was Colonel Tsuji, who was allegedly involved in the Bataan Death March, served with General Yamashita (the Tiger of Malaya) in the Malayan Campaign, and visited Guadalcanal, all in the first twelve months of the Pacific conflict (and later served in the Japanese Diet in the 1970s). His influence on generals was considerable and he affected the course of events to a degree far greater than his rank would normally warrant.

It should be understood that Japan's decision to attack the Allies was not an easy one, and many within Japan, including Emperor Hirohito, had grave reservations. Right up until December 7, the advisability of this action was questioned. However the War Party in Japan was in power. War to them appeared inevitable and the longer the delay, the stronger the Allies, especially the U.S.A., would become. Thus Japan slipped towards her first defeat in 2,600 years as a nation.

Japan's army saw Russia as the primary enemy while the navy viewed America in that role. The army saw the future for expansion in the north, while the navy saw it in the south. Ironically the army led the cabinet that launched a largely naval war in which airpower proved decisive.

This mock-up of Ford Island and Battleship Row was constructed by the Japanese after the attack on Pearl Harbor for use in a propaganda movie.

★★★ ══════ # The Japanese Situation ══════ ★★★

The most important branch of service in the war of the Pacific was the navy and Japan had the best trained force in the world. No other naval force surpassed the Japanese on a combat ship by combat ship basis. But Japan's problem lay in what Japan *had not* trained for adequately—anti-submarine and convoy operations—and the inability of Japan's economy to compete against her enemies in a lengthy war. In a short, quick, and decisive war Japan could survive. The Japanese shipbuilding industry was not set up for mass-production of warships, much needed as escorts for convoys. Japan had a romantic view of war that really did not ad-

dress the tedious need for convoy and anti-submarine work.

Admiral Toyoda Soemu remarked in 1937 to a British officer, "We lag behind in the material agencies of war; we therefore try and keep our personnel equal or superior to that of any other Navy." In the pursuit of this excellence, Japan regularly sent her ships on training missions to the far north. Tougher conditions prevailed there, and for the most part the Japanese practiced out of sight of other nations. Men usually received only three days off a month, thus giving the saw that a typical week was "Monday, Monday, Tuesday, Wednesday, Thursday, Friday, Friday!" It was not unusual to have men, and sometimes ships, lost in these practices.

At the start of the war Japan's fleet had ten aircraft carriers, of which six were large fleet carriers. They were efficient, carrying a large number of aircraft (70–90 per ship), but like the Americans, the Japanese had not adopted the British practice of armoring decks, and thus were vulnerable to damage from the air. With a speed of 30 or more knots, they traveled throughout the Pacific and, as a unit, they were the most powerful single weapon at the start of World War II in the Pacific.

In terms of battleships at the start of the war, Japan had ten that dated from World War I. Heavily reconstructed after the war, they were faster (the *Nagato* and *Mutsu* could reach 26 knots) than America's battleline, but individually they were not superior to America's battleships. The most noteworthy of the ten were the four Kongo class battleships, originally built as battlecruisers. At 30 knots, they could steam with the carriers, and armed with eight 14-inch guns each, they were clearly superior to any American heavy cruiser.

Under construction at the start of the war were several Yamato class superbattleships armed with nine 18-inch guns, weighing 64,000 tons, and moving at 27 knots. The Yamato took 49 months to build and were bigger than any American ship (which were built to be able to get through the Panama Canal). They could fire at such long ranges that they could sink American battleships by literally firing over the horizon. Spotter planes noted the fall of shot.

All the major navies built up 10,000-ton heavy cruisers between the wars. To compare Japanese heavy cruiser capacity with Allied capacity here are statistics for one cruiser from each major nation:

It should be noted that the Japanese knowingly violated the weight restrictions of various pre-war naval treaties, as did Germany, Italy, and the Soviet Union, who never signed any of the naval treaties. Only France, of the Western democracies, exceeded the treaty restrictions on some ship types.

Japan had a large force of older light cruisers built in the early 1920s. Smaller than most Allied light cruisers, they were fast, and one was usually assigned as flagship to a destroyer squadron. A few were built during the war, but were largely unexceptional vessels.

Japan's destroyer force (given meteorological names) totaled 175 ships, and a maximum of 130 destroyers existed at any one point in the war; 129 were sunk. Japan's destroyers excelled in ship-to-ship combat, usually being larger and more heavily gunned (usually 2000 tons with six 5-inch guns) than the Allied ships (1500–1800-tons armed with four or five 4.7-inch or 5-inch guns) and with the secret long lance 24-inch torpedo, which was issued in 1935 to the Japanese fleet (post-Fubuki class destroyer and larger heavy cruisers). They also carried a larger warhead than most Allied warheads (1080-pounds versus the British 21-inch MkIX with its 810-pound warhead and the American 21-inch Mk15 with a 825-pound warhead) and had a longer range and speed (the long lance could cover 21,900 yards at 48–50 knots, the British torpedo 11,000 yards at 41 knots, and the U.S. torpedo 6,000 yards at 45 knots). It should be noted that torpedoes could have longer ranges if they were set for slower speeds; thus the long lance could conceivably travel 43,700 yards if set for a speed of 36–38 knots! As it ran on oxygen, it did not leave a wake and could not be easily spotted. Ironically this torpedo was developed when during a tour of a British ship in the

	ATAGO	HOUSTON	HMAS CANBERRA
	12781 tons	9050 tons	9870 tons
Primary Armament	10 8-inch	9 8-inch	8 8-inch
Secondary Armament	8 5-inch DP*	8 5-inch/25 AA**	4 4-inch AA**
Torpedos	16 24-inch (with reloads)	—	8 21-inch
	35.5 knots	32.5 knots	31.5 knots
	4 to 5-inch belt armor	3 to 3.75-inch belt armor	narrow 4-inch armor belt
	6-inch turret armor	2.5-inch turret face armor	1-inch turret armor

*dual purpose, anti-aircraft as used as surface combat capable
**anti-aircraft

Japanese Mitsubishi divebombers prepare to take-off for the attack on Pearl Harbor. Photograph was taken from a captured Japanese propaganda movie.

1920s Japanese officers noted oxygen equipment and assumed that Britain had oxygen propelled torpedoes. This was in error, as the British had, by that time, abandoned their search for such a torpedo. Japan poured energy into the development of the oxygen propelled torpedo and to the regret of many an Allied sailor was successful. When first used during the Battle of the Java Sea, the Allied commanders assumed that the loss of the R.N.N. *Kortenaer* was due to a mine. Not until the war was over was the long range fully understood by the Allies.

Japan excelled in night combat. This was the form of combat that Japan had used to advantage in the Russo-Japanese War. All of Japan's surface combat ships, including the heavy cruisers and battleships, were combat ready for night actions. Japan had also reconstructed two older cruisers and armed them with 40 long lance torpedoes each. Named the *Oi* and *Kitakami* (5,500 tons, four 5.5-inch guns, 36 knots), they were given unit combat roles. In day actions they fired at extreme ranges, right on the edge of or even beyond the horizon. The possible disruption they could cause to an approaching fleet of older and slower battleships was great. In night actions they were used for following heavy and light cruisers in pushing towards the heart of an enemy fleet, where they would make a massive launching of torpedoes.

For anti-aircraft work Japan's destroyers were adequate, but they lacked the mass of weapons that characterized Allied warships. In submarine work the Japanese ships were only passable, lacking as they did much of the new electronic and sonar equipment.

The Japanese had three types of submarines, a long range cruiser (seven were built), the standard I (or *Kaidai*), type for cooperation with the main fleet, and the RO type for work and coastal work. Several carried midget submarines (46 tons, 19 knots submerged, and armed

The HMIJ *Myoko* is typical of the Japanese cruiser fleet prior to WW II.

This rare photograph was copied from a Japanese propaganda booklet describing the Japanese victories of the first few months of the war.

with two 18-inch torpedoes), first introduced in 1938, and transported the midget submarines used at Pearl Harbor. The I-boat was the most important, given a long range, high speed, heavy-gun armament, and good seakeeping qualities. A typical one, the I-61, weighed 1,635 tons surfaced, had a surface speed of 20 knots (8.5 submerged), and was armed with one 4.7-inch gun, six 21-inch torpedoes, and carried 14 total torpedoes. The most advanced types carried a floatplane, a 5-inch and two 25mm guns, had a range of 14,000 miles at 16 knots, and weighed 2,589 tons surfaced.

The problems with Japanese submarines were several. They were employed with the fleet, instead of being used for sinking transports—a failure of doctrine. They had slow diving times due to their large size. Their hulls were vulnerable to sonar and were poor at maneuvering when submerged, making them easy prey for depth-charge attacks. Habitability was poor (as was true for all Japanese ships, but with subs this is a crucial factor), and with long range missions, this took a toll. Finally, when surfaced, the large conning tower was easily picked up on radar, a problem that led to the sinking of many of them later in the war.

All in all, the Japanese navy was tough, but lacked the ability to absorb losses over an extended war.

The Japanese soldier was daring in attack and tough on the defensive, often willing to die when others would surrender. He was a product of Japan's unique society. The army itself was not rigidly organized (see appendixes). Primarily the infantry divisions had triangular organization (three regiments), but several enjoyed the older four-regiment organization and some of the lesser units (such as garrison units) consisted of stripped down units lacking engineering, artillery, etc. Thus, unlike the American army especially, in a confrontation with a Japanese division, the order-of-battle was not certain.

Japan's army consisted of 51 divisions, and had been tied down in a war in China since 1937 which occupied the full efforts of 21 infantry divisions and a brigade of army air. Facing Mongolia were another two divisions, and in Manchuria was a division of army air with 13 divisions. While Japan and Russia had signed a nonaggression pact, Japan had not withdrawn one unit from Manchuria's Kwangtung Army, because Japan did not trust the Soviet Union. Japan, in an undeclared border incident with Russia, had suffered a terrible defeat at Nomanhan (handed to her by the future Russian Marshal Zhukov) in disputed Manchurian/Mongolian territory and had witnessed the virtual destruction of the 23rd infantry division in 1939.

Her Korean and Home Island garrisons took another 5 divisions as well as a division of army air. Thus, the land forces for the thrust south were limited. However, Japanese strategists had devised a shuttle method whereby as one Allied position was occupied or neutralized, the next one in the chain would be softened up and ready for the invasion from the same forces that had just secured the previous objective.

Often the Japanese advanced in two columns. One column held the enemy by a frontal assault while the second column turned a flank, thus enveloping the enemy. In Malaya the second column often moved amphibiously along the coast to turn the Allied flank and thus force a defeat and retreat. Leading the way for these columns was a reconnaissance regiment (really about battalion strength) which included armored cars, sometimes tanks, and sometimes cavalry. The reconnaissance unit pushed until stopped, and then deployed to identify the enemy front and units involved.

Japanese tactical doctrine called for a battalion front of 1600 yards. A regiment covered about three times this front, and often on the attack two battalions advanced on a front with the third battalion as a reserve unit. Infiltration tactics, learned largely from the 1918 campaign in France, were heavily relied upon. The individual soldier, supported by close artillery and air support, was key to further advances.

Tank units were independent regiments for the most part. Sometimes crews abandoned vehicles and joined assaults on foot if confronted with an obstacle. While one must admire this spirit, well-trained crews were lost. Well directed anti-tank fire destroyed offensive minded Japanese tank assaults. Finally, tanks were held in reserve until the enemy front was clearly viewed, and then used in the breakthrough maneuver.

Japan had many and varied types of artillery.

The Japanese soldier worshiped Emperor Hirohito as a god.

She did possess heavy artillery types, due to her experience during the siege of Port Arthur in the Russo-Japanese War of 1904–05. However, Japan lacked large numbers of heavy artillery comparable to the big 155mm batteries common in the artillery-heavy American army. The use of light mortars was extensive in the Japanese army and offered the opportunity for close-in support.

The individual Japanese committed soldier was often willing to sacrifice his life for his nation and the constant willingness to advance infected the entire army. The Japanese army was primarily an offensive army and with this element of spirit could follow up a victory quickly.

The main defects of such tactics were several. If attacking a well prepared position, the Japanese could, and did, suffer tremendous losses. Once the Japanese doctrine was understood, the Allies were ready for surprise attacks, especially night ones. Relying heavily on men, the Japanese army did not have enough or the right kinds of equipment. Their tanks were inferior, and artillery and ammunition were not sufficient. Japanese motorized divisions, usually with at least one regiment on foot, lacked adequate transportation by Allied standards throughout the war.

While not an independent branch, the air force should be considered a separate entity.

Both the Imperial Japanese Navy and the Imperial Japanese Army maintained independent air forces that, at the start of the war, were on par with the best of the great powers. However, as the war continued, two major flaws appeared. One flaw was that while the Japanese aircraft industry produced a great many aircraft (52,242 combat aircraft were produced in the 1941–45 period), it was not flexible enough to adopt new aircraft designs. This was in part due to the fact that many skilled workmen were drafted by the armed services. A second flaw was that many aircraft were fast, adequately armed, but inadequately protected. Thus, many planes were lost with their crews, when an Allied plane with armor and self-sealing tanks was only damaged.

1942 AIRCRAFT PRODUCTION FIGURES

U.S.A.—49,445 aircraft
U.S.S.R.—25,430 aircraft
Britain—23,671 aircraft
Germany—15,556 aircraft
Japan—8,861 aircraft
Italy—2,818 aircraft

The Allies viewed Japan's aircraft as poor copies of obsolete Allied design, which proved to be a big advantage for the Japanese. The first six months of the war showed just how wrong the Allies were. The Japanese army air force entered the war with approximately 1500 aircraft. Of this total, 650 were committed to action against Malaya (3rd Hikoshidan or Air

During the early months of the war in the Pacific, the Japanese Kate was reliable and effective.

Division) and the Philippines (5th Air Division). This concentration against Malaya was due to the Japanese naval air commitment against the Philippines as the Japanese naval air was better trained for operations across the seas and had long range aircraft.

The Japanese naval air force numbered 3000 airplanes of which 1400 were frontline combat aircraft. Some 503 were assigned to the 11th Koku Kantai (11th Air Fleet), which consisted of the land-based aircraft. At the start of the war, the 11th consisted of three air flotillas, the 21st, 22nd, and 23rd. The rest served on board ships, and included the elite 1st Air Fleet which was the best trained air force unit in the world. It was the force that attacked Pearl Harbor.

The Japanese naval air had been assigned the role of guarding the seas surrounding the Japanese Empire after World War I. Later this force was used extensively in the war against China, so in the early part of the war in the Pacific, American planes did not encounter Japanese army aircraft until the middle of 1943 in the battles in the Central and South Pacific.

The ultimate failure of the Japanese aircraft industry lay in its inability to produce more advanced aircraft quickly as the war progressed. This was combined with poor defensive charac-

teristics of the aircraft. Finally, Japan usually kept units on the frontlines too long and thus all the trained pilots eventually died. The Allies withdrew toughened cadre from time to time to rebuild the units and send veteran pilots back home to help train new ones. As the war went on, the Allies produced better trained pilots and Japan's initial pilot edge eventually was lost.

TOTAL JAPANESE NAVAL STRENGTH AT THE OUTBREAK OF WAR

Classification	STRENGTH AT START		UNDER CON-STRUCTION	
	No.	Ton.	No.	Ton.
Battleships	10	301,400	4*	256,000
Aircraft Carriers	10	152,970	4	77,860
Heavy Cruisers	18	158,800	—	—
Light Cruisers	20	98,855	4	44,700
Destroyers	112	165,868	12	27,120
Submarines	65**	97,900	29	42,554
Others	156	490,384	37	57,225
TOTAL:	391	1,466,177	90	503,459

*Four Yamato class super battleships. Two, the *Yamato* and *Mushashi* would be completed while one would be completed as the aircraft carrier *Shinano* and the fourth would be cancelled, after work had started, in March of 1942. Three further "super-Yamatos" were projected.

**21 were small (usually about 1,000 tons), or older submarines built in the 1920s.

Captured Japanese photo taken on deck of aircraft carrier before the Pearl Harbor attack shows crew sending off a divebomber squadron.

American destroyers, like the USS *Sims* shown here, were sturdy vessels, but suffered from faulty torpedoes in the first phase of the war.

The American Situation

The American situation on December 7, 1941, was not as a position of dominance in the Pacific. But nonetheless it was a seemingly strong position. The main prop of American strength was the U.S. Navy.

At the start of the war the U.S.A. had a battleship-oriented navy which was engaged in an immense naval buildup, Congressman Carl Vinson's two-ocean navy rearmament program. During the 1920s and much of the 30s the U.S.A. had neglected her navy and had not built up to the limits allowed under the Washington and London treaties. This was due to finances, as well as to pacifist tendencies that

swept the country (and other Western democracies) after the dreadful losses of World War I.

Also affecting the growth of the navy was the impact of General Billy Mitchell. A radical advocate of air power and a man who made a strong impression on Admiral Yamamoto when Yamamoto was assigned to Washington D.C. in the 20s, Billy Mitchell had an effect far beyond that of any other general. The influence of his writings was not slight. This was the Billy Mitchell who said, "If a naval war were attempted against Japan, . . . the Japanese submarines and aircraft would sink the enemy fleet long before it came anywhere near their coast" and "Air power has completely superseded sea power or land power as our first line of defense." While possibly true in today's world, Billy Mitchell was far ahead of his times.

Fortunately, in spite of reduced appropriations, pacifists, Billy Mitchell, and the scrapping of many battleships, the navy remained strong and filled with enterprise. Still, there was the conservative hand of innovation on the U.S. Navy which could be traced to the battleship admiral mentality.

The navy was dominated by the "gun school." It was normal to have the two top positions in the U.S. Navy held by a battleship admiral. The United States Naval Institute Proceedings (the oracle of the navy), during the three years prior to Pearl Harbor, did not publish *one* article suggesting that the aircraft carrier would supersede the battleships as the backbone of the navy. When construction of the new two-ocean fleet began in 1936, battleship construction was way ahead of aircraft carriers, though considering the age of most of the

existing battleships, this was not surprising. The newest battleship in 1936 was completed in the mid-20s!

The conservative navy brass recognized that airpower affected navies, and as early as 1939 they saw a need for additional anti-aircraft gun protection. When the war in Europe broke out, it quickly became apparent that the British anti-aircraft cruisers (converted World War I light cruisers of the C class—4,290 tons, eight 4-inch guns, 27.5 knots) were worth their weight in gold. From this would come the U.S. Navy's Atlanta class anti-aircraft cruiser (6,718 tons, sixteen 5-inch guns, eight 21-inch torpedoes, 32.5 knots) as well as a steady addition of anti-aircraft guns on the capital ships. Even by the time of Midway, the navy's large ships were being covered with extra anti-aircraft gun positions.

In terms of material at the start of the war, the U.S. Navy had a powerful battleship force made up of older battleships capable of 21 knots. While slower than the Japanese battle-

B-25s on the flight deck of the USS *Hornet* before the historic raid on Tokyo. The *Hornet* was typical of America's carrier fleet with a displacement of 19,800 tons and a crew of almost 3,000.

line, they were more heavily armored than the Japanese and were very accurate in their gunnery practice. Secondary roles for the battleships were only partially explored, with shore bombardment envisioned as a possible role, but high explosive shells were still lacking for the battleships except for a small supply left over from World War I. Separate task forces for specific operations were being used, but only in a limited fashion. In 1941 the battleship was still the key and all other ships were auxiliaries to them. With the arrival of the first fast (27 knots) battleships laid down in 1937, the U.S. Navy was able to construct the powerful task force concept which evolved into the dominating power in the Pacific War. The new U.S. fast battleships lacked adequate subdivision and their armor was on the slim side, but they had excellent 16-inch guns, and the armor plate was modeled on the German *Wotan hart* (samples of which were found in a U.S. Steel subsidiary in the 1930s, apparently through industrial espionage).

At the start of the war America had six fleet carriers, and one other, the *Ranger*, a smaller aircraft carrier that stayed in the Atlantic for the duration. Though dominated by the battleship school, the aircraft carrier did receive a great deal of attention in the interwar period. As the war approached and the eventual twenty-six Essex class carriers were started, it was realized that an interim carrier was needed. The Essex class did not really come on stream until 1943 and 1944. Initially carrier escorts (conversions from merchant ship hulls) were seen as part of the answer, but eventually President Roosevelt intervened and pushed for the conversion of the Cleveland class CL hull to light carriers. Nine such conversions occurred, and all were in service by 1943. As with so much of America's war effort, large quantities using similar designs were the keynote of her building program.

Probably the biggest deficiency in the cruisers built was the lack of torpedo armament. The gun school so dominated the navy that torpedoes were limited to destroyers. However, on a 10,000-ton treaty limit, the navy built some excellent gunnery platforms. The rapid-fire (6 to 10 rounds per minute per gun), 6-inch gun carried on the light cruisers of the Brooklyn class (9,767 tons, fifteen 6-inch guns, eight 5-inch

guns, 32 knots) gave a tremendous broadside punch, especially in a close range night action. Such a ship, at night, was probably superior to a heavy cruiser armed with eight to ten 8-inch guns firing three to five rounds a minute. The advantage of the heavy cruiser was in daylight action when the heavy cruiser had a longer range, as well as a slightly more accurate shell due to the heavier weight and better armor penetration at long ranges.

America's destroyers were sturdy little vessels, but, again, inferior on a one to one basis to Japan's. Averaging about 1600 tons, armed with four or five 5-inch guns, eight to sixteen 21-inch torpedoes, and steaming at about 35 knots, they had only one advantage: there were lots of them. Not until the Fletcher class came into service would the navy have a destroyer that could match Japan's best. America's destroyers suffered from faulty torpedoes well into 1943. As anti-aircraft platforms and for anti-submarine warfare work, America's destroyers were quite good.

America's submarine arm was strong, though it too was armed with a torpedo that shared the flaw with the destroyers. Interwar submarine designs were based on the German U-boats of World War I, specifically the U-135. They had a long cruising radius. This allowed for deep penetration into the vast Pacific Ocean. A typical submarine was the *Perch*, launched in 1936. She displaced 1,330 tons (1,997 when submerged), had six 21-inch tubes, one 3-inch deck gun, and could steam at 18.8 knots on the surface and 8 knots when submerged. Range at 10 knots was 11,000 nautical miles. By the end of the war, the effect of the navy's submarines was decisive.

The United States Navy neglected night tactics for ships larger than destroyers. It did not believe capital ships should engage in night actions, and thus did not train for night actions. Admiral J.O. Richardson, who preceded Admiral Kimmel in command at Pearl Harbor, attempted in 1940 to train in this area, due in part to the lessons of war at sea learned by the British against the Italian and German navies. The battle to Matapan was an excellent lesson. At Matapan, in early 1941, three British battleships fired at night at 5,000 yards and were instrumental in sinking three heavy cruisers of the Italian navy. The fleet maneuver resulted in "a

Motor torpedo boats, or PT boats, offered all the advantages of speed in a lightweight craft, but were vulnerable to fiery explosions when hit.

confused night battle between the two fleets, with some near collisions, undesired illuminations, and missed gunnery and torpedo opportunities." That night tactics were not an essential part of training before the war was due in part to the approaching adoption of radar which was thought to be a panacea for night action confusion.

The American army was not the best army in World War II. Furthermore, the units sent to the Pacific Theater were, for the most part, second rate. This situation was due in part to the antimilitary traditions of the American republic dating back to the American Revolution. In the interwar period there was a strong wave of anti-

militarism which affected the army. Fundamentally, the army was dominated by conservative officers who pushed the artillery arm and maintained a nonflexible infantry force. Somewhat like the British army in these respects, the American army was capable of changing and growing, and thus becoming by the end of the war, a decisive force for victory.

The United States Marines were a much more aggressive force than the army and had studied the problems created by a war in the Pacific. Amphibious operations were required in the Pacific and the U.S.M.C. had the plans and prototype equipment ready for such operations.

The American armed forces deployed, in the

course of early 1942, four National Guard divisions, second rate units at this point in the war, to the Pacific Theater; the 41st and 32nd to Australia in part to allow Australian troops to remain in other theaters, and the 37th to Fiji in support of New Zealand. In March, the 27th division (four instead of the usual three regiments) joined the 24th Hawaiian division, the only complete regular division in the Pacific, in Hawaii. The 1st Marine was preparing to go to New Zealand, later to Guadalcanal.

The garrison in the Philippines consisted of one incomplete regular division (the Philippine division). Two reserve divisions and ten national divisions made up of Filipinos rounded out the garrison. Unfortunately, none of the Filipino divisions were properly trained or equipped.

An American infantry division totaled 15,245 men in 1941. Consisting of three regiments, there were three light artillery battalions, and one medium artillery battalion. A full strength

Grumman TBF-1 Avengers flew from carriers and could carry bombs, depth charges or torpedoes ("tin fishes").

division had 1,834 vehicles, twelve 155mm guns, thirty-six 105mm howitzers, eight 75mm guns, sixty 37mm anti-tank guns, thirty-six 81mm and eighty-one 60mm mortars. Each of the three battalions in a regiment had a headquarters company, a heavy weapons company, and three rifle companies. As with so much of America's war effort in 1941 and 1942, the army was not complete in equipment or training—the U.S.A. was simply not ready for war.

The main army decision after Pearl Harbor was to reinforce the various outposts in the Pacific—from the Panama Canal to Alaska—and halt the Japanese advance. The main effort was against the Axis powers in Europe. The process of stemming the Japanese advance required more resources than first realized.

By May of 1940 the Army Air Corps was authorized to expand to 54 air groups totaling 4,000 tactical aircraft and over 200,000 men. By the autumn of 1941, 84 groups were contemplated. By December 7th, 1941, the Army Air Corps broke down as follows:

ARMY AIR CORPS

	GROUPS
Heavy Bombardment Groups	14
Medium Bombardment Groups	9
Light Bombardment Groups	5
Fighter Groups	25
Observation Groups	11
Transport Groups	6
	70

As can be seen, the goal of 84 air groups was still a paper figure and even the 70 air groups here listed were understrength and still contained obsolete aircraft.

President Roosevelt, in May of 1940, called for 50,000 planes a year annually from America's manufacturing sector. Programs were established to produce 50,000 pilots a year. It was this effort which overwhelmed the Axis in the end.

TOTAL ALLIED NAVAL STRENGTH IN THE PACIFIC

	BATTLESHIPS BATTLE CRUISERS	AIRCRAFT CARRIERS	HEAVY CRUISERS	LIGHT CRUISERS	DE- STROYERS	SUB- MARINES
Britain and Dominions	2	—	3	13	6	1
Netherlands	—	—	—	3	7	15
U.S.A. Asiatic	—	—	1	2	13	33
U.S.A. Pacific	8*	3	13	9	67	27
TOTALS:	10	3	17	27	93	71

*two older battleships, the *New Mexico* and *Idaho*, were transferred in January of 1942 to the Pacific from the Atlantic. Two additional new ones, the *North Carolina* and the *Washington* had just been completed and were working up in the Atlantic.

U.S. NAVAL CONSTRUCTION

	1941	1942	1943	1944	1945
Battleships	3	3	1	1	—
Battlecruisers	—	—	2	—	—
Aircraft Carriers	—	3	5	9	6
Light Aircraft Carriers	—	3	6	—	6
Escort Carriers	2	15	25	35	8
Heavy Cruisers	—	2	2	3	4
Light Cruisers	6	8	7	12	4
Destroyers	27	119	98	61	56
Destroyer Escorts	25	306	105	—	—
Submarines	15	41	67	78	20

Please note that these ships also had commitments in the Atlantic, especially the escort ships, though the need for larger modern combat ships for use against German and Italian navies was present for much of the war.

For perspective, in 1940, with Great Britain on the ropes, CNO Harold Stark stated that Japan had twelve battleships under construction, and naval intelligence reported that Italy and Germany had built or were building 16 battleships. Even Franco's Spain was considering laying down some Italian design Roma battleships!

Several American projects were cancelled as the war progressed; for example, plans for five Montana class battleships armed with twelve 16-inch guns, due to a perceived lack of armor-making facilities. To help alleviate this blockage, the profit margin limit in the Vinson-Trammell Act for the two-ocean navy was removed, as well as the minimum wage law for armor-producing steel companies. Similar measures were established for the shipbuilding industry.

The U.S.A. naval construction program built 1300 ships by a workforce of 42,000 men and women.

It must also be remembered that throughout this early part of the war America was busy preparing new designs, primarily in response to the incredible weapons produced by Nazi Germany. But by looking to the future, America assured the Allies that new and better aircraft, like the Mustang or B-29, would be developed as the war progressed.

The *Prince of Wales* of the King George V Class was moderately armed with only two four-gun turrets and one two-gun turret.

★★★ The Commonwealth Situation ★★★

The historian H.P. Willmott said of Great Britain's policy on the eve of war with Japan, "In the place of a deliberately conceived strategy reigned confusion, unreality, and weakness, shrouded by wishful thinking." Frankly, Great Britain, as well as the Commonwealth, was thinly stretched, and the war in Europe had Winston Churchill's attention firmly riveted. Further, the seeds for unrest lay ready in the colonial possessions, especially India, where a well established independence movement was already growing.

Looking to the Far East, the British Empire had positions scattered throughout: Hong Kong, Malaya, Burma, the Commonwealths of Australia and New Zealand, the Solomons and Gilbert Islands (as well as island outposts stretching across the Pacific), and the jewel of India, second most populated region of the world.

What did Britain have to face Imperial Japan? The Royal Navy was already heavily committed against the Axis in Europe and losses had been heavy. The Royal Navy believed in ships of moderate dimensions, for the most part. Her battleships of the *Price of Wales* type were probably the weakest modern battleships built after World War I. The British Government believed that the naval treaties would continue to exert a deadening hand on naval construction. Thus, this new class of modern battleship was armed with the smallest gun (14-inch) of all modern battleships. It weighed in at 35,000 tons and could steam at 29 knots. Still, this class was a powerful addition to the British navy.

Britain's carriers were well built ships. Their armored decks allowed them to suffer damaging dive-bomber hits which knocked out American or Japanese carriers. However, British carriers usually carried about one-half the number of planes as the Japanese and Americans.

Royal Navy cruisers and destroyers were ships of moderate dimensions, but, as all British and Commonwealth ships, were well crewed.

Britain had heavily developed night combat tactics as a direct outgrowth of experience against Germany in World War I. The British, along with the Germans and Japanese, were the best experts at surface night combat at the start of World War II, especially when employing capital ships in that role.

The big advantage that Britain had was that her crews were well trained and filled with veterans of two years of war, a war that saw numerous operations at sea. The disadvantages were that the British held a faulty perception of the Japanese navy and the Royal Navy was stretched very thin. The Japanese proved to be very tough opponents, possibly the toughest in the war, and stretched the Royal Navy even thinner.

The Dutch navy operated only small battleships, such as the one shown here, which were originally designed as coastal defense ships for service in the East Indies.

The Commonwealth Army

BRITAIN'S ARMY COMMITMENTS

	UK	Middle East	Persia & Iraq	Malaya**
Armored Divisions (UK)	6	3	—	—
Infantry Divisions (UK)	21*	2	—	—
Dominion Infantry Divisions	2	6	—	1
Indian Infantry Divisions	—	2	3	2
TOTALS	29	13	3	3

*This excludes nine country divisions, similar to militia divisions stationed in Australia. In 1941 the 18th British division was on its way to the Middle East.

**The 1st Burma division was made up of locally raised troops and some Indian units, and by January of 1942, the 17th Indian Division. The 17th was a new unit, training was lacking (six weeks worth in many cases) and many of the valuable cadres had been "milked" for other units of the rapidly expanding Indian army.

The Australians had several militia divisions training throughout Australia by early 1942, which were considered to be about half the value of one of the regular Australian divisions. It should be noted that a full strength Australian division had seventy-two 25-pounders, much heavier gunning than a comparable U.S. division. There is no question that at this point in the war the Australian regular divisions were better trained for combat than any American unit (or British), with the possible exception of the U.S. Marines. Dudley McCarthy, the official Australian historian, said of the Americans that there was ". . . some lack of realism in the outlook of the newly-arrived formations. Staff work seemed defective and training methods somewhat unpractical."

India, too, made a valuable contribution to the war effort. While her best units, the 4th and 5th Indian, served in the Middle East and Africa, and proved equal (and sometimes superior) to comparable European troops, India now had to face an enemy rapidly approaching her eastern border.

India had to deal with a domestic independence movement and some pro-Japanese sentiment throughout the war. India virtually lacked a navy, though she did manage to put to sea and man various sloops for convoy duty in the course of the war, and her air force was virtu-

ally nonexistent. India made important economic contributions as well.

It was with her army that India made the largest contribution, quadrupling her army between 1939 and 1942. Yet in 1941 she did not have one modern armored car or tank. Anti-tank training was deficient. None of her divisions sent to Malaya had their organization and equipment third brigade. The Indian army was lacking in support and technical units (especially artillery) of all sorts, officers, and had to be concerned with the Northwest frontier (the Afghan border), as well as internal security.

INDIAN ARMY EXPANSION

1939	4th Indian, North Africa
1940	5th Indian, Cyprus (with the fall of France the 6th Persia, 7th, 8th Iraq, 9th Malaya and 10th Persia were formed up).
1941	11th Malaya, 14th, 17th, 19th, 20th, and 34th were being formed in India.

Units were stationed outside India in location noted in fall of 1941. The formation began of three armored brigades, equipped with cruiser tanks, which would debut in 1943 and would be attached to various headquarters in India on the Burma border.

In terms of airpower, the situation was even worse as virtually no modern aircraft existed in the Far East, compounding the underestimation of the Japanese ability to use airpower well. Airfields in India and support roads were totally lacking on the frontier with Burma. Finally, the manufacturing ability in India and Australia was extremely limited. In a word, the Far East was a vulnerable part of the British Empire.

The Dutch contribution must be mentioned because the Dutch navy was competent, though small, and her submarines inflicted losses to the Japanese. Their supreme commander Vice-Admiral Helfrich got the nickname "ship-a-day Helfrich" largely due to the success of the Dutch subs.

Unfortunately the Dutch army was made up largely of Indonesians, many who resented Dutch rule. The Dutch air force in the Dutch East Indies consisted of about 34 P-40s, 31 Buffalos, 36 Glenn Martin bombers, and about 22 older fighters. Too few and too old.

USS *Phoenix* burns following the attack on Pearl Harbor.

THE WAR
IN THE
PACIFIC

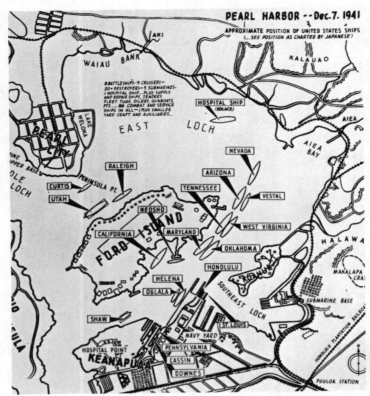

Map shows the position of ships surrounding Ford Island on the morning of December 7, 1941.

Air Raid Pearl Harbor — This is No Drill

The attack on Pearl Harbor was masterminded by the Japanese Admiral Isoroku Yamamoto. A strong air advocate, he had been instrumental in equipping the Japanese naval air force with powerful and long range aircraft, as well as helping facilitate the construction of the world's largest aircraft carrier fleet—ten carriers at the start of the war. Yamamoto spent time in Washington, D.C., in the 1920s, where he gained the reputation as an excellent poker player—the bluff was a trademark of his play.

As late as 1937 the fleet doctrine for aircraft carriers for Japan was the same as the American: providing an air umbrella for the surface fleet as it advanced towards the enemy. But, as Chief of the Naval General Staff Admiral Osami Nagano, who studied English at Harvard (as had Yamamoto), indicated after the war, the concept of employing the carriers to project fire power deep into the enemy territory was learned from the Americans. This concept became official Japanese doctrine in 1938. With this doctrine change, Yamamoto was given the weapon to achieve his policy goals.

Yamamoto's goal was to hurt the American fleet enough so that it would be incapable of influencing the Japanese strike south into Southern Asia. If key capital ships, especially American aircraft carriers, were damaged or sunk, then the American fleet would not intervene while Japan secured her key resources needed to fuel the Japanese war economy. A successful attack on Pearl Harbor would achieve this. Further, in 1940 the British had attacked the main Italian fleet at Taranto and had scored a marked success by surprising the Italians in harbor. This was done with one carrier. Why not six?

There were three important problems that needed to be addressed in this attack. First, the Japanese carriers were going to be used in the attack against the Philippines. So, the long range naval aircraft, especially the new Zero fighter, were moved to Formosa. With their long range, air raids against Luzon Island in the Philippines could be properly implemented, and could be escorted by the landbased Zero. Secondly, the Pearl Harbor attack force had to get to the Hawaiian Islands. The Japanese tanker fleet could accomplish this although the Japanese carriers could only have a small escorting fleet. Finally, to achieve sure success, surprise was the key. Tactical surprise was an element to be gained at the time of the actual raid.

While Yamamoto devised the concept, Commander Minoru Genda prepared the overall plan, and Genda's friend Commander Mitsuo Fuchida worked out the details. It was Genda who wanted to employ high level planes to drop modified 16-inch shells from the Nagato class battleship against the American ships at Pearl Harbor. Fuchida worked out the details that they attacked at 3,000 meters (9,843 feet), instead of the usual 5,000 meters (16,404 feet). The latter altitude would be above anti-aircraft fire, while the former would allow the bombs to just penetrate the armored decks of the American battleships.

Fuchida also disapproved of the conventional nine plane formation and adopted a five-plane formation:

The overall Japanese plan called for the fighters to sweep in, and if command of the air was achieved, to attack and strafe the air installations. Then torpedo planes with special fins allowing them to drop torpedoes in the shallow waters of Pearl Harbor would attack the aircraft carriers present. Dive bombers would then roar in to destroy the carriers so that they could not be possibly salvaged, as the Italian battleships at Taranto had been. If carriers were not present, and it was not thought they would be, then the planes would attack the battleships.

U.S.A. LAND BASED AIRCRAFT IN HAWAII ON DECEMBER 1, 1941

	QUANTITY	
MODERN BOMBERS		
B-17Cs and B-17Ds	12	
A-20As	12	
OBSOLETE BOMBERS		
B-18A	33	
MODERN FIGHTERS		
P-40C	12	
P-40B	87	
P-40E	39	
P-36A	14	
MISCELLANEOUS ARMY		
Cargo, Transport, Etc.	22	
NAVY LANDBASED AIRCRAFT		
At Kaneohe airfield—PBYs	36	(some miscellaneous craft too)
At Ford Island—misc. including shipboard scout planes	33	
AT EWA MARINE AIRFIELD		
Wildcats	11	
Vindicator SB2U-3s	32	
Miscellaneous aircraft	6	

Of the Army Air Corps, 143 of the planes were usable, while 88 were under repair at the time of the attack. Some 87 were usable after the attack, while 79 of the planes under repair were left after the attack. The navy lost 27 PBYs, while the Marines lost or had severely damaged 9 Wildcats, 18 Vindicators and 6 utility planes. Total U.S.N. air losses were 92, and 31 damaged. Included are planes flying from *Enterprise* during and after attack, several damaged and shot down by friendly anti-aircraft. At the start of the attack there were a total of 394 planes on Oahu.

JAPANESE PEARL HARBOR STRIKE FORCE

FIRST AIR FLEET
1st CARRIER DIVISION: *Akagi* (fleet flagship) and *Kaga*
2nd CARRIER DIVISION: *Soryu* and *Hiryu*
5th CARRIER DIVISION: *Zuikaku* and *Shokaku*
1st DESTROYER SQUADRON: CL *Abukuma* (5,570 tons, seven 5.5-inch guns, eight 24-inch torpedoes, 35 knots) Flagship destroyers *Isokaze, Urakaze, Tanikaze, Hamakaze, Arare, Kusumi, Kagero, Shiranuhi,* and *Akigumo* (2,370 to 2,490 tons, six 5-inch guns, eight 24-inch torpedoes with reloads, 35 knots)

SUPPORT FORCE
3rd BATTLESHIP DIVISION: *Hiei* and *Kirishima*
8th CRUISER DIVISION: *Tone* and *Chikuma* (13,320 tons, eight 8-inch guns, eight 5-inch guns, twelve 24-inch torpedoes, five scout planes, 35 knots)

SHIP LANE RECONNAISSANCE UNITS
SUBMARINES: *I-19, I-21,* and *I-23* with 5 midget submarines.

The second wave would not contain torpedo bombers as their losses would be too high with a by then fully aroused American enemy firing from anti-aircraft gun positions. The second wave would work over the island defenses instead. The Japanese goal was to sink all carriers and at least four battleships. American land based air was to be smashed.

The commander of the attack force was Vice Admiral Chuichi Nagumo, who was not the best choice for this role. An admiral of average abilities, he was uncomfortable with carrier airpower. He was a battleship admiral and had no previous hands on experience with carriers before being given that command. A perfectionist, he also had a tendency to take counsel with his fears. Genda always blamed the Japanese Personnel Department for assigning Nagumo to this position.

As the Japanese attack force moved across the Pacific there were two threats to the surprise factor. One was a Russian freighter which was sighted early in December during the approach to the Hawaiian Islands. To this day, the English speaking public does not know what the Russian freighter radioed to the Soviet Union that evening when she checked in with Vladivostok. Also, there was the American Ultra operation. This was the U.S.A. intelligence service operation in which Japanese codes were broken and the Japanese mail was being read.

Ultra revealed that Japan was about to launch an attack against the Netherlands East Indies, British possessions, and the U.S.A. However, in Washington, it was never perceived that Pearl Harbor itself was to be attacked. What was expected, by America's leaders, was an attack against America's possessions in the Far East, principally the Philippines and Guam. Sabotage by the 157,907 people of Japanese blood on Pearl Harbor was the main concern of the local Hawaiian commanders. Thus, General Short, the army commander, ordered that all planes be massed close together at the various island airfields to easily guard against sabotage. They would turn out to be easy targets for the attacking Japanese aircraft.

There is no doubt that Americans had failed to properly prepare against attack on Pearl Harbor. Until 1940 the American fleet was based on the West Coast. In that year, Washington decided to move the fleet to Pearl as a "message" to Japan. The admiral commanding, James O. Richardson, was incensed over this decision and twice journeyed to Washington in attempts to get this decision changed. Instead, Richardson was relieved of his command and Admiral Husband B. Kimmel was appointed.

American strategy was based on what they expected Japan to do, not on what Japan was *capable of.* This was fueled by the perception that Japan was not very capable. A cardinal error. Finally, proper equipment and enough of that equipment was not present on the Islands at the time of the attack. Richardson had seen this as a major problem. Radar had just arrived on Oahu, but was not properly used and was still very new. So new was radar that when a set revealed approaching enemy aircraft on December 7, the report was ignored. PBYs and other long range reconnaissance aircraft were too few and could not properly cover all approaches to Pearl Harbor. America had failed to go to war production soon enough, and the weapons and planes that were produced often went to the Philippines or to the Atlantic Theater, or to the Allies. Finally, there was a failure to anticipate an attack. Admiral King commented, on the American attitude as an "unwarranted feeling of immunity from attack . . . seems to have pervaded all ranks at Pearl Harbor, both Army and Navy."

So across the Northern Pacific, outside normal shipping lines, steamed the approaching Japanese task force loaded with more than 350 aircraft on the way to strafe, bomb and torpedo. Unfortunately for the Japanese, all the American carriers were absent that morning from Pearl Harbor, although the *Enterprise* (19,875 tons, 18 fighters, 36 torpedo bombers—usually only 18 on board—37 dive bombers, and 5 utility aircraft, eight 5-inch guns, 32.5 knots) with Admiral Halsey on board was approaching harbor and was scheduled to tie up before the attack, but was delayed. The signal to attack on December 8, 1941 (Japanese time), was received on December 2 when 940 miles from Midway Island. The message was "Climb Mount Niitaka." (Mount Niitaka is the highest

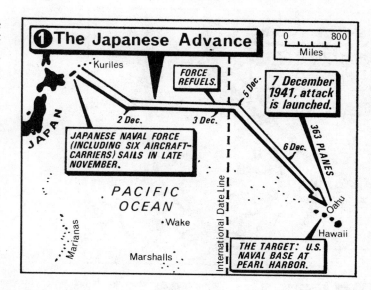

MIDWAY DESTRUCTION UNIT
Destroyers *Ushio* and *Sazananmi*

FLEET TRAIN
Eight tankers and supply ships

JAPANESE AIR ATTACK AGAINST PEARL HARBOR

Of 185 planes scheduled for the attack in the first wave, 183 took off. They were:

43 Zero Fighters
49 Kate Horizontal Bombers
51 Val Divebombers
40 Kate Torpedo Bombers

Two additional fighters tried to take off, but one crashed on launch and a second one was forced back due to engine trouble.

The second wave launched:

36 Zero Fighters
54 Kate Horizontal Bombers
78 Val Divebombers

One Val had to return to the carriers due to engine trouble. Fighters were always the first to lead, while the torpedo bombers were always the last to rise from the deck.

mountain in Formosa, which was the highest point in the Japanese Empire in 1941.)

The opening round began not with planes, but with midget submarines. While unsuccessful in this attack, and disappointing throughout the war, the Japanese launched five midget submarines early in the morning towards the harbor entrance. All were lost, one by the destroyer *Ward* on patrol off the harbor at about 6:45 A.M. on December 7, 1941. The sub's conning tower was sighted by a PBY on air patrol. The reaction of the observer was "My God, a sub in distress." But it was in the defensive sea area in which all subs were to be attacked and sunk if submerged. The *Ward* closed, fired on it, depth charged it, and reported that it had sighted and sunk a submarine in the defense sea area. Some of the officers were concerned that they had attacked an American sub, while the ensign on the PBY, William Tanner, assumed his career would be forever maimed for following orders.

The first Japanese wave of the torpedo planes and horizontal bombers attacked the battleships at battleship row along Ford Island. The fighters, after securing control of the air, abdicated by the Americans, strafed the various airfields to assure control of the air. A flight of Vals were detailed to work over the naval aircraft at Ford Island. Hickham and Wheeler airbases, both army, received attention too. The second wave worked over the airfields again.

So the attack began.

The reaction to the Japanese attack on this

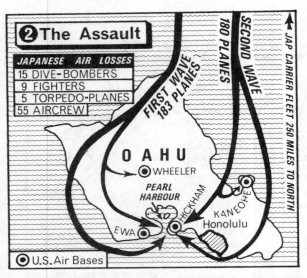

② The Assault

JAPANESE AIR LOSSES	
15	DIVE-BOMBERS
9	FIGHTERS
5	TORPEDO-PLANES
55	AIRCREW

FIRST WAVE 183 PLANES

SECOND WAVE 180 PLANES

JAP CARRIER FLEET 250 MILES TO NORTH

OAHU

⊙ WHEELER

PEARL HARBOUR

HICKHAM

KANEOHE

Honolulu

EWA ⊙

⊙ U.S. Air Bases

The first wave of the Japanese air attack targeted the ships along Battleship Row off Ford Island. Many ships anchored closer to the mainland were not hit, such as the one shown here, the USS *Narwhal*.

Because the radar system was new, it was thought to be unreliable. So when incoming planes were detected, they were ignored. Here a Japanese plane flies over Pearl Harbor.

Another plane, and this one flying lower.

Early in the morning, Japan sent five midget submarines into Pearl Harbor. The attack was unsuccessful and all the submarines were lost before they entered the harbor.

"Day that will live in infamy" had its humorous moments. Initially some Americans thought this was a drill. Seaman Robert Osborne, based with a utility plane squadron on Ford Island, couldn't understand why American planes were bombing. He remembered thinking that "Somebody is going to catch it for putting live bombs on those planes." One of the seamen on the doomed *Arizona* saw the approaching enemy planes and remarked, "This is the best goddamn drill the Army Air Force has ever put on!" The message went from the fireroom of the battleship *California* to the head on the *Nevada*, "This is a hell of a time to hold general drills." Commander Herald Stout of the destroyer-minelayer *Breese* had standing orders that no general quarter drills would be held before 8 A.M. on Sunday. When the alarm sounded he left his breakfast to chew out the officer of the watch. On board the battleship *Oklahoma* the PA system announced, "Real planes, real bombs; this is no drill!"

American destroyer leaves Pearl Harbor to patrol the defensive sea area during the attack.

Captured Japanese photograph was taken from the air during the attack on Pearl Harbor. The ships anchored off the tip of Ford Island can be clearly distinguished. From left to right: the *Nevada*, the *Arizona* and *Vestal*, the *Tennessee* and *West Virginia*, and the *Maryland* and *Oklahoma*.

Watertender Samuel Cucek looked into the head on the destroyer tender *Dobbin*, called to Fireman Charles Leahey, "You better cut that short, Charlie, the Japs are here."

Chief Petty Officer Albert Molter, gardening at his Ford Island residence, thought a drill was in progress, until Esther, his wife, called to him, "Al, there's a battleship tipping over."

Colonel William Farthing was in the control tower of Hickam Field, the main Army Air Corps base near Pearl, when he saw a line of planes approaching and begin diving. Farthing assumed they were Marine planes from Ewa Airbase. He remarked to Colonel Bertholf, "Very realistic maneuvers. I wonder what the Marines are doing to the navy so early Sunday?"

Rear Admiral William R. Furlong, on board the ammunition ship *Oglala*, paid little attention to the planes until he saw a bomb drop from one of them. Furlong thought, "What a stupid, careless pilot, not to have secured his releasing gear." As the plane turned and the red meatballs on the wings were seen he shouted, "Japanese! Man your stations." His next order flashed to all ships in the harbor was "All ships in harbor sortie!"

The first ten minutes of the attack brought virtually no resistance from the American fleet. It allowed the Japanese to wreck their most

Taken moments after the photograph opposite, this shows hits on the *Arizona*, *West Virginia*, and *Tennessee*.

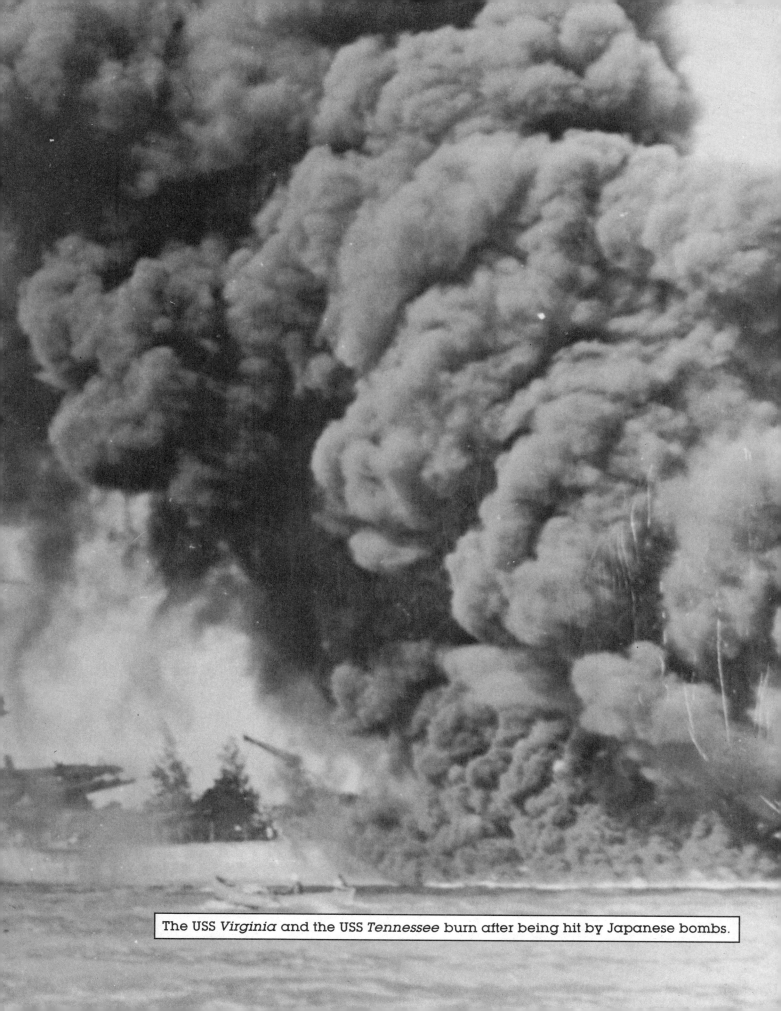

The USS *Virginia* and the USS *Tennessee* burn after being hit by Japanese bombs.

USS *Oklahoma* lays capsized in shallow water after the attack.

grievious blows against the anchored battle-ships off Ford Island.

The *Oklahoma* (29,067 tons, ten 14-inch guns, twenty 5-inch guns, 20.5 knots) took three torpedo hits and began to list to port. One more torpedo slammed into her. She continued her heavy list and then capsized, a horrible fate for such a ship, and the many men who died, locked in the dark bowels as she turned upside down and oxygen slowly ran out . . . dragged across the bottom of a barnacle encrusted hull . . . the *Oklahoma* capsized eight minutes after the attack began.

The *West Virginia*'s officer of the deck, Ensign Roman L. Brooks, thought that the *California* had suffered an accidental internal explosion when he saw an explosion coming from her. Actually, it was one of the first bombs to hit Ford Island, and the *California* was in line with it, but Brooks ordered "Away fire and rescue party!", thus bringing hundreds of men up on deck and avoiding certain death when the first torpedoes hit. The *West Virginia* took six torpedo hits and two bomb hits and was sunk.

Captain Mervyn Bennion remarked at the start of the Japanese attack to his Marine orderly "This is certainly in keeping with their history of surprise attacks." Bennion suffered a stomach wound and died during the attack, although conscious to the end. He was one of the 103 lost and 52 wounded on board that day. Lieutenant Claude Ricketts and Boatswain Mate Billingsley saved the *West Virginia* from the fate of the *Oklahoma* by working the knobs and levers that counterflooded against the flooding caused by the torpedo hits. These two men who knew what to do saved the lives of hundreds of men.

The *Tennessee*, protected from torpedoes because she was inboard of the *West Virginia*, received just two bombs hits, although the debris from the explosion of the *Arizona* hurt her. The *Tennessee* lost only five men and twenty one wounded. The battleship *Maryland* suffered even less, being hit by two bombs and losing only four men and fourteen wounded.

The *California* (34,858, twelve 14-inch guns, twenty 5-inch guns, and 20.5 knots, sistership of *Tennessee*) was badly damaged. While hit by only two torpedoes and two bombs, she was prepared for inspection on Monday—most of

When the initial alarms were sounded, many men looked to the skies with disbelief. However, two successive waves of Japanese air attacks proved the reliability of the early warnings. Spectacular explosions often followed direct hits on ships, such as shown in the photograph of the USS *Shaw*.

her watertight compartments had been opened up or the doors had been loosened. Thus, in an "unbuttoned" state, the *California* flooded easily, and slowly sunk so that by December 10 she was settled on the mud of the bay bottom. She also suffered from severe oil fires and lost a total of 98 men killed and 61 wounded.

The *Nevada* was one of the more fortunate of battleships that day, actually getting underway and attempting to sortie to sea. In the initial few minutes of the attack she suffered one torpedo hit forward and two bomb hits. Ensign Joseph K. Taussig, Jr., used the anti-aircraft on the *Nevada* so well that little other damage was done initially, though he was personally wounded in the leg. By 8:50 A.M. the *Nevada* cast off and began to proceed towards the harbor entrance.

The Japanese, seeing the *Nevada* underway, tried to sink her in the harbor entrance, thus bottling the American fleet up, but, though hitting her five times with bombs, the *Nevada* beached herself in a safe position. Fifty died on her, with 109 wounded.

The only other battleship present was the *Pennsylvania*, only slightly damaged, in drydock with two destroyers, both severely damaged in the attack.

Chaplain Howell M. Forgy served on the *New Orleans* (10,131, nine 8-inch guns, eight 5-inch guns, 32.5 knots) at Pearl Harbor. He remembers:

the clang-clang-clang continued
stubbornly, and the shrill scream of the

The USS *Nevada* moved away from burning ships as salvage and rescue teams went toward the damaged ships in search of survivors. When the Japanese saw the *Nevada* underway, they went after her, hitting her five times.

bo'sun's pipe beeped through the speaker. "All hands to battle stations! This is no drill! This is no drill!"

But I wasn't buffaloed. . . . This must be some admiral's clever idea of how to make an off-hour general quarters drill for the fleet realistic. . . . I ran to the well deck, where I could get a clear view of the harbor. Off to our starboard quarter, about five hundred yards, the mighty *Arizona* was sending a mass of black, oily smoke thousands of feet into the air. The water around her was dotted with debris and a mass of bobbing, oil-covered heads. I could see hundreds of men splashing and trying to swim.

Others were motionless.

Flashes of orange-red flames snapped out of the anti-aircraft guns, bright against the jet clouds ascending all along battleship row. The cage-like formast of the *Arizona* poked through the smoke at a crazy, drunken angle. The *Weavie*—that's what we called the *West Virginia*—looked as though her back had been broken. She was sagging amidships, and her bow and stern angled upward.

Forward of the *Weavie* the *Oklahoma*'s main deck was disappearing beneath the water. She was rolling on her side, and her big bottom was coming up. I could see hundreds of her crew jumping into

The USS *California* was badly damaged after being hit by two torpedoes and two bombs.

The flag still flies.

Damage off Ford Island was mostly done in the first minutes of the attack. The USS *Arizona* is in the foreground; Ford Island, on the right.

The USS *Shaw* was hit with three bombs which exploded her forward magazine. In the explosion, the dry dock was badly damaged.

the water. Dozens of others were crawling along her exposed side and bottom, trying to keep up with the giant treadmill.

I wondered if the devil himself could have immuned these planes against our shells. What was this new, horrible, evil power that turned Pearl Harbor into a bay of terrible explosions, smoking ships, flames, and death? . . . A long ribbon of black crepe trailed out behind it as a plane disappeared. It crashed in the backyard of (the) Naval Hospital. We got one! They could be hit!

I felt better. . . . I guess I shouted and screamed as loudly as any one. Mike Jacobs, master at arms, was standing near me. He grinned at the string of smoke in the sky and drawled, "I guess chaplains can cuss like bo'sun's mates when they have to."

When the *Arizona* (sistership to the *Oklahoma*) blew up at Pearl Harbor, it was not due to a bomb down the stack, but a bomb that hit the forecastle alongside the second main turret. It pierced the deck and exploded the main magazine. As Walter Lord described it, ". . . a huge ball of fire and smoke mushroomed 500 feet into the air. There wasn't so much noise—most of the men say it was more a 'whoom' than a 'bang'—but the concussion was terrific. It stalled the motor of Aviation Ordinanceman Harand Quisdorf's pickup truck as he drove along Ford Island. It hurled Chief

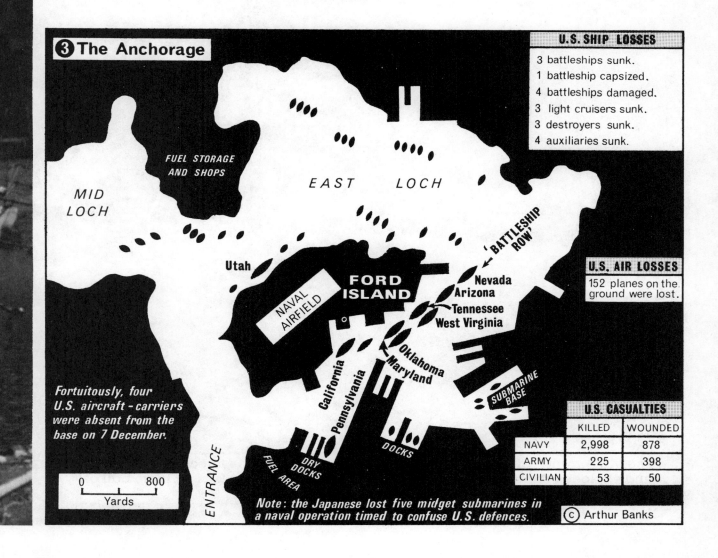

❸ The Anchorage

U.S. SHIP LOSSES

3 battleships sunk.
1 battleship capsized.
4 battleships damaged.
3 light cruisers sunk.
3 destroyers sunk.
4 auxiliaries sunk.

FUEL STORAGE AND SHOPS

EAST LOCH

MID LOCH

Utah

FORD ISLAND

NAVAL AIRFIELD

'BATTLESHIP ROW'

Nevada
Arizona
Tennessee
West Virginia

U.S. AIR LOSSES

152 planes on the ground were lost.

California
Pennsylvania

Oklahoma
Maryland

SUBMARINE BASE

DOCKS

Fortuitously, four U.S. aircraft-carriers were absent from the base on 7 December.

ENTRANCE

FUEL AREA

DRY DOCKS

U.S. CASUALTIES		
	KILLED	WOUNDED
NAVY	2,998	878
ARMY	225	398
CIVILIAN	53	50

0 — 800
Yards

Note: the Japanese lost five midget submarines in a naval operation timed to confuse U.S. defences.

© Arthur Banks

The USS *Arizona* (above) was blown up when a bomb hit the forecastle and exploded the main magazine. An eyewitness described it as "a huge ball of fire and smoke (that) mushroomed 500 feet into the air."

On the other side of Ford Island, the USS *Utah* (above) and the USS *Raleigh* (below) were torpedoed and bombed. The USS *Utah* capsized while the *Raleigh* was held afloat by a repair barge.

Albert Molter against the pipe banister of his basement stairs. It knocked everyone flat on Fireman Stanley H. Rabe's water barge. It blew gunner Carey Garnett and dozens of other men off the *Nevada*. . . . Ensign Vance Fowler off of the *West Virginia*. Far above, Commander Fuchida's bomber trembled like a leaf."

Rear Admiral Isaac C. Kidd was killed, along with Captain Franklin van Valkenburg, just after the quartermaster had reported to the captain a bomb hit. A moment later "the ship was shaking like an earthquake had struck it, and the bridge was in flames." Firefighting continued until 10:32 when she was finally abandoned. Casualties on the *Arizona* were the most of any ship lost that day, a total of 1103 killed and 44 wounded out of 1511 on board on December 1. She had taken one torpedo hit and eight bomb hits.

Captain Cassin Young, winner of the Medal of Honor, of the repair ship *Vestal*, afire from two bomb hits earlier, was anchored next to the *Arizona* when she blew up. Over 100 of the 466 men on board were literally blown overboard from the resulting explosion! The same explosion also put most of the burning fires out. Orders to abandon ship were issued, but countermanded as an oil-covered Cassin Young came up to the officer of the deck and inquired, "Where the hell do you think you're going?" The reply of "We're abandoning ship" brought a "Get back aboard ship! You don't abandon ship on me!"

On the light cruiser *Detroit*, sistership to the *Marblehead* and *Raleigh*, the 3-inch anti-aircraft guns had protector caps on the shells. The men manning the anti-aircraft guns had to bang the shells against the gun shield to knock the protector caps off.

The Marine barracks emptied and for hours they fought with machine guns and rifles as well as patrolling the base. In the process, it was noted that food had not been sent out to the troops, and the cooks and messmen had grabbed rifles and were in the field. Some enterprising Marine opened the brig and the prisoners became prisoners-at-large and cooked! It worked.

The army had two divisions, the 24th and the 25th, on the island of Oahu. Many of the troops joined in the defense that day, and some

When the USS *Oklahoma* took three torpedo hits, it listed to port and capsized in eight minutes. Behind the *Oklahoma*, the USS *Maryland* sits upright but damaged.

died. Unfortunately their anti-aircraft batteries had only training ammunition available, and men of the 27th Infantry regiment remember the one sergeant who refused to issue guns—because he could not release guns without orders from the adjutant.

The *Christian Science Monitor* had a correspondent, Joseph Harsch, in Honolulu on the 7th. Harsch woke up his wife that morning and told her, "Darling, you often have asked me what an air raid sounds like. Listen to this—it's a good imitation." They fell back to sleep a bit later! It was the same Harsch who had interviewed Kimmel the day before. Kimmel had told him, when Harsch asked Kimmel if Japan would attack America in the Far East, "No, young man, I don't think they'd be such damned fools."

As the *Enterprise* and her task force entered Pearl that night, Admiral Halsey surveyed the damage done. Finally he growled, "Before we're through with 'em, the Japanese language will be spoken only in hell!"

Total losses in life for the Americans that day were 2,403 killed, and 1,178 wounded. All eight battleships were sunk or damaged, along with three light cruisers, three destroyers, and four auxiliary craft. The Japanese lost six fighters and fourteen dive bombers. Part of the failure to shoot down more planes was due to poor high altitude anti-aircraft fire. Much of that fire exploded *behind* the planes due in part to the American prewar training methods—training called for towing a target sleeve at speeds no greater than 127 m.p.h. The fire control director could only follow a target moving at 150 m.p.h.

Planes and hangars were bombed during the attack. Photos show a destroyed B-17 (above) and Hangar #5 (opposite above) burning near Hickam Field.

In this photo taken during the attack near Base Hospital #2, Ford Island and burning ships can be seen across the harbor.

No Japanese aircraft in the attack that morning flew that slowly.

Two questions arose from the action that day: Was a second attack by the Japanese air units feasible and were the targets the correct ones? Genda suggested another attack to Nagumo after the second wave of planes returned to the carriers. Genda wanted the primary targets of a second attack to be dockyards and fuel tanks. An "occasional ship" would be an extra. Interestingly enough the proposal was *not* for another attack that day, but the following day. This was because the Japanese did not know where the American carriers were, but they did know that some land planes remained for a possible counterattack. Genda wanted time for further intelligence to come in. Secondly, the Japanese planes had been rearmed with weapons against ships and to change weapons in the afternoon would mean too long a delay during short daylight hours of December. Another attack was feasible, but Nagumo, pleased that he had accomplished his orders, returned home, complacent that he had few losses for such a tremendous victory. Preserving Japan's strongest weapon was important to him. Never again would the Japanese be in such an advantageous position. The war might have turned out differently. It was not unlike winning a great victory in a battle but not following up with a firm pursuit to destroy the remaining enemy forces. Admiral Nimitz said of the failure of Japan to follow up the first attack, "The fact that the Japanese did not return to Pearl Harbor and complete the job was the greatest help to us, for they left their principal enemy with the time to catch his breath, restore his morale, and rebuild his forces."

As far as targets go, most authorities agree that the fuel tanks should have been priority targets. The destruction of the fuel (4,500,000 barrels of oil were present) at Pearl Harbor would have effectively moved the American fleet back to the West Coast and have affected American submarine operations adversely. The submarine arm was left untouched, a grave error, as they could immediately go over to the attack. Ensign Taussig always wondered why the ammunition at West Loch was not bombed. The *Nevada* alone had 1,440 14-inch shells stored there with 2,880 seventy-pound bags of smokeless powder (she was being furnished new projectiles).

The final error by Japan in choice of targets was Pearl Harbor, itself. This surprise attack unified the United States and overnight ended all talk of isolationism. It did not leave America divided or dismayed, but unified the country in a way that no other overt move could have done. Rear Admiral Chuici Hara, commander of the 5th carrier division, remarked that Roosevelt should have given the Japanese a medal for the attack! The attack insured that the war was fought to the bitter end. The only way Japan could have justified the attack would have been if at least one or more American carriers had been present on December 7th at Pearl.

There were many tragedies yet to be enacted after the air raid. Internment camps for Japanese nationals and even U.S. citizens followed. Colonel Cornelius C. Smith (U.S.M.C.) told of a Filipino-American coming by his headquarters on December 10. The Filipino wanted to see the general. The then Sergeant Smith said that the general was busy and to talk to him instead. With a grin on his face, the Filipino related how he had "Got four Japs in the truck, no good man, I kill them." They were there, in the truck. The Filipino then said that he "Got six more under house," and he did. The Japanese had been his neighbors on Oahu.

Army and navy planes were destroyed in the attack. This photo shows a demolished army amphibian plane. More than 80 navy planes were destroyed in the attack.

American casualties were 2,403 for the one-day attack.

Mass graves were quickly filled.

General Douglas MacArthur

The Fall of the Philippines

The Japanese viewed the Philippines as an important enemy bastion lying on their flank to South Asia. If Japan did not go to war with the U.S.A., then at any point if America came into the war, Japan's vital shipping lanes would be threatened. So, even though the Philippines were not that rich in resources, Japan felt she must attack and take the Philippines. One benefit to Japan would be the use of the southern islands in this vast archipelago. From those islands Japan would move air power in and begin the attack against the Dutch East Indies.

The situation in the Philippines was unique and fascinating at the beginning of the war. The main battle was fought on Luzon, the largest island, where the capital, Manila, is located. Originally, under the Rainbow warplans, the garrison in the Philippines fell back to Bataan Peninsula at Manila Harbor, and turned it into a fortress, which held for six months. The American fleet was supposed to appear from the east to save the situation. In reality, most thoughtful leaders looked at the garrison in the Philippines as a forlorn hope.

In April of 1941 General Douglas MacArthur, retired from the American army but in command of the Philippine army preparing for independence under the presidency of Manuel

Quezon, introduced a new war plan for the Philippines. MacArthur felt that with large reinforcements, especially in long range and over-rated B-17 bombers and fighters (the P-40E), that he could hold Luzon, the main island, and cause havoc to the Japanese with the new B-17s. Another advantage to holding the Philippines was that from there the army could be expanded without limits, unlike America's home armies still under pre-war congressional restraint. When MacArthur advocated that older World War I equipment be sent to help this rearmament effort, it was implemented.

MacArthur had the support of the American Asiatic Fleet made up of Admiral Thomas C. Hart's flagship the heavy cruiser *Houston*, one old light cruiser, and thirteen World War I four-piper destroyers (named for their distinctive smokestacks). These forces headed south so they would not be overwhelmed by Japanese air and sea power. Also present were various small craft, including PT boats and seventeen submarines. The submarines could have been a decisive weapon, especially against slow Japanese transports, if the torpedoes worked. For almost two years the torpedoes ran too deep and would not explode, if lucky enough to hit, when impact was directly at 90 degrees on the target. They only exploded at acute angles. What made the situation worse was that it was not recognized as an ordnance problem and was blamed on the submarine commanders and their tactics and lack of ability!

On December 7th, in the Philippines, were thirty five B-17s (with thirteen due to arrive shortly), 107 P-40Es (700 mile range, 6 MGs, 354 m.p.h.), and a few more than seventy older fighters (mostly P-35As). The biggest advantage, or so the Americans thought, with having the P-40Es, was that there were no Japanese fighters that had the range to escort Japanese bombers from Formosa. Thus, the Japanese would be forced to establish airbases on Luzon before adequate fighter protection appeared.

This was an incorrect assumption, as the Japanese Zero, with the naval air forces, based in Formosa, could fly to strategic American airfields at Clark and range over most of the north-central portion of Luzon. All the Zeros not on carriers were based on Formosa. This meant that Japan did not need carriers for oper-

ations against Luzon, but could employ them against Pearl Harbor.

The army situation looked promising for MacArthur. He had a regiment of Marines, the 4th, though MacArthur never used it except for garrison work. He had a division of regulars in the form of the Philippine scouts (primarily long service and very loyal Filipinos, about 10,233 officers and men) and a second reserve division of retired constabulary and scouts. There also existed ten Philippine divisions, each of 7500 men. The latter, however, were newly mobilized, the third regiment of each division having only been called up a few days before the war started. They were also poorly equipped, especially in artillery and machine guns. (The rifles, old Springfields, were overly large for the dimunitive stature of the average Filipino soldier.)

Additionally, MacArthur had the 192nd and 194th Tank Battalion (each consisting of Company A, B, and D) of 54 Stuarts each (12.23 tons, one 37mm gun, two MGs, 51mm armor, 36 m.p.h. crew of 4). Also formed were two provisional self-propelled units made up of 75mm guns mounted on trucks. Douglas MacArthur could field a fair amount of artillery, including 155mm field guns. Finally, he had a fortress at Corregidor which, as long as it held out, made Manila Harbor a bottle with Corregidor the cork—the Japanese could not use Manila until Corregidor was captured.

Most of this force was based on Luzon, although three Filipino divisions and minor units were based on other islands in the Philippine archipelago. A small but interesting battle for Mindanao transpired between Japan and the Filipino-American army in April and May of 1942. Facing the Filipino-American force was the Kawamura detachment and Kawaguchi detachment.

The Japanese navy totally dominated this area of the Pacific, and with the loss of the *Prince of Wales* and *Repulse* on December 10, had no fears of losing it, even temporarily.

In the air the Japanese army fielded the 5th Air Division and the Navy based the 21st and 23rd Air Flotillas. Also present at Kagi Airfield in Formosa was the 1001st Air Transport Unit and the 1st and 3rd Yokosuka Special Naval Landing Force. Numbering 849 men each, with

Typical Japanese Independent Units Used in the Philippines

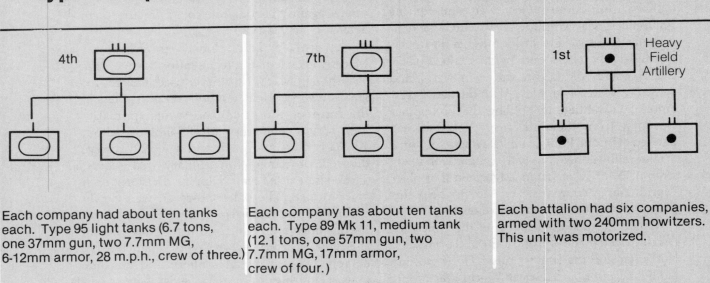

4th

Each company had about ten tanks each. Type 95 light tanks (6.7 tons, one 37mm gun, two 7.7mm MG, 6-12mm armor, 28 m.p.h., crew of three.)

7th

Each company has about ten tanks each. Type 89 Mk 11, medium tank (12.1 tons, one 57mm gun, two 7.7mm MG, 17mm armor, crew of four.)

1st Heavy Field Artillery

Each battalion had six companies, armed with two 240mm howitzers. This unit was motorized.

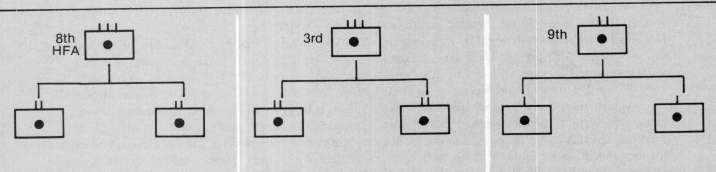

8th HFA

The 8th had a total of sixteen 100mm pieces, horse-drawn.

3rd

The 3rd Independent Infantry gun regiment had two companies with each battalion. Each company had four 37mm type 94 guns, horse-drawn.

9th

The 9th Independent Heavy Artillery battalion had each motorized company armed with two 150mm type 89 guns.

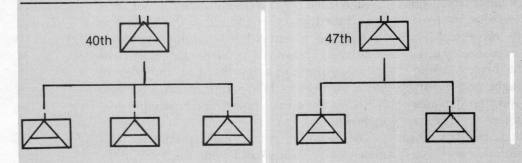

40th

Each company had four 75mm Type 88 anti-aircraft guns.

47th

Each company had four 75mm type 88 anti-aircraft guns.

These are typical units used in the Philippine campaign by Japan. Note that not all sources agree. For example, some show the 1st heavy fired artillery as having twenty-four 150mm howitzers.

Later, in February, after General Homma was stalled in front of Bataan, the Japanese Imperial Headquarters sent the 4th infantry division, and more independent units to aid General Homma. The 4th was poorly equipped (it still had cavalry for reconnaissance), and 11,000 men.

5TH AIR DIVISION

4th Air Brigade

50th Air Regiment (3 fighter squads)	36 Nates (390 mile range, 2 MGs, 292 mph - obsolete)
8th Air Regiment (1 reconnaissance squad)	9 Babs (1,491 mile range, 1 MG, 298 mph)
(3 light bomber squads)	27 Lilys (1,230 mile range, 3 MGs, 661 pound bombload, 298 mph) 2 Dinahs (1,537 mile range, 1 MG, 375 mph - reconnaissance)
16th Air Regiment (3 light bomber squads)	27 Anns (1,056 mile range, 2 MGs, 661 pound bomb load, 263 mph - older than the Lily)
14th Air Regiment (3 bomber squads)	18 Sallys (932 mile range, 6 MGs, 1,653 pound bomb load, 268 mph - Hurricanes and P-40s had advantage on the Sally)

Attached to 5th Air Division

24th Air Regiment (3 fighter squad)	36 Nates
76th Independent Air Squadron	9 Babs
10th Independent Air Unit 52nd Independent Air Squadron	9 Sonias (660 mile range, 3 MGs, 441 pound bomb load, 263 mph - popular well protected ground support aircraft)
74th Independent Air Squadron	12 Marys (826 mile range, 2 MGs, 661 pound bomb load, 263 mph - obsolete)

11TH AIR FLEET

21st Air Flotilla (based on Formosa)

Kanoya Air Group (bombers)	27 Bettys (3,749 mile range, 3 MGs, 1 20mm cannon, 1,764 pound bomb load or torpedo, 266 m.p.h.)
1st Air Group (bombers)	36 Nells (2,722 mile range, 3 MGs, 1 20mm cannon, 1,764 pound bomb load or torpedo 232 m.p.h. - older version of Betty. Design initiated by Yamamoto in 1933), the long range of the Nell was a real surprise to the Allies.
Higashi-ko Air Group (reconnaissance)	27 Mavis - based at Palau (2,981 mile range, 3 MGs, 1 20mm cannon, 211 m.p.h. - extended range to 3,779 miles.)
1001st Air Unit (transports)	25 Tina (Nell style) transports - for Yokosuka Special Naval Landing Force (Japanese Marines) paratroops (1 MG, 216 m.p.h.)

23rd Air Flotilla

Takao Air Group (bombers)	54 Bettys
Thainan Air Group (fighters)	54 Zekes (1,160 mile range, 2 MGs, 2 20mm cannon, 331.5 m.p.h. - the Zero was the best with an extended range of 1,930 miles. Some 837 were built by March of 1942
	6 Claudes (746 mile range, 2 MGs, 270 m.p.h. - the plane the Zero replaced. The light aircraft carriers Ryujo, Hosho, and Zuiho and garrison areas began the war with this plane.)
(reconnaissance)	8 Babs
3rd Air Group (fighters)	45 Zekes
	7 Claudes
(reconnaissance)	7 Babs

Because of the vast geographical position of Japan's theater, the Imperial Japanese Navy and Army had a constant need for long range reconnaissance aircraft. Ranges are given for normal distances, but extended ranges were commonly used with reduced bomb loads and/or weight. For example, the Sally was used for attack in central Luzon from Formosa with a range of 1,680 miles.

THE ANATOMY OF A JAPANESE INVASION

What follows are a series of charts showing what the Japanese directed towards the Filipino-American army under General Douglas MacArthur in the first five months of the war. From the first air raids on December 8, 1941, to the fall of Corregidor Island, the long and bloody struggle for control of the Philippine islands consumed blood, time, and treasure. Yet, the Japanese mustered an army and air force that was not all first rate, but in actuality a mixed force of first, second, as well as third rate units.

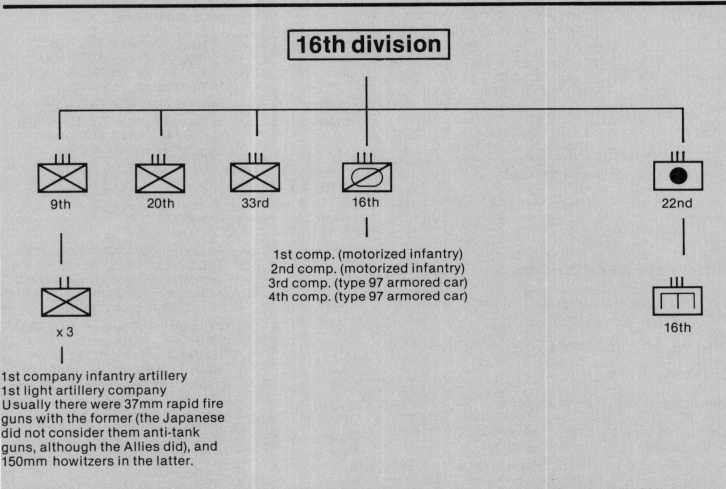

16th division

9th   20th   33rd   16th   22nd

x 3

1st comp. (motorized infantry)
2nd comp. (motorized infantry)
3rd comp. (type 97 armored car)
4th comp. (type 97 armored car)

16th

1st company infantry artillery
1st light artillery company
Usually there were 37mm rapid fire guns with the former (the Japanese did not consider them anti-tank guns, although the Allies did), and 150mm howitzers in the latter.

Each infantry battalion has three infantry companies, one machine gun company, and a battalion atillery platoon, the latter containing two 70 mm howitzers. The 70 mm had a range of about 3,000 yards firing a 8.3 pound high explosive shell.

One battalion of each regiment was mounted on bicycles.

The 22nd Field Artillery Regiment was made up of three battalions, the 1st being motorized, while the 2nd and 3rd were horse drawn.

Numbering about 2,000 men, the 1st had 12 75mm field guns with a range of 13,300 yards firing high explosive armor piercing shrapnel, or smoke. The 2nd and 3rd had twenty four 105 mm howitzers between them with a range of 14,200 yards, firing high explosives only.

The 16th Engineer Regiment consisted of two companies, the first being motorized, the second on foot.

Support units include transport, medical, ordance, water purification,

headquarters (usually 300 men), and veterinary.

Please note that the recon regiment and engineer regiment were regiments in name only and in actual size were much smaller in size. The former numbered either 440 or 650 men (sources vary). Each infantry regiment in the 16th had 2,850 men each.

Type 97 armored car or tankette, weighed 4.25 tons, had one 37mm, four 12mm armor, 26 m.p.h., and a crew of two.

48th division

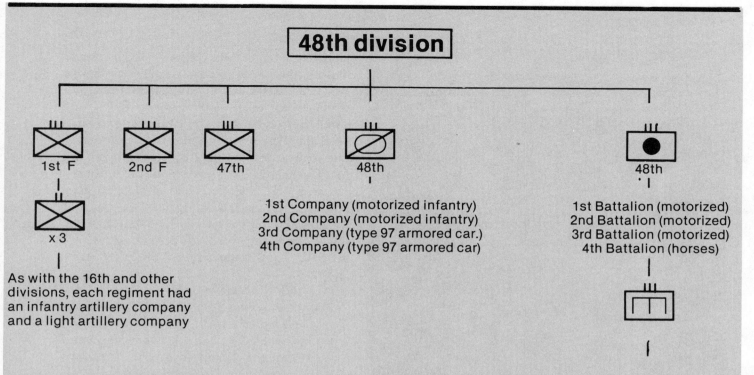

1st F	2nd F	47th

48th

48th

x 3

1st Company (motorized infantry)
2nd Company (motorized infantry)
3rd Company (type 97 armored car.)
4th Company (type 97 armored car)

1st Battalion (motorized)
2nd Battalion (motorized)
3rd Battalion (motorized)
4th Battalion (horses)

As with the 16th and other divisions, each regiment had an infantry artillery company and a light artillery company

The 48th was an elite division and was considered by Japanese standards to be a motorized unit. Each infantry battalion had four infantry companies, one machine gun company and one battalion

artillery platoon. The 48th could move one third of her infantry by truck, one-third by bicycle, while the final third marched. Wartime strength in the invasion of the Philippines was 15,663. It was used

in the invasion of Java and spent the rest of the war there.

F = Formosa-Consider the armament of the 16th as typical.

65th brigade

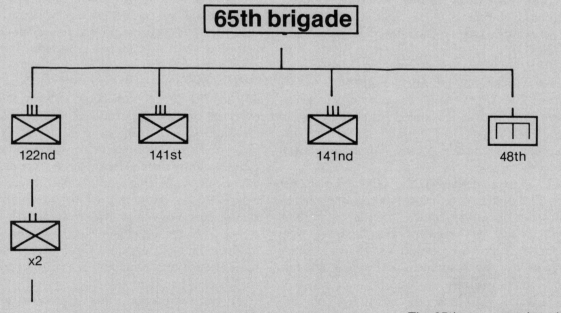

122nd	141st	141nd	48th

x2

Each regiment, note only 2 battalions, had a field-gun company, a light artillery platoon. Equipment would tend to be older marks. Each battalion had three infantry companies and a machine gun company.

The 65th was a garrison brigade and would resemble a landwehr unit. The 65th numbered 7,300 and was entirely on foot. Though a second line unit, it was used heavily at Bataan after the 48th division was withdrawn for operations in the Dutch East Indies.

Vice President Sergio Osmena left the Philippines with President Manuel Quezon and General MacArthur. Osmena later returned to the Philippines as president with MacArthur.

750 of them being combat troops, they were Imperial Japanese Navy parachute troops. These units were saved for use in the Dutch East Indies.

The Japanese army attacking MacArthur's army was actually inferior in numbers by a factor of 2 to 1, yet the Japanese army was a veteran force with a clear objective solidly planned for. It also ended up dominating the air and sea, sapping the morale of the Filipino-American force.

The Japanese planned to open the war against the Philippines with an air raid against various airbases on Luzon, but as it was night there when Pearl was bombed, the Japanese were concerned that they would not gain a surprise against the American airforce. But luck and fate took a strange turn.

It was fogged in on the morning of the 8th over Formosa, so the Japanese could not leave for the attack. With nervous apprehension the Japanese feared that by the time they would be able to leave for the raid, the Philippines would certainly be aware of the attack on Pearl and would be alert for an air attack . . . yet the Japanese caught many planes on the ground that morning and inflicted terrible losses on the American Army Air Corps that morning, destroying fifty three P-40s, eighteen B-17s, and about thirty other aircraft. Tactical surprise had been complete with bombing attacks at Clark followed up with an hour of strafing by 84 Zeros. The Japanese lost seven planes. The American army was equipped with anti-aircraft guns that had ammunition dating to 1932—much of the ammunition were duds, and "most of the fuses were badly corroded" according to Colonel Sage, commanding the 200th Coast Artillery.

Why did this disaster occur?

The post-mortem will probably never completely reveal all the truth, but part of the problem lies with the relationship between MacArthur, the Philippines, and President Quezon. MacArthur had been raised by his father (Arthur MacArthur, an American Civil War hero at Chattanooga and governor-general of the Philippines) in these islands at the turn of the century, and loved that nation. Quezon hoped briefly that he could declare neutrality for the Philippines, thus sparing that country the impact of war. MacArthur, aware of this, possibly wanted to see neutrality turned into reality, and his orders said that he was not to do anything until " . . . Japan commit(s) the first overt act".

So, when word of the air raid on Pearl Harbor arrived, MacArthur could still say that no overt act of war had occurred, yet, against the Philippines. The army air commander, Major General Lewis H. Brereton, wanted to attack Formosa immediately, but could not get permission from MacArthur and his staff. Meanwhile a Japanese army air raid on the northern portion of Luzon did cause the American Air Force to rise from the airfields in Central Luzon .

Over the next few days the Japanese gained total control of the air and sea, in preparation for making landings.

The Japanese faced a major problem in that they lacked sufficient ships to land troops in the more vital Malaya invasion *and* conduct major landings on Luzon. So, the initial move was to land small detachments on the northern portion of Luzon, in sparsely populated, mountainous terrain, with few and poor roads, left virtually undefended by MacArthur. In the first two weeks of the war, the Japanese were able to consolidate these early gains and bring air units onto Luzon.

With the invasion of Malaya accomplished, ships were moved northward to pick up the bulk of the 48th and the 16th divisions. The 48th landed between the 22nd and 24th of December at Lingayen Gulf, north of Manila, while the 16th came ashore at Lamon Bay on the 24th, to the south of Manila. The Japanese plan called for an advance towards Manila and a battle of encirclement, a favorite strategy learned from von Moltke in the 19th century and employed in the Russo-Japanese War of 1904–05. MacArthur had deployed his troops, the I and II Corps, at various landing points along the coast.

The landing on the north side of Lingayen Gulf, involving eightly-five transports with supporting warships including two battleships, witnessed almost the entire 48th Division coming ashore with both tank regiments. The Tanaka Detachment hit the American flank at the same time as the landing to provide distraction as the Japanese came ashore. Four Filipino divisions faced the Japanese with a understrength Philippine Scout cavalry regiment, the 26th, the latter horsed and with some light armored scout cars.

The invading Japanese army was a veteran force with a well planned objective. This photo, depicting the march on Manila, was taken from a Japanese propaganda booklet entitled "Victory on the March."

The infamous Navy Hotel near the Cavite Navy Base, a popular sailors' hangout, was destroyed in the invasion.

What is interesting about this landing is that it came as no surprise, other than that it came on December 22, instead of in January. It was a logical landing point and maneuvers had been conducted in that area many times. Homer Lea in his prophetic *The Valour of Ignorance*, written in 1909, mapped the exact spot for invasion by the Japanese. Yet the official historian of the campaign, Dr. Louis Morton, wrote later, "Despite the warning, the Americans seem to have been ill prepared to drive off the invaders."

The main problem was that the Filipino troops were simply not capable of engaging in combat in a mobile environment. For example, the 71st Division advanced with a battery of self-propelled 75mm guns against the Japanese. They did not execute their maneuver rapidly,

and instead were attacked by the 4th Tank Regiment and 48th Reconnaissance Regiment. The tanks were a threat that the 71st had little defense against, and so they fell back and Baguio, the Philippines' summer capital, fell.

Next the Japanese moved to consolidate their invasion and push southward. They accomplished this quite easily, with only the 26th Cavalry offering any serious resistance. The 26th covered the withdrawal of the Filipino divisions, and in the words of General Wainwright, "Here was true cavalry delaying action, fit to make a man's heart sing. Pierce (the commander) that day upheld the best traditions of the cavalry service." The 26th was also reduced in half due to fighting losses. The Japanese used the 4th Tank Regiment as a point unit, and the

The Cavite Navy Base across the bay from Manila was nearly destroyed during the Japanese attack. In the area of the bell behind this church 70 unidentified casualties were discovered.

Torpedoes were stored in the submarine base at Cavite.

Damaged street in the old walled city in Cavite.

Filipino-American Army had virtually no weapons to stop it. The effect on morale of the continuous retreat, without proper weapons to stop the enemy, and no hope for relief was devastating.

To the south on Luzon, at Lamon Bay, the 20th Regiment of the 16th Division in 24 transports landed on 23rd of December. Some air support came from the Japanese seaplane carrier the *Mizuho* (12,150 tons, six 5-inch guns, 24 floatplanes, 22 knots). Also supporting was the Japanese force that had landed at Legaspi. It had covered the 150 miles from that port city and appeared on the flank of the Filipino 51st Division. The 51st resisted, but was forced to fall back, primarily due to the pressure of the 16th Reconnaissance Regiment. Total Japanese losses were 268 killed and wounded and 7,000 men of the 16th Division were ashore.

The rapid advance of the Japanese on the 23rd and the 24th of December, and intelligence information that 80,000 to 100,000 Japanese troops had landed, convinced MacArthur that he could not defeat the enemy on the beaches as he had hoped. Therefore an order to retire to Bataan was issued. Insufficient stores were rushed there, something that could have been accomplished earlier in the campaign. Manila was declared an "open city," and the Japanese entered Manila before the end of December. Yet

General Homma lands on the coast at Lingayen Gulf on December 24, 1941. Four years later General MacArthur returned to the Philippines to liberate the island from the Japanese. The famous photographs which depict MacArthur's return landing are ironically similar to this one.

The Japanese advance south to Manila was supported by the 4th tank regiment.

before the withdrawal was complete, several short sharp actions were fought as the Filipino-American army fell back to one river after another on the island of Luzon. The Japanese advanced down the central valley, with another prong racing down on the western side of the valley.

In the south the Filipino 51st steadily fell back suffering losses the entire way. It had to hold long enough to allow Manila to be emptied of supplies, but it also had to be able to retreat fast enough when called upon to race through the city and slip into Bataan on the north side of Manila Bay. Manila acted as a bottleneck. Con-

sidering the green troops and lack of equipment, this operation was successfully carried out and no major units were cut off in the withdrawal into Bataan. This was due in part to the Japanese belief that with the fall of Manila the war in the Philippines would be over.

Thus, the Japanese did not expect much resistance from the Filipino-American army after Manila fell, and were surprised, in a series of sharp bloody actions, before Bataan, to find an enemy that was no longer retreating.

The fight began as Malaya fell quickly, and General Homma's Japanese 14th Army was mired in a slow siege of the peninsula which incurred high losses to both sides. A student of the campaign, H.P. Wilmott, said General Homma had "the three most successful generals in history . . . . Their names were Hunger, Disease, and Despair."

The "battling bastards of Bataan" kept the smaller Japanese army checked, defeating their attacks from both frontal and flanking amphibious operations. Eventually, the 4th Division was sent as a reinforcement to the 14th Army. The lack of food, medicine, ammunition, and

supplies took their toll. Bataan had to surrender, leaving Corregidor holding out, but for how long?

There had been a command change. MacArthur, along with President Quezon, was ordered out to Australia. The actual journey began on March 12, 1942, with the famous PT-boat (54 tons, four 21-inch torpedoes, 39 knots) ride to the southern islands and an eventual flight to Australia. In Australia, feeling terribly threatened by an advancing and victorious enemy,

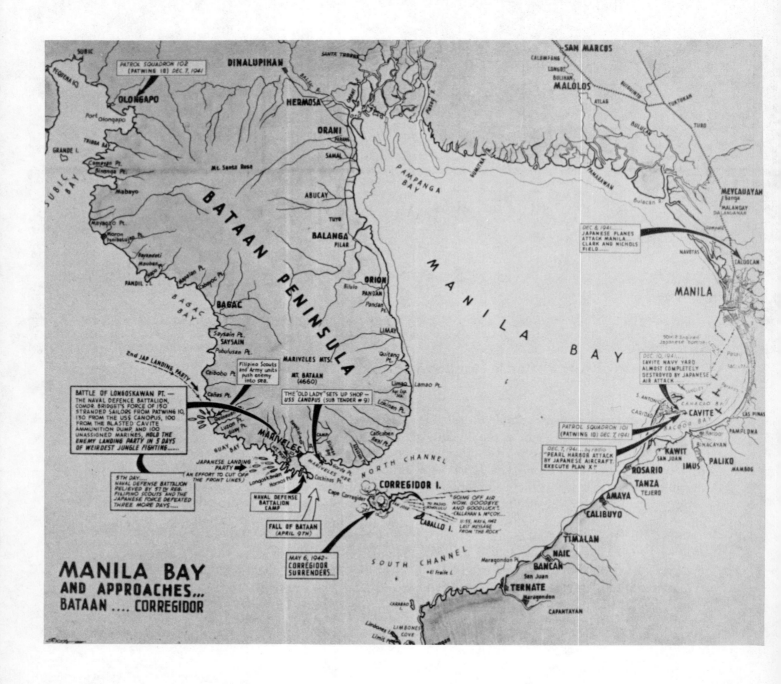

Japanese morale was high during their assault on the Bataan peninsula.

During the Death March, prisoners carried dead and dying comrades whenever possible. Many prisoners were shot along the road or left to die in the jungle.

MacArthur symbolized the commitment America had made to the defense of Australia, a defense that Great Britain had failed in. General Douglas MacArthur's reception by Australia was both strong and positive. MacArthur's determination to fulfill his "I shall return" promise stood largely on the base that Australia gave him.

Bataan eventually fell on April 9th, and 78,000 men became prisoners. Thousands died in the Bataan Death March to prisoner of war camps. Many Japanese acted in callous and barbaric fashion towards the half starved prisoners; many who fell by the wayside were shot. Food and water was scanty, but some prisoners did escape into the bush to fight on.

For Corregidor, with thousands living on short rations in tunnels, under frightful bombardment, the end was inevitable. In May of 1942 Japanese troops, and three tanks, landed on the island. On the 6th General Wainwright, commanding since MacArthur's departure, surrendered the entire archipelago, including Filipino-American troops fighting elsewhere in the Philippines.

When Bataan fell in April, 78,000 men became prisoners. The forced march of the prisoners to their prison camp was so severe that thousands died in what is known as "The Bataan Death March."

There are two key points about the fighting in the Philippines. First, General Douglas MacArthur, although he received the Medal of Honor for this campaign, conducted it very poorly. His planes were caught on the ground, his fortress redoubt was inadequately prepared, his strategy in allowing Japanese forces to consolidate their position in the north combined with his inability to deal with a smaller enemy army. But, he learned from his errors, and in the next few years established beyond a doubt that he was one of the most brilliant generals that America has ever produced.

Secondly, the Filipino-American army had been unable to stop the Japanese, an enemy that for most of the campaign was never greater than nine battalions in strength. The Japanese timetable was not affected greatly, and although General Homma's career in the Japanese army was finished, Japan had depleted few resources to capture these islands.

The fighting in southern Bataan was fierce. Here Japanese flame-thrower captures a blockhouse in the main defense line at the tip of the peninsula.

General Wainright, tired and exhausted, surrenders on May 6 to General Homma on the front porch of a house on Bataan.

Members of a guerrilla band known as the ''Scorpions'' were evacuated from a small island off the Philippine mainland several weeks after the fall of Manila.

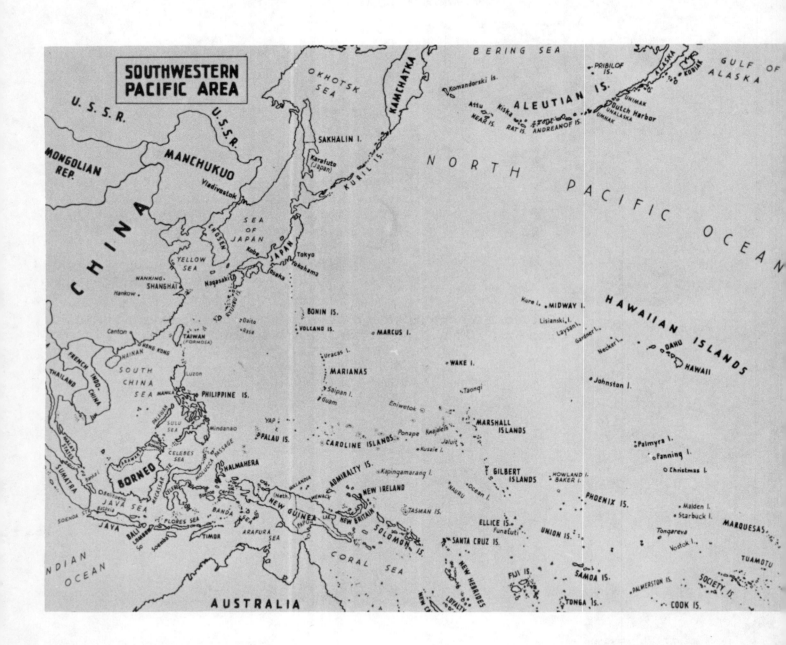

The Malayan Campaign

Winston Churchill noted that the fall of Malaya, and the surrender at Singapore, was the " . . . worst disaster and largest capitulation in British history." Though the British outnumbered the Japanese forces in overall numbers, the Japanese were facing second rate units that were poorly equipped and trained for static warfare, and for the most part, suffered from inept leadership, lack of air and sea support, and were supported by an almost feudal society with a civil administration unable to properly aid the military. Field Marshal Wavell wrote in a dispatch two days after Singapore fell, "The trouble goes a long way back; climate, the atmosphere of the country (the whole of Malaya has been asleep for at least 200 years), lack of vigour in our peacetime training, the cumbrousness of our tactics and equipment, and the real difficulty of finding an answer to the very skillful and bold tactics of the Japanese in this jungle fighting."

Malaya itself was an obstacle. The climate, high humidity, heat, and rain is such that it takes a minimum of two months for troops to get used to it. The heavy rains on this peninsula create swamp-like conditions in vegetation-chocked rivers and streams. Mountains peaking at 7,000 feet run down the center of the island, inhibiting movement. The west coast of Malaya (i.e., furthest away from Japan) had most of the population and ports, but both coasts had important ports that needed to be protected from Japanese landings. Allied strength was also dispersed by the need to garrison rear areas of civil unrest in the various airfields (built often in spots that the RAF wanted them in, but not where the British army, which had to defend them, wanted them located), airfields with an inadequate number of planes of obsolete types.

The sought-after jewel of Malaya was the naval base and seaport of Singapore. Sitting on the Straits of Malacca, it was a base into which Britain had poured resources for twenty years, so that the British fleet would have a naval base which it could operate if engaged in a war with Japan. Lord Jellicoe, the former commander of the British fleet at the battle of Jutland, and key point man in getting the base of Singapore started, concluded in 1919 that, "the safety of the bases of Colombo and Singapore is vital to Australia and New Zealand; and the safety of Sydney and other naval bases in the South Pacific, and of Singapore and Colombo, is of the greatest importance to India." Jellicoe had earlier stated that "Japan is as much a bogey to India as it is to Australia." As for Australia, Jellicoe rightly concluded that *it must be recognized that Australia is powerless against a strong naval and military power without the assistance of the British Fleet.* (Jellicoe's italics). So the construction of a base at Singapore was recommended to protect both colonial India and the underpopulated and immense Australian

ORDER OF BATTLE FOR JAPANESE 25th ARMY

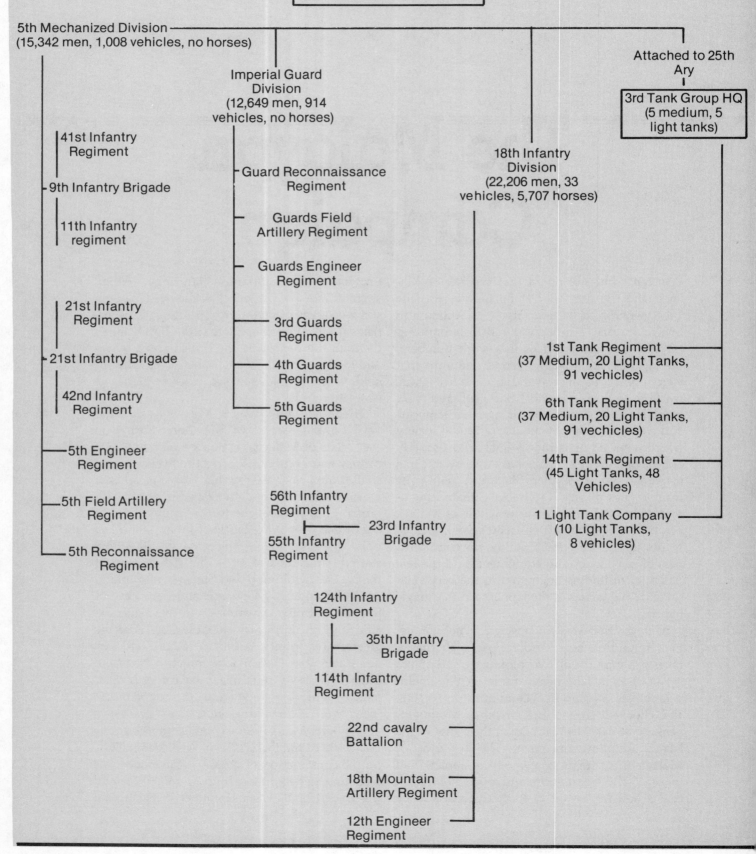

3RD AIR DIVISION
(used for Malaya operation)

3rd Air Brigade

59th Fighter Regiment (3 fighter squads.)	36 Oscars (745 mile range, 2 MGs, 308 mph)
27th Light Bomber Regiment (3 light bomber squads)	27 Lilys
75th Light Bomber Regiment (3 light bomber squads)	27 Lilys
90th Light Bomber Regiment (3 light bomber squads)	27 Lilys

7th Air Brigade

64th Fighter Regiment (3 fighter squads)	36 Oscars
12th Heavy Bomber Regiment (3 heavy bomber squads)	27 Sallys
60th Heavy Bomber Regiment (3 heavy bomber squads)	27 Sallys
98th Heavy Bomber Regiment (3 heavy bomber squads)	27 Sallys

12th Air Brigade

1st Fight Group (3 fighter squads)	36 Nates
11th Fight Group (3 fighter squads)	36 Nates
81st Reconnaissance Regiment	9 Babs & Dinahs

15th Independent Air Group

71st Independent Reconnaissance Squad	9 Sonias
73rd Independent Reconnaissance Squad	9 Sonias
89th Independent Reconnaissance Squad	9 Idas (767 mile range, 2 MGs, 216 mph)
12th and 20th Anti-aircraft Regiments Attached	

11TH AIR FLEET

22nd Air Flotila (based near Saigon)

Genzan Air Group	36 Nells
Takao Air Group detachment	12 Claudes
Mihoro Air Group	36 Nells

Detached from the 21st Air Flotilla

Kanoya Air Group	27 Bettys

Detached from the 23rd Air Flotilla

Tainan Air Group Detachment (Yamada Unit)	25 Zeke or better known as Zeros with 6 Babs attached.

Stationed at Rong Sam Lem Bay (Near the Thailand border) were the three Seaplane Tenders *Kimikawa Mara* (15 seaplanes), *Sanyo Maru* (8 seaplanes), and *Sagara Maru* (8 seaplanes). The various ships carried another 25 scout planes.

continent from invasion by Japan. Its loss would expose Australia to raids or invasion and would open the Indian Ocean to attack. Malaya also contained 38% of the world's rubber and 58% of the world's tin.

Vice Admiral Ugaki, the chief of staff to Admiral Yamamoto, drew a list in December of 1941 of what Japanese forces in Southern Asia hoped to achieve. Those goals were:

1) The destruction of the enemy fleet.

2) The destruction of enemy bases and the securing of Japanese bases.

3) The encouragement of anti-British movements in India.

4) An East-West link-up between the Axis powers.

It should be noted that Japan at this time envisioned an independent Arabia and India liberated by Axis forces. The capture of Singapore was a key step in the implementation of these goals. Only the halting of the Japanese army on the Burma-India border and the defeat of the Japanese navy at Midway could halt the implementation of these goals.

The first step in the seizure of Malaya was the occupation of French Indochina, more important than the Burma Road in supplying the Nationalist China forces at this stage of the war. So when France fell to Nazi Germany in 1940, the Japanese took that opportunity to seize Indochina in a bloodless move, a move completed by July of 1941. It was this seizure that brought about the trade embargo by the Allies against Japan which was the final straw forcing her to attack Pearl Harbor.

To conduct the attack against Malaya, Lieutenant General Tomoyuki Yamashita was chosen to command the 25th Army. Yamashita graduated fifth in his class at the Military Academy at Hiroshima in 1908. Probably the most brilliant Japanese general of the war, his campaign and victory in Malaya was one of the most outstanding campaigns of World War II. Thus he earned the title of "Tiger of Malaya." Yamashita finished the war in command of the main Japanese army on Luzon in the Philippines, beaten by MacArthur, but he was not conquered by him. He surrendered with the end of the war. However, the atrocities committed in Malaya by troops under his command were his death sentence at the war crimes trial after the war.

Four divisions were assigned to the 25th Army, but Yamashita, because of the problems entailed with supplying four divisions, asked only for three. Yamashita was assigned the excellent 5th (motorized—by Japanese standards and having four instead of the usual three regiments), the 18th and the Imperial Guard divisions. It should be noted that the guard division was actually a newly trained formation without recent combat experience and was not highly regarded. Further, the commander of it, Takuma Nishimura, represented another faction within the Japanese army than the faction that Yamashita was from. To complicate matters further, Prime Minister General Tojo, who resented Yamashita's army-wide popularity, assigned Colonel Tsuji directly to Yamashita's staff to keep an eye on Yamashita. This was done after Tsuji had completed his vital assignment of preparing the plans for the campaign.

Colonel Tsuji had thirty officers on Hainan Island in China and Formosa (Taiwan today) planning the campaign against Malaya. The environment in South China prepared these officers for the Malayan climate and the conditions they would have to fight in. Various units in the campaign were preparing on Hainan and Formosa as early as April of 1941. After the Japanese victory in Malaya, due in part from this planning, Colonel Tsuji remarked, "For the first time in history, an army carried out a blitzkrieg on bicycles!" For intelligence, the Japanese used over 180 officers who in turn recruited locals, for preparing for the invasion of Malaya. The German Abwehr (Secret Service) commented on this level of preparation as being even more thorough than when the Nazi Germany planned the invasion of Norway in 1940.

Also to assist in the campaign, Yamashita had the 3rd Tank Regiment, three engineer regiments (needed to repair the numerous destroyed bridges of Malaya), and two additional regiments of heavy artillery. The 3rd Air Division of the army assisted, and the Japanese navy also gave aid beyond transporting the initial invasion force.

Facing the invading Japanese army was the more numerous but inferior British army under the intelligent but uninspiring Lieutenant General Arthur E. Percival. The overall commander

Allied Naval Strength in the Far East on December 17, 1941

EASTERN FLEET BASED AT SINGAPORE

Vice-Admiral Phillips, commanding

Battleships
Prince of Wales

Battle Cruisers
Repulse

Light Cruisers
Danae, Dragon, Durban, *and the* Mauritius *(refitting at port)*

Destroyers
Electra, Express, Tenedos, Vampire, Scout, Thanet, *with the* Encounter, Jupiter, Stronghold, Vendetta, Isis *refitting at port*

EAST INDIES SQUADRON AT CEYLON

Vice-Admiral Arbuthnot, commanding

Battleships
Revenge

Light Aircraft Carriers
Hermes *refitting*

Heavy Cruisers
Exeter

Light Cruisers
Enterprise *refitting*

AUSTRALIAN AND NEW ZEALAND SQUADRONS

Rear Admiral Crace, commanding

Heavy Cruisers
Canberra *(Australia on route from South Altantic)*

Light Cruisers
Adelaide, Perth, Achilles, Leander, *with the* Hobart on route from the *Mediterranean*

Destroyers
Le Triomphant *(Free French) and the* Stuart *and* Voyager *refitting*

NETHERLAND EAST INDIES FLEET

Vice-Admiral Helfrich, commanding

Light Cruisers
De Ruyter, Java *and* Tromp *(*Sumatra *out of commission at Surabaya)*

Destroyers
Van Nes, Bankert, Witte de With, Kortenaer, Piet Hein, Evertsen, *and* van Ghent

UNITED STATES ASIATIC FLEET BASED IN THE PHILLIPINES

Admiral Hart, commanding

Heavy Crusiers
Houston

Light Cruisers
Boise *and* Marblehead

Destroyers
Pope, John D. Ford, Paul Jones, Stewart *(which was captured at Surabaya in March 1942 and served as a Japanese warship)*, Bulmer, Barker, Parrott, Whipple, Alden, Edsall, John D. Edwards, *with the* Peary *and* Pillsbury *refitting.*

Additionally, the British had 1 submarine refitting, the Dutch 14 (one refitting) and the Americans 29 (four refitting)

---

of the Far East, with Singapore as headquarters, was Air Marshal Sir Robert Brooke-Popham. At Singapore were the 1st and 2nd Malaya Infantry brigades. Primarily fortress troops, they were insurance against a coup d'main against Singapore itself and manned the powerful Coast Defense Batteries. A brigade is roughly the equivalent of a Japanese regiment. The 8th Australian Division made up of two instead of the usual three brigades, along with the 12th Indian Brigade guarded the mainland areas near Singapore. In the north of Malaya along the border with Thailand and at various northern coastal ports, in prepared and fortified positions, was the III Indian Corps, commanded by General Heath, made up of two divisions, the 11th and the 9th, of four brigades, with a fifth additional brigade as a reserve unit. It was the III Corps that first felt the brunt of the Japanese attack. None of the troops were properly trained.

Before the war the British command requested 100 tanks, but they were not forthcoming. Britain, during this campaign, was unable to send any tanks to Malaya, in part due to Churchill's feeling that this would be a dispersal of strength. It also was evidence of a general attitude towards the potential Japanese enemy. One battalion commander in Malaya remarked to Brooke-Popham while reviewing the commander's battalion, "Don't you think they are worthy of some better enemy than the Japanese?" Brigadier Stewart, who commanded the 12th Indian Brigade, also commented to Brooke-Popham that, "I do hope, Sir, we are not getting too strong in Malaya, because if so the Japanese may never attempt a landing." Less than a year later, Stewart's brigade was chased by the 4th Guards Regiment and eight tanks for a fortnight before escaping—Stewart's brigade did not enjoy support from the air and was frequently attacked.

The saddest situation was in the air for the British. Pre-war studies stated that it was desirable to have 582 planes based in Malaya—336 would be the bare minimum required to defend Malaya—and on December 7th, 1941, Britain disposed of 246 airplanes. Of these 246 planes, 88 were disabled, and of the remaining 158 planes, the most modern fighter was the overweight Buffalo. The 36 torpedo planes were obsolete bi-plane Vildebeestes with a maximum speed of 137 m.p.h.! The Vildebeestes were "archaic and rickety bi-planes with fixed landing gear, masses of rigging wires and braces, and open cockpits." One pilot was quoted as saying that, "It was noted among the British crewmen after the war began that some Japanese casualties might have been caused when Japanese pilots caught sight of the Vildebeestes and laughed themselves to death." In the course of the campaign some Hurricane fighters (970

miles, 12 MGs *or* four 20mm cannon, 342 m.p.h.) arrived, but it was a matter of too little too late. It could be argued that the lend-lease shipment of Hurricanes to Soviet Russia fighting for her life against the savage German invasion of 1941 sealed the doom of Singapore and the garrison stationed there. Planes destined for Russia obviously could not go to Malaya as well.

The British were not blind to the threat of Japan, although they certainly underestimated it. Churchill said in September of 1940 that "The Naval Intelligence Division are very much inclined to exaggerate Japanese strength and efficiency." However one of the inadequate actions taken by Churchill in 1941 was to reinforce the British navy in the Far East. Force Z was created, made up of the new fast battleship *Prince of Wales* (36,727 tons, ten 14-inch guns, sixteen 5.25-inch guns, 28 knots), and the fast older reconstructed battlecruiser *Repulse* (32,000 tons, six 15-inch guns, nine 4-inch anti-

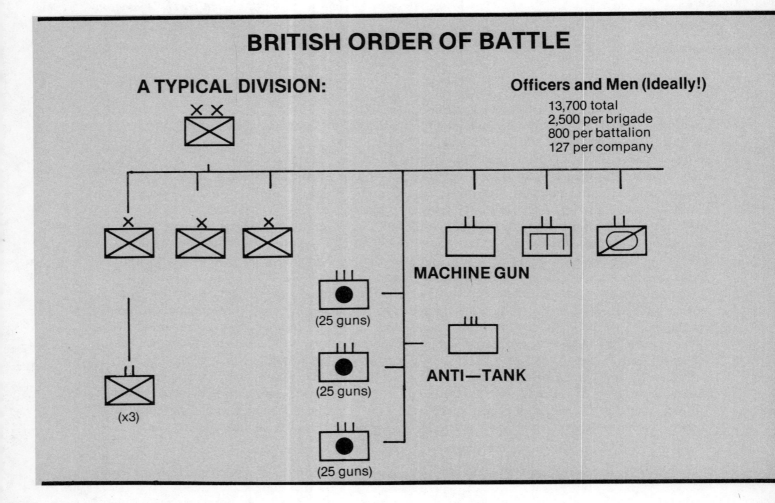

BRITISH ORDER OF BATTLE

A TYPICAL DIVISION:

Officers and Men (Ideally!)

13,700 total
2,500 per brigade
800 per battalion
127 per company

(x3)

(25 guns)

(25 guns)

(25 guns)

MACHINE GUN

ANTI—TANK

BRITISH ORDER OF BATTLE IN MALAYA ON FEBRUARY 8, 1942

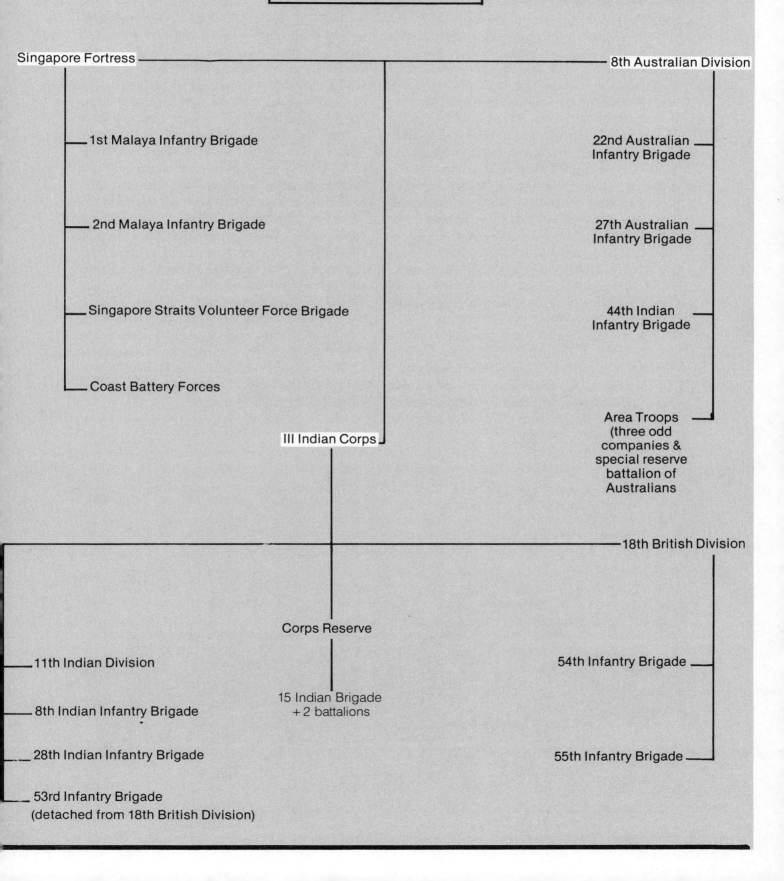

**H. Q. MALAYA COMMAND
LT. GEN. PERCIVAL** —— 12th Indian Brigade (reserve)

Singapore Fortress

— 1st Malaya Infantry Brigade

— 2nd Malaya Infantry Brigade

— Singapore Straits Volunteer Force Brigade

— Coast Battery Forces

III Indian Corps

8th Australian Division

22nd Australian Infantry Brigade

27th Australian Infantry Brigade

44th Indian Infantry Brigade

Area Troops (three odd companies & special reserve battalion of Australians

18th British Division

Corps Reserve

11th Indian Division

15 Indian Brigade + 2 battalions

54th Infantry Brigade

8th Indian Infantry Brigade

28th Indian Infantry Brigade

55th Infantry Brigade

53rd Infantry Brigade (detached from 18th British Division)

ship guns, and six 4-inch anti-aircraft guns, 28 knots). The fleet carrier *Indomitable* (23,000 tons, twelve Fulmar fighters, nine Sea Hurricane fighters, twenty-four Albacore torpedo planes, 30 knots) was due to go with them but was grounded in a fog in Kingston, Jamaica, and no other suitable carrier was available. So Force Z was forced to rely on land based air, probably that of another service, i.e., the RAF, and not British Naval Air units. This was a key to the destruction of Force Z by the Japanese. In addition to Force Z, the British navy at Singapore fielded three old D class light cruisers (4,850 tons, six 6-inch guns, twelve 21-inch guns, 27 knots) and six destroyers. Sadly for the British Empire, only one submarine was present in the Far East and that one was under refit. The omission of such a valuable defensive weapon was a terrible blow to the defense of this region, especially since British submarines were reasonably capable craft, unlike the American submarines at that stage of the war.

The strategy behind the sending of this force was twofold. If the Japanese invaded Malaya, Force Z could be used, with proper land based air cover, to attack the enemy invasion convoy. Churchill actually felt that the Japanese were unable to invade Malaya and that Force Z was of value in destroying the Japanese battlecruisers which Churchill feared would be unleashed against British Far East trade routes. As Churchill stated, "I cannot feel that Japan will face the combination now forming against her of the United States, Great Britain, and Russia, while already preoccupied in China . . . . Nothing would increase her hesitation more than the appearance of the force mentioned (25 August, 1941) . . . and above all of (*the Prince of Wales*). This might indeed be a decisive deterrent." Churchill's employment of Force Z was "that kind of vague menace which capital ships of the highest quality, whose whereabouts are unknown, can impose upon all hostile naval calculations." Churchill felt that Force Z could lose itself among the islands of Southern Asia and with its high speed could run from a strong enemy or "catch and kill anything" weaker. Churchill was taking a leaf from the employment of the German Kriegsmarine in which the battleship *Bismarck* or *Tirpitz* tied down many Allied warships in the Atlantic. This tying down, coupled with the American fleet, would be a force that Japan could not defeat, or so Churchill thought.

The aircraft carrier *Indomitable* was supposed to join the battleship *Prince of Wales* and the battlecruiser *Repulse* to support Force Z but was grounded in a fog in Jamaica. Force Z was left to rely on inadequate land-based air support—a fatal mistake.

Before the attack on Pearl Harbor, a large Japanese convoy was sighted heading south. The Japanese tried to give the impression that the convoy was on its way to Thailand, but at a certain point it was obvious that it was proceeding towards the coast of Northern Malaya and the extreme southern coastal tail, or Kra Peninsula, of Thailand. It was at this point that the Japanese vice-admiral, Jisaburo Ozawa, ordered a shadowing British Catalina flying boat to be shot down. This was on December 7th—on that side of the International Date Line was almost a full 24 hours before the attack on Pearl Harbor—it was the first hostile act of the war about to begin in the Pacific.

Direct air support was limited as this was some distance from Japanese airbases in Indochina, near Saigon. The 5th Division was putting ashore, and at Kota Bharu, a Malayan coastal town, was engaged with the 9th Indian Brigade. The invasion fleet was almost forced to withdraw by attacks from the Vildebeestes! The lack of proper air cover for the Japanese invasion fleet, and the loss of one transport, give an indication of what might have occurred if the British air units had been up to minimum strength with modern aircraft. Losses amounted to about 500 men for the 5th division, virtually all these occurring at Kota Bharu, but the entire division was ashore within 24 hours either in Northern Malaya, or heading towards the Thai-Malaya border. The British never planned for such a quick landing of hostile forces in Malaya. Thai resistance to the Japanese invasion, which also involved the seizure of the capital of Bangkok, lasted about 24 hours.

British reaction to the invasion was to dispatch Force Z, made up of the *Prince of Wales* and *Repulse* with four destroyers, to engage the enemy transports. If Force Z had been delayed even just two days, it would have had strong additional reinforcements including the Dutch light cruiser *Java*, the heavy cruiser *Exeter*, and others. The hard driving Admiral Tom Phillips, the new admiral in charge of the fleet in the Far East, who sailed with and commanded Force Z, was under the impression that in terms of air opposition, he would meet only Japanese army air units supporting their invasion. Phillips thought these planes were armed with the incorrect type of weapons, i.e., ground attack weapons and not armor-piercing bombs and torpedoes. So, Phillips moved quickly in the hopes of disrupting the invasion of Malaya. Phillips had had a desk job for most of the war and lacked modern combat experience. He was noted in the British navy for arguing that a battleship with room to maneuver, given an adequate anti-aircraft armament, could survive air attacks. Phillips just before the war felt that the torpedo hitting percentage in combat from torpedo planes would be less than 15%. It proved to be 22% against his two capital ships! British intelligence intimated that the Japanese forces were made up of the rebuilt fast battleship, *Kongo*, three heavy cruisers, two light cruisers and 20 destroyers. In actuality Phillips was faced with two Kongo class battleships, seven heavy and three light cruisers, and twenty-four destroyers. The overall Japanese naval command was under Vice-Admiral Nobutake Kondo. A gunnery specialist, he was a cautious man of few brilliant qualities. The immediate convoy escort force was under, in the words of Professor Marder, the "first-class fighting admiral, and the Navy's foremost tactician" Vice-Admiral Ozawa.

In London, on December 9th, Admiralty officials were discussing sending Force Z to the American West Coast to join with the remnants of the American battleship fleet, or to "vanish among the innumerable islands, exercising a vague menace as rogue elephants." By then it was too late, Force Z had gone to sea. Phillips hoped to surprise the Japanese, get in among the enemy convoys in the Gulf of Siam off Northern Malaya, or possibly engage the lone *Kongo*, then retire before hastily organized long range bombers could attack Force Z. Phillips was convinced that no torpedo plane could operate *very* effectively beyond a radius of 200 miles, as that was the British experience. In actuality, the Japanese did operate at a radius of 1,000 miles with the requisite skill required. Finally, Phillips sailed hoping that he would receive fighter protection. Phillips was *not* promised this support, and indeed he did not receive it as air losses during the first two days of war were substantial and there was a lack of communication on Phillip's part. Wishful thinking by Phillip brought about the loss of Force Z.

The Japanese knew by early December that

the *Prince of Wales*, and possibly her sister ship the *King George V*, was present at Singapore. Yamamoto had decided, on this basis, to move a unit of the highly trained and skilled Kanoya Air Corps from Formosa to the Saigon area. The Genzan and Mihoro Air Corps, stationed in Indochina, were good units, but lacked the training against ship targets that the Kanoya Air Corps had undergone over the years. The Kanoya Air Corps was especially skilled at torpedo drops in shallow water, which was a common characteristic of the waters around Singapore.

Kondo knew that Force Z possessed radar, and he was intimidated by the modern *Prince of Wales* with its aura of an unsinkable battleship. Kondo proposed that the British enemy be attacked with bombs and torpedoes by day and by a destroyer attack at night.

When Force Z proceeded to sea on December 9, it moved north as originally planned, but was sighted, both by Japanese air as well as submarine forces. With surprise thus lost, Phillips turned back towards Singapore when a false report arrived telling of an invasion at Kuantan in central-south Malaya. Phillips turned Force Z towards its port in hopes of catching a Japanese

invasion force in the act of landing. Phillips did not inform Singapore of this change in plans and though a force of Buffalo fighters was standing by to give escort, it was not sent until too late. (In January of 1942 when Singapore was under attack from Nells and Bettys the Buffalo fighters were relatively ineffective against them.)

Meanwhile the Japanese organized a strike of eighteen planes from the Kanoya, seventeen planes from the Genzan, and eighteen planes from the Mihoro Air Groups. Weather conditions on the 9th of December were so bad that all the planes had to return, although not before three of them had sighted an enemy force at night and dropped flares over it—it was Ozawa's flagship the heavy cruiser *Chokai* Ozawa present with his five heavy cruisers (*Chokai*, *Kumano*, *Mikuma*, *Mogami*, and *Suzuya*), with two light cruisers (*Kinu* and *Yura*), and four destroyers nearby in separate squadrons. Ozawa did not except airpower alone to sink these enemy capital ships so he intended to attack at night with his force. At 8:30 P.M. Ozawa was 50 miles from Force Z. By 9:20 this range fell to between eight and twenty-two

The *Kongo* battlecruiser had been recently reconstructed with increased armor protection and reboilered for more speed when she joined the Japanese force off Malaya.

miles. A night action between the *Prince of Wales* and the *Repulse* against five Japanese heavy cruisers probably would have been strictly decided on a basis of who saw whom first, although Admiral Phillips was tactically a lightweight next to Admiral Ozawa.

Kondo ordered Ozawa to fall back for several reasons. First, the Japanese force had not trained together and was hastily thrown together, and second, the destroyers were low of fuel. Third, weather conditions were not good and the Japanese feared the new weapon called radar rumored to be on the British ships (it was). Finally, Ozawa realized that the British force was now no longer heading for northern Malaya, but towards the south central Malaya area. Ozawa could not account for the reason the enemy was heading in that direction and was therefore understandably suspicious. Kondo decided to order the withdrawal of Ozawa, and instead of running the risk of defeat in detail to the British, he ordered a concentration of all key surface combat units. Kondo's decision to concentrate the entire fleet, lead by the battleships *Kongo* and *Haruna*, gave him the possibility of engaging the enemy in the morning. They concentrated that night and headed south at 24 knots. Early in the morning Force Z was sighted by air reconnaissance and orders were issued for an immediate air attack.

The first wave was of sixteen Nells armed with torpedoes and nine Nells armed with one 1,102-pound bomb each of the Genzan Air Corps. The second wave was of eight Nells armed torpedoes, eight Nells armed with two 551-pound bombs each, and seventeen Nells armed with one 1,102-pound bomb each of the Mihoro Air Corps. The final wave, from the Kanoya Air Group, was of twenty-six Bettys armed with the most modern torpedo available to the Japanese. All planes departed for the attack on Force Z between 6:25 A.M. and 8:00 A.M.

Japanese air tactics called for a simultaneous attack by both horizontal bombers and torpedo planes. It was recognized that the bombs in question were too small to penetrate the decks of the British battleships, but the resulting "confusion in the target ship through the damage caused by hits" made it easier for the attacking torpedo planes. At this point the Japanese knew that larger bombs were needed for harming battleships, and used such weapons at Pearl Harbor by converting 16-inch shells to bombs. But that weapon was available only in limited numbers and none were available in this Southern Theater of the war.

Torpedoes cause more damage when set for a deeper depth. The ideal position to hit a battleship is as deep as possible, but to set a torpedo too deep will allow it to possibly go under a target ship and thus miss altogether. In the approaching action, the Kanoya Air Corps, which scored the most torpedo hits, set their torpedoes for an in between setting of four meters (about thirteen feet) which was ideal for cruisers, but not the ideal six meters for battleships. So, if the setting had been for battleships instead of for cruiser targets, it could be assumed that the resulting damage would have been greater than it was.

The Japanese expected losses to be about one-third of the planes involved in the attack. The Japanese as they went in thought they were going in against two King George V battleships. They lost just three planes in the battle against Force Z, although several more were damaged. When compared to the losses of the Bettys against the *Lexington's* Task Force in the February 1942 battle off Rabaul, one can gain a sense of what the lack of good fighter cover meant.

The first attack took place from the nine bombing Nells of the Genzan Air Corps in which the bombers mistook the little destroyer *Tenedos* (1,090 tons, three 4-inch guns, four 21-inch torpedoes, 36 knots–built during World War I) for a battleship and wasted their attack. All bombs missed with none falling closer than 100 yards from the tenedos. Mistakes like this occurred throughout the war on both sides.

The air units were despairing of finding Force Z when a reconnaissance plane located the force and made the proper signals. By 11:00 A.M. the first attacking planes arrived over Force Z and began launching their attacks. Ideally the Japanese planes would have concentrated and launched an attack as a complete unit, but having been in the air for hours, they were concerned about their fuel and so went in as they arrived on the scene.

The first attack began at 11:13 A.M. with unbelievable noise created by 5.25-inch dual-purpose guns, Oerlikons, Bofors, and the

Captured Japanese photo shows the fatal attack on the *Prince of Wales* and the *Repulse* off the Malay peninsula.

"chattering, ear-splitting rhythm of the multiple pom-poms." The attacks were against the *Prince of Wales* and the *Repulse*, and some damaged planes dropped bombs on the destroyers.

The bombers came in at about 9,750 feet to 13,000 feet. Torpedo planes attacked from heights higher (32 feet to 100 feet) than the Royal Navy torpedo planes, launching their torpedoes at 325 to 1300 feet from the target ship.

The first attack by the Mihoro Air Corps scored one bomb hit on the plane hanger of the *Repulse*. A small fire resulted which was quickly extinguished. The second attack included the *Prince of Wales*. Torpedo planes of the Genzan group came in low and as the torpedo officer of the *Prince of Wales* remarked to Admiral Phillips, "I think they're going to do a torpedo attack," to which Admiral Phillips replied, "No they're not. There are no torpedo aircraft about." The attack scored two torpedo hits on the port side of the *Prince of Wales* which damaged the boiler rooms and slowed her to 15 knots speed. Flooding was severe and counterflooding (to correct the list of the ship) placed the ship low in the water. The steering control was damaged and all the 5.25-inch dual purpose guns were placed out of combat from electrical failures and flooding damage.

The third attack from units of the Mihoro group against the *Repulse* missed. Captain William Tennant of the *Repulse*, with help from the navigating officer, H.B.C. Gill, avoided this attack by "steaming at 25 knots . . . . I maintained a steady course until the aircraft appeared to be committed to the attack when the (ship's) wheel was put over and the attacks providentially combed." Calm orders for 30 degree turns first to one side then 30 degree turns to the other side was the standard procedure that kept the *Repulse* free of torpedo hits, . . . until the Kanoya Air Corps arrived.

The fourth attack at 12:20 P.M. was deadly. Six of the incoming twenty-six Bettys attacked the crippled *Prince of Wales* and scored four hits on the starboard side, correcting the list from the first attack, but dooming the vessel. Her speed dropped to about 9 knots. The *Repulse* was simply overwhelmed. Tennant describing this attack, "I found dodging the torpedoes quite interesting and entertaining until in the end they started to come in from all directions and they were too much for me." The first hit slowed her to 15 knots and jammed her rudder, this letting the next four hits rip her side open. Orders for abandoning ships were forthcoming at 12:25 P.M. In five minutes both ships were on their last legs. By 12:33 P.M. the *Repulse* had capsized and then, as described by Lieutenant John Hayes, "She reared into the vertical as the stern disappeared. Just the bow, half gray, half reddish bottom color, hung for a moment in a last defiant gesture to the sky; then that too slid back into a cauldron of bubbles while the water blackened from oil in convulsive eddies, and the *Repulse* was gone."

Two additional attacks scored only one bomb hit on the *Prince of Wales*, but that bomb hit knocked out additional boiler rooms. There were 18,000 tons of water on board the *Prince of Wales*, speed was reduced to 6 knots, and losses were heavy. At 1:15 P.M. The ship was ordered to be abandoned. One sailor was heard to remark to a friend, "Come on, chum, all them explosions 'll have frightened the blinkin sharks away." They then jumped into the water. Phillips, and Captain Leach who had fought the German battleship *Bismarck* with the *Hood* in May of 1941, both went down with the *Prince of Wales*. Some 513 men from the *Repulse* and 327 men from the *Prince of Wales* died in the attack.

As for Admiral Phillips' decision to remain on board and die with his flagship, one senior officer stated later, "Tom Phillips would have had great difficulty in facing the situation if he had survived, and for that reason many officers would sympathize with his decision not to leave the ship." The problem with this decision is that it was a personal decision that overlooked the context of the situation. Phillips commanded the Far Eastern naval forces, and not just Force Z. His hard driving nature might have helped in saving the situation in Malaya and possibly he could have learned lessons quickly enough to make up for ignorance displayed at this point in the war. A tough call, but it is quite understandable why Phillips made the decision he did.

The loss of the *Prince of Wales* and *Repulse*, coupled with the Pearl Harbor raid, caused the status of surface ships, and especially battleships, within the American and British navies to be viewed by many as useless except for convoy duty. Coupled with a steel shortage, the construction of battleships in America was severely curtailed, while in Britain the Lion class battleship was delayed (later cancelled) because of cost and questions of its effectiveness. Later surface naval battles redeemed the value of the battleship as well as gave it new roles as anti-aircraft platforms and shore bombardment duties.

Admiral Sir Dudley Pound said in 1943 of the destruction of Force Z, that "we all under-rated the efficiency of the Japanese air forces, and certainly did not realize the long ranges at which they would work." The British *Daily Mail* wrote, "There has been a tendency to underrate their machines and airmen. We should hear no more of that." Admiral Ugaki noted that, "Nothing more brilliant than this remarkable success . . . by destroying the *Prince of Wales* it may be said that we have avenged the *Bismarck* in the Far East, on the opposite side of the earth." The upshot to all of this was that Japan's confidence in victory in Malaya was enhanced, while there was a corresponding loss of morale for the troops in Malaya. There no longer existed a strong naval force to contest the command of the sea at Singapore. Singapore was now a beleaguered fortress.

The Japanese were ashore and consolidating their position in Thailand in just three days from the start of the war. A reinforced regiment of the 5th Division was pushing down the eastern coast of Malaya towards Singapore. This force captured Kuantan on December 30th from elements of the Indian 9th divisions. But it was on the west coast where the real fighting occurred.

The problems facing the rest of the III Indian Corps were several. It only had three brigades to defend northern Malaya and the prize of Penang, a small island city and seaport. Originally it had planned that the 11th Indian Division would enter Thailand and seize strategic defensive positions, including the ports invaded by Japan. This plan, Operation Matador, did not occur except for an abortive advance contested by Thai troops. So the Indian troops, primed for an advance, suddenly found themselves on the defensive. They were deployed at Jitra in defensive positions, waterlogged from recent rains which covered several important airfields, and were supposed to offer resistance for up to three months.

The other two regiments of the 5th Division advanced towards Jitra and began an immediate night attack on the 11th. The 5th Reconnaissance "regiment" (about 300 men), supported by ten medium tanks, pushed in, capturing a anti-tank battery that was unmanned—the troops were sheltering from the rain and were not warned. The advance was halted, largely from attacks by famed Indian Gurkha and British infantry battalions. The Japanese responded by moving units around the flank and employing their artillery with good effect. By the evening of the 12th the British were retreating. Over 3,000 Indian troops surrendered (the 15th Indian Brigade was reduced to a quarter of its strength), and in the insuing blunders, over three hundred trucks and armored cars, fifty field guns, and fifty heavy machine guns were lost to the Japanese. A position meant to last for weeks had fallen in thirty-six hours of fighting to two Japanese battalions and a company of tanks. The effect of this defeat so early in the campaign, coupled with the destruction of Force Z can not be underestimated. Further, with the fall of the nearby airfields, with runways in good repair, the Japanese Army Air, with its short range aircraft, could now be properly employed. Yamashita had written in his diary on

November 10, "If Indian troops are included in the British forces defending Malaya, the job should be easy." This was in part due to the lack of adequate equipment and training, but it was also due to the fact that the Indian troops had been "milked" over the first two years of the war for other units stationed mostly in the Middle East. This practice was now being paid for in full.

The III Indian Corps under General Heath fell back steadily, holding at various positions and managing to conduct a reasonable retreat with attendant heavy losses and loss of morale. Part of the reason the defense failed was that too often the front was too long. At Jitra one British brigade covered a front of six to seven miles. Nor must the east coast of Malaya be compared to the mountains or west coast of Malaya. The east coast was not jungle, but was filled with plantations and a good road network. So it was fairly open terrain. The British probably should have used small forces to tripwire the Japanese advances, fortifying key river crossings to slow up advances, and then strongly counterattack against the isolated Japanese spearheads. The Japanese typically practiced what they learned to call the "Fishbone Attack." A tank force advanced up the road, then turned its turret to one side and fired at enemy positions in adjacent plantations. Meanwhile, the artillery opened on those same positions so that there was incoming fire from two separate directions. Usually only a few weapons were capable of dealing with the tanks, and usually they were sited in the wrong spots! The name was derived from the tanks being like the ribs on a fish's backbone, steadily moving down a road, with the Japanese artillery being the backbone.

The Imperial Guard now came up and both the 5th and the Guard pushed south. The 18th still had not arrived and was marching up from ports in Thailand. Penang fell on the 19th. With it a tremendous amount of shipping was captured. This allowed the Japanese to employ a new weapon against the retreating British forces—amphibious operations. Incredible as it sounds, and lacking any supporting warships on that side of Malaya, the Japanese were constantly outflanking British positions as they drove south from the seaward flank. Japanese

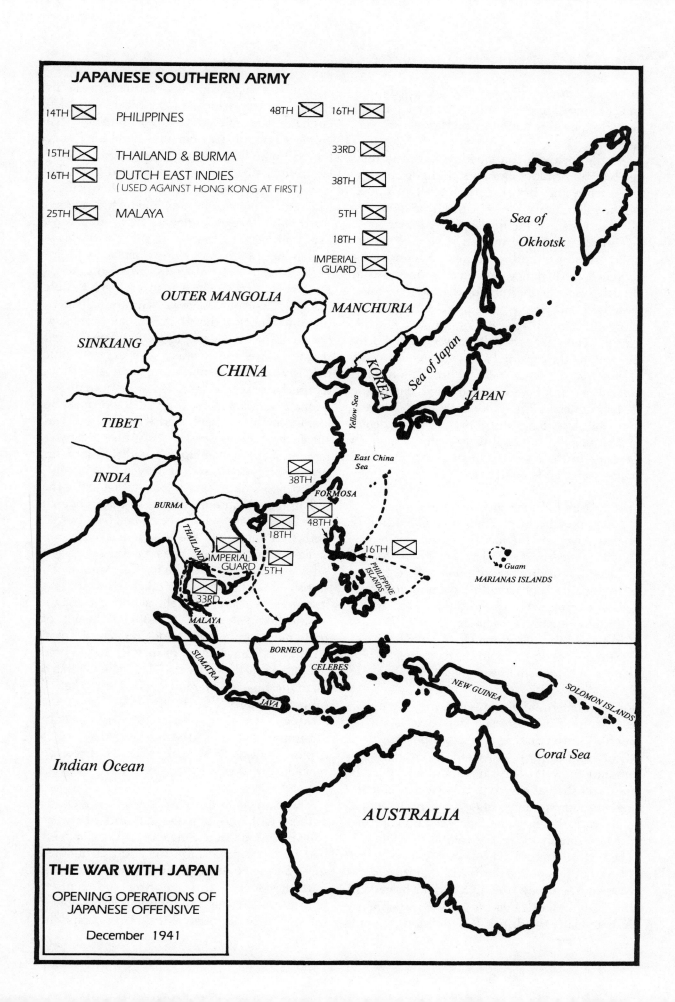

JAPANESE SOUTHERN ARMY

14TH ☒ PHILIPPINES

15TH ☒ THAILAND & BURMA

16TH ☒ DUTCH EAST INDIES
(USED AGAINST HONG KONG AT FIRST)

25TH ☒ MALAYA

48TH ☒   16TH ☒

33RD ☒

38TH ☒

5TH ☒

18TH ☒

IMPERIAL
GUARD ☒

OUTER MANGOLIA

MANCHURIA

SINKIANG

CHINA

KOREA

Sea of
Okhotsk

Sea of Japan

JAPAN

Yellow Sea

TIBET

INDIA

BURMA

38TH ☒

East China
Sea

FORMOSA

THAILAND

18TH ☒

IMPERIAL
GUARD ☒

5TH ☒

48TH ☒

16TH ☒

PHILIPPINE
ISLANDS

Guam

MARIANAS ISLANDS

33RD ☒

MALAYA

SUMATRA

BORNEO

CELEBES

JAVA

NEW GUINEA

SOLOMON ISLANDS

Indian Ocean

Coral Sea

AUSTRALIA

THE WAR WITH JAPAN

OPENING OPERATIONS OF
JAPANESE OFFENSIVE

December 1941

airpower was also employed. Airpower did not inflict many casualties and the damage inflicted was insignificant, but effect on morale was certain.

As the Japanese continued to advance, they received tremendous amounts of important supplies from the British Army itself. Dubbed "Churchill rations," they came from two key sources. One was the British Army which in its retreat often failed or did not have time, to destroy accumulated supplies. Secondly, a scorched earth policy, such as the one used in Soviet Russia at the time of the German invasion, was not implemented in Malaya (or in most of Southern Asia during the Japanese advance). The Allies thought they would shortly be retaking the captured areas. There was also a feeling that the Asian colonial population could not survive if this were implemented. Finally the British Official History points out another reason. In describing the work of the "denial teams" busy in the final days destroying goods of value to the enemy, it points out that these teams were hindered. These teams

> . . . were however greatly handicapped,
> when they began the denial of plant and
> machinery, by the fact that some persons
> with vested interests did their utmost to
> delay the destruction of their property
> by lodging appeals with local authorities.
> Some firms, whose head offices were in
> Britain, Australia, or India, even
> appealed to their home Governments.
> Some went so far as to obstruct the
> work of the denial teams.

Ruthless determination was lacking in the British Army. The end result was that Japan received help during the campaign from "Churchill rations" as well as an immense amount of war booty and huge stockpiles of resources such as tin, coal, rubber, manufacturing and refining units, after the fighting ended.

By early January the Japanese had captured Kuala Lumpur, today the capital of Malaysia. The 11th Indian Division was virtually destroyed at this point, but British reinforcements were on their way (the 45th Indian Brigade of the 17th Indian Division arrived on January 3rd, and later the British 18th division), and the Australian 8th division was about to make its stand. The commander of the theater, Brooke-Popham was relieved of his command by a younger general, Lieutenant-General Sir Henry Pownall who had seen action during the fall of France in 1940. Percival had decided to cut his losses by withdrawing to the southern tip of Malaya (the state of Johore) and let his untested Australians have their chance. But in some ways Percival failed in this too. He split the 8th Australian into two parts, reinforcing each with inferior British and Indian troops, and ignored the fact that the Australians were very flexible troops. Lieutenant-General Gordon Bennett, the commander of the 8th Australian, wanted to try some more aggressive tactics. Bennett felt that what was needed was less reliance on static defensive positions, and more aggressive counterattacks once the Japanese were committed. Bennett was not allowed a real opportunity to implement his concept, and when the 8th was surrendered he escaped to Australia. Bennett's reputation, by escaping when the rest of his troops surrendered, was destroyed. It is interesting to note that Yamashita felt that both the Indian and Australian troops in the campaign were second rate, which they were. The best of both were serving in the Middle East.

The entire Southern Asia area was set up as a separate theater in which the Americans, British, Dutch, and Australian pooled their resources. General Wavell, who first fought against Rommel in 1941, was offered the post of Supreme Commander, and remarked upon accepting, "I have heard of men having to hold the baby, but this is twins!" The Allies suffered many defeats and were disbanded with the fall of Java in early March of 1942. Part of the strategy was for two returning veteran Australian divisions, the 6th and the 7th, to deploy in Java. Events, however, occurred too quickly for this part of the Allied plan to succeed.

The Australian 8th Division set up a classic ambush with one company at a bridge between Kuala Lumpur and Singapore. The Japanese had faced no opposition for about a hundred miles and were literally riding bikes six abreast with no scouts and ignoring rudimentary precautions. About three hundred were allowed through to be disposed by the troops behind the ambush. The bridge was then blown. As the Australian official history reported it, "the charge hurled timber, bicycles, and bodies skyward in a deadly blast. Almost simultaneously, Duffy's three platoons hurled grenades among the enemy and swept them with fire from Bren guns, Tommy guns, and rifles." The Australians fell back to a river position on the Muar and were prepared to fight there to hold the southern tip of Malaya.

However, the Japanese recovered, and pushing south with their two divisions on a broad front, managed to establish themselves on the opposite bank of the river. They also faced the newly arrived 18th Division, and, again, outflanked the river by a amphibious operation. The entire time, even with 52 new Hurricanes present, the Japanese commanded the air, which meant that movement of Allied troops was largely limited to night marches. With this final position turned, the British were forced to retreat into Singapore itself. In the process the commander of the 9th Indian Division was killed in an ambush and before the only causeway connecting Singapore to the mainland was blown up on January 31st, two entire Indian brigades, the 22nd and the 45th, were destroyed through aggressive Japanese advances.

Singapore normally held 550,000 people in 1941, but by February of 1942 over 1,000,000 people were present, many being refugees. The island is 220 square miles, and has 70 miles of coastline. The distance from the island to the mainland varies from 600 yards to 5,000 yards, but troops had to be posted all around the island with the Japanese having mastery of the sea. Most of the heavy guns set up for coast defense between 1934 and 1941 were incapable of firing towards the mainland, and could only aid in defense against heavy warships at sea. The Japanese did not need such warships so the guns were of little value.

Present on the island, facing the twenty-seven battalions of the three Japanese divisions were twenty-one Indian battalions, thirteen British battalions, six Australian, two Malayan, and three volunteer units of Singapore volunteers. There were also two British and one Australian machine gun battalions and one reconnaissance battalion. Training and strength varied radically from unit to unit.

Over the next few days, artillery bombarded the Allied positions and air attacks were usually three a day. Virtually all remaining Allied air units were withdrawn from Malaya. Percival also guessed wrong as to where the main Japanese attack would come from. The Japanese set up a feint with the Guard to the east, while they attacked with the 18th and the 5th in the west. The deception worked.

On the evening of February 8th the Japanese, with 440 guns and 200 rounds per gun opened fire and using 100 motorboats and 200 collapsible launches came across. Some 4,000 men were in the first wave and by the morning of the 9th most of the 5th and the 18th were on the island. The attack fell against the 8th Australian and weak 44th Indian Brigade and they simply were too few to stem the Japanese tide. The Japanese continued pushing and by the 14th had reopened the causeway and been joined by the Imperial Guard. The Japanese were starting to run low on artillery shells and the British resistance, especially from their artillery, was hurting. One Japanese staff officer was concerned that it would be themselves and not the British who might have to surrender!

Percival wanted the fight, but his subordinates in a conference, including Bennett, felt that the troops were worn out and surrender was the best course to be adopted. The following exchange is recorded. Percival stated, "There are other things to consider. I have my honour to consider and there is also the question of what posterity will think of us if we surrender this large Army and valuable fortress."

General Heath retorted, "You need not bother about your honour. You lost that a long time ago up in the North (of Malaya)."

Percival wanted to continue on and gave orders to do so, but by the 15th recognized that the large civilian population was suffering, especially from lack of water. Food reserves were down to two days.

A ceasefire was arranged for on the 15th of February. The British were to surrender unconditionally.

The total number of British troops lost numbered 138,708, of which about 67,700 Indians, 38,500 British, and 18,500 Australians were captured. The Japanese victory produced a tremendous amount of war booty. Captured items included about 630 field artillery pieces, 54 fortress guns (some would be later used at Tarawa), 1,800 trucks, over 3,000 machine guns, and much more. So not only did the Japanese get the help of "Churchill rations," but in the end they took most of the British equipment. The Japanese suffered 9,656 killed or wounded in the campaign in fighting an average of two engagements a day and advancing an average of about fourteen miles a day, largely on foot and bicycle. The Japanese repaired an average of five bridges a day during their advance.

For Britain, the fall of Singapore coincided with the famous "Channel Dash" in which several large Nazi Germany warships successfully raced up the Channel to Germany from the ports in France. Parliament was upset and there were calls for a shake-up in the war cabinet. Interestingly enough, considering that this was the greatest surrender of troops in the history of the British Empire, there never was a formal inquiry as to why this disaster occurred, in marked contrast to the congressional hearings on the Pearl Harbor defeat.

The Emperor of Japan, Hirohito, wrote of the victory,

> Our army and navy working in close co-operation in Malaya, have resolutely carried out difficult maritime escort tasks, transport duties and landing operations, and in the teeth of tropical diseases, and enduring intense heat, they have harried and hunted a strong enemy and broken through his defenses at every point, capturing Singapore with the speed of the gods, and destroying Great Britain's base in East Asia.
>
> We express our profound esteem for these deeds.

The Emperor thereupon renamed Singapore "Shonan" or "the radiant South." The first three days after the fall of Singapore the Japanese Kempei, with the aid of two battalions of infantry from the 5th Division, entered the city and large numbers of Chinese residents were taken, and many of them executed. Their alleged crime was supporting the Nationalist Chinese in the ongoing war with Japan in China. It is interesting to note that the numerous acts of brutality by the Japanese in this campaign, and later towards the prisoners, are virtually ignored in the Japanese Official History of the war. It is as if by not mentioning it, or not addressing these immoral and illegal acts, that they did not exist. Ironically, Japanese conduct towards Russian prisoners in the Russo-Japanese war of 1904–05 was quite good, but the war prior to that, the Sino-Japanese War of 1894–95 also witnessed numerous atrocities by the Japanese against the Chinese. What made World War II different? Was it because the enemy were morally inferior in Japanese eyes and thus it was allowable to brutalize the enemy, even if they were helpless prisoners? Is it something to do with the psychological theory of a repressed people in a repressive society going outside and letting loose?

There are many reasons for this disaster to the British Empire. First was the fact that the Japanese enemy was underestimated and the troops defending Malaya were poorly trained, poorly equipped, and poorly led. Secondly, proper fortifications were not built (almost £40,000 was not spent on fortifications that had been allocated in 1939, and was not even known to Percival!). The bridges could have been more adequately prepared for demolishing and fortifications placed before December 7, 1941. (One of the top British Engineer officers on the scene suggested this course of action, but it was not implemented properly.) Thirdly, racism on the part of the British was obvious to the people of Malaya. Indian officers, even with the same rank as white officers, rode in different train cars by law. When Penang was evacuated only the Europeans were actively evacuated; the local Indian, Malay, and Chinese populations were ignored and left to the invaders. The attitude problem affected the labor troops as well. If properly exploited, the native population of Malaya could have been used for preparing fortifications, but wages were grossly low. Pay was allocated on a basis of race: Tamil Indians were paid less than Chinese, etc. It should be noted that 25,000 of the captured Indian troops, out of 67,000 total, joined the Indian National Army (the INA was set up by the Japanese as a puppet army) to fight the Allies later in World War II on the Indian border with Burma.

The Fall of Guam, Rabaul, and Wake

As the campaign in Malaya and the Philippines unfolded, important matters were developing in the Pacific. Guam fell easily to the Japanese. A physically large island, lacking an adequate garrison, virtually unfortified due to the provisions of the Washington Treaty of 1922, Guam was struck from the air on December 7, 1941. The Nankai or South Sea Detachment made up of the I, II, and III battalions of the 144th Regiment (detached from the 55th division), reinforced with one battalion of mountain artillery, and a company each of cavalry, engineers, transport troops and field anti-aircraft, took the island on the 10th of December.

From Guam, this same Japanese force left for Rabaul, escorted by a minelayer division on December 14. Distant cover was provided by four fleet carriers (*Akagi*, *Kaga*, *Shokaku*, and *Zuikaku*, escorted by two fast battleships, two cruisers, and seven destroyers) returning from the Pearl raid. The South Sea Detachment, commanded by the slight, balding Major General Tomitaro Horii, numbered 4,886 men and officers. At Rabaul, approximately 1,600 Australians who knew they were unsupported, and with meager coast defense and air defense at their disposal, suffered air attacks while waiting for the Japanese invasion.

On the evening of January 23, 1942, the Japanese landed at Rabaul and all key points fell quickly. The garrison of the 2/22nd Battalion of the 23rd Brigade, with a small number of men from the New Guinea Volunteer Rifles, achieved but one small check when some of the Japanese,

landing at night, came ashore talking, laughing, striking matches, and at one point showing a flashlight, moved directly into a wired ambush complete with Vicker's machine guns. But eventually this position was outflanked and overwhelming numbers took Rabaul. Kavieng, across from Rabaul on New Ireland, fell the following day to about half of the 2nd Maizuru Special Naval Landing Force (500 troops). This unit had been picked up at Truk earlier. The following day the rest of the Maizuru and all of the Kashima Special Naval Landing Force consolidated the position at Kavieng.

Thus one of the most magnificent harbors in the South Pacific passed into the hands of the Japanese Empire. From this fortress base enemy task forces went forth over the remainder of 1942 and into 1943. It was never retaken by the Allies as it was not needed in the Allied leapfrogging operations of the future months. Plans for moving against New Guinea began.

The one seed left that would keep the Allied struggle alive in these waters was the establishment of the Coast Watchers. Australia had planted two commandos of 25 men each in New Guinea and the Solomons. Over the next two years these men, along with the regular troops that took to the bush instead of surrendering, as well as most of the local native population, developed a communications network (and rescue service) that was extremely valuable in aiding the Allied cause.

But it was earlier at Wake that Japan received her first check and American men distinguished

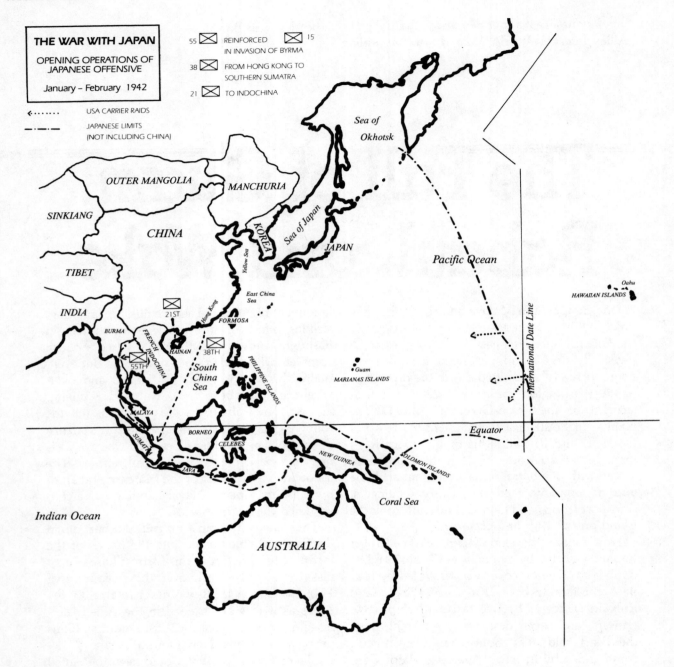

THE WAR WITH JAPAN

OPENING OPERATIONS OF
JAPANESE OFFENSIVE

January – February 1942

55 ⊠ REINFORCED ⊠ 15
IN INVASION OF BYRMA

38 ⊠ FROM HONG KONG TO
SOUTHERN SUMATRA

21 ⊠ TO INDOCHINA

←······· USA CARRIER RAIDS

——— JAPANESE LIMITS
(NOT INCLUDING CHINA)

themselves.

Wake Island is really three small atolls separated by narrow channels around a lagoon, and it is far from any other significant island in the north-central Pacific Ocean. It was a Pan American clipper refueling site and a small military base. The main garrison consisted of about 40% of the First Defense Battalion (447 men) and 60 navy men. Coast defense guns included six 5-inch guns, twelve 3-inch guns, and some .50 and .30 caliber machine guns. A coast defense battalion at this time was new (established in 1939) and did not have a tight organization, but, instead, did offer some resistance to small raiding forces.

The approaching Japanese force consisted of Rear Admiral Sadamichi Kajioka on his flagship the light cruiser *Yubari* (3,141 tons, six 5.5-inch guns, four 24-inch torpedoes, 35 knots, the prototype for all Japanese heavy cruisers built in the 1920s and the 1930s), with six old destroyers covering patrol craft carrying 450 special naval landing forces of the 2nd Maizuru units. Additional fire support was given by the 18th Cruiser Squadron made up of the *Tenryu* and *Tatsuta* (3,948, four 5.5-inch guns, six 21-inch torpedoes, 33 knots), two sisterships that were Japan's oldest cruisers in service, definitely a second string attack. Two Maru transports carried the garrison troops for the island after occupation.

Wake was first attacked by thirty-six twin-engine Nell bombers, of the 24th Air Flotilla, on the 8th of December and air attacks continued through the 10th. They destroyed seven of the few Marine Wildcat (F4F-3s) fighters on the island, as well as generally inflicting damage on everything. The Japanese thought that they had softened up the island. The Japanese were about to come to understand the old naval adage about ships not liking to attack forts.

The Japanese force approached with three light cruisers (the *Yubari* was leading the two others) followed by six destroyers. Two Marus and two patrol craft in two separate groups flanked the main column. The Japanese began firing on the island at 5:22 A.M. at 6,000 yards range. The Marines did not return fire and allowed the Japanese column to approach. At the start of the third pass, with oil tanks now afire and the residential area under bombardment—but not the hidden guns, and with the range being about 3,000 yards—the Marines opened fire.

The *Yubari* came under heavy fire, but was not hit. A smokescreen was ordered as well as an immediate retirement. One of the patrol craft carrying the assault troops was hit, the engine disabled, and the boat drifted ashore. As the retirement continued one of the Marus was hit and so Kajioka ordered three of his destroyers to attack the offending 5-inch gun battery (the six 5-inch guns were divided into three separate batteries). The *Hayate, Oite,* and *Mochizuki* (each 1720 tons, four 4.7-inch guns; first two have six 21-inch torpedoes, the latter six 24-inch torpedoes with four reloads, 37 knots) screened the Marus by charging the offending battery and making more smoke. The *Hayate,* leading the attack, was hit squarely by about six successive 5-inch rounds and blew up with no survivors, killing 168 men. She thus became the first major fighting ship lost by Japan since the start of the war. The *Oite* and *Mochizuki* retired with the former suffering some damage and nineteen casualties.

The attack continued without great results (only one Marine died that day) when four remaining Wildcat fighters came into view at 7:24 A.M. The Wildcats strafed the Japanese ships, which forced the final retirement of the Japanese force. The Wildcats continued to attack, shuttling between Wake's airfield to get additional ammunition, and the Japanese force, when they scored their biggest success of the morning by hitting the destroyer *Kisaragi* on her depth charges setting off a tremendous explosion and sinking her with all hands (150 men).

The Japanese thus retreated minus both troops and ships—the *only* instance in World War II when a sea invasion was turned back by the defenders.

The defenders, in sending a message to Pearl of the successful attack, sent it in code. As was usual they included filler to throw off the enemy code breakers. The filler from this message established one of the great myths of the war: "Send us . . . more Japs!"

There appear to be three major "might have beens" in the Pacific War at this time: What would have happened if Japan had concentrated her main effort to knock out Great Britain by heavy attack into the Indian Ocean basin? What would have happened if Japan had won or even gained a draw in the battle of Midway? What might have happened if the American Wake Island operation had not been cancelled midcourse?

America's soul was stirred when she read that valiant Wake Island had withstood the Japanese onslaught. Coming but a few days on the heels of Pearl Harbor and disasters throughout the Pacific rim, Wake Island caught America's attention and Admiral Kimmel thought he saw an opportunity for achieving a vital victory.

A relief force was sent escorted by a task force built around the fleet carrier *Saratoga*. The *"Sara"* carried eighteen Marine Buffalo fighters to the island. With them was the supply ship *Tangier,* loaded with supplies for the island. At worse, the *Tangier* would be run aground at

Wake, permitting some supplies to get through. To cover this force was Halsey and the *Enterprise*'s task force.

Finally, the *Lexington*'s task force raided Japanese-held Jaluit Island as a diversion. Afterwards, this force headed towards Wake to support the *Sara*'s task force.

Meanwhile the Japanese advanced towards Wake Island with an overwhelming force, but a force unaware of any actual American relief expedition. The invasion force had had her losses replaced and slightly strengthened. The main air support came from Admiral Abe's *Hiryu* and the *Soryu* (the carrier division commanded by Rear Admiral Tamon Yamaguchi, one of Japan's best, and most aggressive), but escorted by only the heavy cruisers *Tone* and *Chikuma* (13,320 tons, eight 8-inch guns, twelve 24-inch torpedoes, 35 knots and five scout planes), and two destroyers. A surface force under Rear Admiral Goto commanding four of the oldest Japanese heavy cruisers and three destroyers covered the invasion force by steaming to the east of Wake Island.

So what happened?

Admiral Kimmel was relieved in the midst of a major operation, the relief of Wake, by a stodgy Vice Admiral Pye, the battleship division commander. Pye remained in command until Admiral Nimitz, then in Washington D.C., could arrive in Hawaii.

Vice Admiral Fletcher, in effective command of the relief force, was never a jack rabbit on the offensive, and was constantly refueling in all of his operation. Delay followed delay, and the relief force was still distant from Wake Island on December 23, when the Japanese began landing on the island. But, before this second invasion attempt, the American naval forces had been recalled by Pye. At 5 A.M. on the 23rd, Wake Island radioed:

"The enemy is on the island. The issue is in doubt."

The island fell that evening.

The Fall of the Indies

The Dutch, in many ways, were the most loyal and helpful ally in that part of the world because they depended on the larger powers to protect their last major bastion of strength. They lived up to their national reputation of being a stubborn and determined people; they fought their ships to the end and fought as best they could on land. Unfortunately for the Dutch rulers of this archipelago, the native populations were not the most willing of subjects. An independence movement was alive, led by future President Sukarno, but the Dutch were largely insensitive to it. Major guerrilla warfare was prevalent at the turn of the century, and memories had not faded.

The value of the vast and populous Dutch East Indies lay in the tremendous oil wealth of the islands, primarily Borneo, divided between Britain and the Netherlands. Strategically, these islands offered a barrier for any enemy approaching from the Indian Ocean or the Australian continent. To gather intelligence about the islands, the Japanese relied on visiting ships, business operations, as well as one unusual source—a brothel catering to upper class Javanese homosexuals who were highranking officials within the Dutch administration.

The Japanese strategy entailed several southward thrusts from bases in Southern China, Indochina, the southern Philippine Islands, and Palau One thrust aimed towards Malaya and British-ruled Borneo; a second thrust, down through the center towards Dutch Borneo; and the third to Celebes, with an eventual aim towards the Spice Islands. This multi-front advance allowed for the possibility of periodic checks, although Japanese strength was too overwhelming to be halted for long.

The first check, and first Allied surface action victory of the war in the Pacific occurred in the central area as Japanese ships advanced south towards Balikpapan. Guarded by only 200 Dutch soldiers, the 56th Regimental Combat Team would capture this oilfield and port easily.

Attrition started when the invasion force arrived off the port, with B-17s damaging two transports. Then the Dutch submarine *K-XVIII* came in close and torpedoed the *Tsuruga Maru*. This submarine attack caused Rear Admiral Nishimura to deploy his flagship the *Naka* (5,595 tons, seven 5.5-inch guns, eight 24-inch torpedoes, 35 knots) and ten destroyers (*Yudachi, Harusame, Samidare, Murasame, Suzukaze, Kawakaze, Umikaze* and *Yamakaze* (1,980 tons, five 5-inch guns, eight 24-inch torpedoes, 34 knots) and the *Natsuguma* and *Minegumo* (2,370 tons, six 5-inch guns, eight 24-inch torpedoes, and 35 knots; all these de-

Vast oil fields made the Dutch East Indies valuable to the Japanese.

stroyers carried torpedo reloads) seaward to hunt for subs. Nishimura had no warning of an approaching enemy surface force—cloudy weather kept air reconnaissance to a minimum.

As soon as war had been declared, the U.S. Asiatic Fleet had been withdrawn to the Dutch East Indies. Shortly thereafter the remaining U.S. Army Air Corps bombers in the Philippines were evacuated to the Indies as well. Rear Admiral Glassford was dispatched with the light cruisers *Boise* and *Marblehead* with the old four pipers *John D. Ford*, *Parrott*, *Paul Jones*, and *Pope* (1,190 tons, four 4-inch guns, twelve 21-inch torpedoes, 32 knots; in 1942 these destroyers were twenty years old). Unfortunately the *Boise* struck an uncharted rock and had to return to base while the *Marblehead* developed engine trouble and could not make better than 15 knots speed, so she was unable to participate in the night attack on the Japanese anchorage. If the cruisers had been employed in the attack, they most likely would have acted as gunnery support ships for the destroyers to fall back on after the destroyers launched a torpedo attack.

So Commander Paul Talbot took his ships in for the first surface engagement for the U.S.A. since 1898. His orders over voice telephone were simple and direct: "Torpedo attack; hold gunfire until the 'fish' are gone; use initiative and prosecute the strike to the utmost."

The Americans attacked boldly, after steaming by Japanese destroyers that did not properly handle recognition lights in identifying the attacking American ships. At 3:16 A.M., with enemy transports outlined by burning fires of the oilfields, the Americans fired their first twelve

torpedoes, but missed the mark. The destroyers' second advance through the transports yielded better results: three Marus were sunk by torpedoes with an assist from some gunfire. The *Ford*'s gunnery officer described this part of the action as "draw-shooting at its best. As targets loomed out of the dark at ranges of 500 to 1,500 yards, we trained on and let go a salvo or two, sights set at lower limits, using the illumination from burning ships."

The *Patrol Boat No. 37* (850 tons, two 4.7-inch guns, 18 knots with stern modified to land one Daihatsu landing craft), guarding the transports along with the *No. 36* and *No. 38*, was sunk by gunfire and torpedoes from the *Pope* and *Parrott* at the end of the action. Yet, after two passes through the enemy transports, the formation of four destroyers was getting scattered, so orders were issued to head home concluding the action at 3:50 A.M. A short pursuit by the *Naka*, *Minegumo*, and *Natsugumo* failed to catch the retiring destroyers. In the battle, one hit was scored on the *Ford* wounding four men. Glassford signaled the returning destroyers in the morning with a "well done"!

Palembang, in Sumatra, was a key airfield and oilfield in southern Sumatra. The island was defended by seven Dutch battalions (on an island larger in land area than Japan itself) and a depleted British Hurricane fighter squadron. On February 14, the day before Singapore surrendered, the Japanese attacked with part of the 1st Raiding Regiment, 380 parachute troops. These troops were armed with rifle and bayonet (30 to 40 rounds of ammo), grenades, 2-inch knee mortars, pistol, and hand grenades. As a fierce battle was fought at the airfield, the Japanese

The light aircraft carrier *Ryujo* repeatedly attacked Admiral Doorman's force causing it to retire until dawn. During the retreat, Doorman lost the *Van Ness*.

pushed the *38th Division* towards a landing on the island.

Vice Admiral Jisaburo Ozawa was covering the 38th, as well as threading his way through the vast exodus of Allied troops and civilians taking any boat possible to flee Singapore. Ozawa had the light carrier *Ryujo*, his flagship the heavy cruiser *Chokai*, the heavy cruisers *Mikuma*, *Mogami*, *Suzuya*, and *Kumano* (the latter four were sisterships, 12,400 tons, ten 8-inch guns, eight 5-inch dual purpose guns, twelve 24-inch torpedoes [with reloads], and 34 knots), the old light cruiser *Yura*, and the destroyers *Shirakuma*, *Ayanami*, *Isonami*, *Shikinami*, *Murakuma*, *Shirayuki*, and *Hatsuyuki*. Advancing towards him to engage in battle was Admiral Doorman with the light cruisers *De Ruyter*, *Java*, *Tromp*, the british heavy cruiser *Exeter* (8,390 tons, six 8-inch guns, four 4-inch anti-aircraft guns, six 21-inch torpedoes, and 32 knots), the Australian light cruiser *Hobart* (7,105 tons, eight 6-inch guns, four 4-inch anti-aircraft guns, eight 21-inch torpedoes, and 32 knots), Dutch destroyers *Banckert*, *Kortenaer*, *Van Nes*, *Van Ghent*, and the American destroyers *Bulmer*, *Barker*, *Parrott*, *Stewart*, *Pope*, and *John D. Ford* (all the American destroyers were four pipers). Unfortunately, the *Van Ghent* hit an uncharted rock and sank, distracting the *Bankert* to look for survivors. Faced with repeated air attacks from the *Ryujo*, with only four more hours of daylight, Doorman decided to retire and not risk a night action. Doorman, while facing a slightly superior enemy, had the opportunity to attack and disperse an invasion convoy. Doorman himself is quoted as saying history would condemn his decision to retire. Thus an interesting "might-have-been" passes into history. Doorman lost the *Van Nes* to air attacks on the 17th of February while retiring.

Meanwhile, the 38th Division, after some delay, completed the landing at Palembang. Southern Sumatra fell. Later, the Imperial Guard captured northern Sumatra.

The Japanese began moving into high gear during January with the campaign in Malaya going smoothly, the Philippine position consolidating, and the victory at Pearl Harbor neutralizing the American threat. As a prelude to the capture of Java, the Japanese began moving south, capturing strategic positions in the outlying islands.

The eastern advance opened inauspiciously on January 4 when a surprise B-17 raid on the crowded harbor of Davao in Mindanao hit the second turret of the heavy cruiser *Myoko* with a 250-pound bomb and killed or wounded 64 men, sending her to Japan for repairs until February 26.

During the first week in January of 1942 the Japanese began moving the 21st and 23rd Air Flotillas, of about 150 planes each, into the southern Philippine Islands. They gave proper air support for the move into Borneo and the capture of the key airfield at Menado on north end of Celebes Island, the unusually shaped large island with the four arm-like projections in the north central section of the Dutch East Indies. The position was guarded by approximately 1500 troops although fewer than 400 were regular troops. The Japanese attack was in three dimensions.

The invading force was covered by the 21st Air Flotilla and the Eastern Force. The attack consisted of a sea landing by the Sasebo Combined Special Naval Landing Force, which was the 1st and 2nd Sasebo. Strength was about 1600 men organized into six infantry companies and two machine gun companies. The third dimension was supplied when the 1st Yokosuka was air-dropped. This paratroop unit, which started the war in Formosa, was flown in twenty-five Tinas (a modified Nell bomber, of which twenty-five were present in Formosa on December 8, 1941) in two waves. The first wave was of two companies numbering 334 men, and a second wave, reusing the same planes, of 185 men. The light machine gun company was not employed in this landing. Winds were strong and the drops were made from too high an altitude, but these Japanese Marine paratroops did siphon valuable Dutch troops away from the landing beaches.

The Allies launched a minor retaliation from the air, but the attack was simply overwhelming. By the 24th of January the airfield was being used by the 21st Air Flotilla, with two immediate effects. It cut off the Allied ability to fly air units to the Philippines and it moved the Japanese operational air radius south by 300 miles. (This same process was repeated over the next month at Kendari on Celebes Island and at

The reconstructed aircraft carrier *Akagi* was one of four Japanese to launch an air raid against the Australian port of Darwin.

Ambon Island in the fabled Spice Islands).

The next move was a massive air raid by most of the force participating at Pearl Harbor. The target was the Australian port Darwin, a minor port, in the desolate and underpopulated Northern Territories. It was vital in early 1942 as a base through which troops, planes, and supplies were funneled to the Dutch East Indies. It was the closest port and airfield to the Dutch East Indies in Australia.

The Japanese decided to launch three attacks. Two would be invasions; one to Timor, one to Bali, the closest large island to the west of Java, which contained an airfield for ferrying airplanes onto Java; and an air raid against Darwin from four fleet carriers, the *Akagi*, *Kaga*, *Hiryu*, and *Soryu*, and supporting warships.

Surprise was not secured on this attack. As the seventy-one Val divebombers, eighty-one Kate torpedo planes armed with bombs, and thirty-six Zeros approached, they were sighted from a coast watcher base manned by aborigines. Still, the warning time was very limited. Unfortunately for the Australians, their only defensive aircraft were a handful of wretched Wirraways and a flight of ten P-40s on the way through to Java. Some of the pilots had as little as twelve hours of flight time! Against the veteran Japanese Zero pilots they were "meat on the table," and in the course of the raid all ten P-40s in the flight were lost for one Zero and one Val destroyed, both to anti-aircraft fire. Captain

T. Minto of the *Manunda*, a freighter at Darwin, recalls

the wharf was burning near its inner end; *Barossa* and *Neptuna* at the wharf both appeared to have been hit and *Neptuna* was on fire. *British Motorist*, off our bow, was sinking by the head. *Meigs* was on fire aft and sinking. *Mauna Loa* was down by the stern with her bow broken. . . . (the) American destroyer (*Peary*) was on our port side, a solid mass of flame with burning oil all round her and what was left of the crew jumping into the burning oil. We manned our motor life-boat with four of a crew and went to their rescue and eventually picked up over thirty badly burnt and wounded men.

About fifty-four landbased bombers roared in from Kendari and Ambon after the carrier planes hit *Darwin*, to add to the damage. The old four piper *Peary* was sunk, the harbor damaged, and about 250 men killed. Eight ships, including the *Peary*, were lost as well as valuable stores. The effect on morale was heavy, and even today the Australians remember this raid as the most major attack ever launched against their mainland. The Australian War Memorial at Canberra contains a special section devoted to it.

The attack against Bali was particularly

aggravating as it was directly across from the western tip of Java. The Japanese were finding that their airbase on Celebes and Borneo suffered during the wet season, and they hoped, rightfully, that Bali would be drier so they could operate their land based aircraft close to Java and more often. The Japanese sent in two transports carrying an infantry battalion from the 48th Division (the Kanemura Detachment) protected by the light cruiser *Nagara*, and the destroyers *Oshio*, *Asashio*, *Michishio*, *Arashio*, *Wakaba*, *Hatsushimo*, and *Nenohi*. The Allies, as too often in this campaign, were out of position and undertaking several operations at one time. In retrospect, the Allies would have done better to have maintained a strong *united* naval force so that when a vulnerable Japanese convoy was sighted, the Allied force could have proceeded resolutely in an attack. As it was, Doorman had some ships on the east end of Java, some covering an aborted convoy to Timor, and a small force at Surabaya and Tjilatjap (a port on the south side of Java). He ordered the force at Surabaya (light cruisers *de Ruyter* and *Java*, the destroyers *Piet Hein*, *Ford*, and *Pope*) to go in first at night against the Japanese escort, followed by the Tjilatjap force of the light cruiser *Tromp* and destroyers *Stewart*, *Parrott*, *John D. Edwards*, and *Pillsbury*. Finally, a third group of eight Dutch PT-type boats went in, although they did not find any targets.

Thus came about the Battle of Badung Straits, easily one of the worse battles fought by the Allies in World War II. The Japanese had successfully completed their landing and were in the process of departing the waters by February 19. Only the *Asashio* and *Oshio* (2,370 tons, six 5-inch guns, eight 24-inch torpedoes with reloads, 35 knots) were present with one Maru damaged from a bomb earlier in the day. The *de Ruyter* (6,450 tons, seven 5.9-inch guns, 32 knots) followed by the *Java* (6,670 tons, ten 5.9-inch guns arranged so only seven could fire on the broadside, 30 knots) went in first, trailed by the *Piet Hein* (1,310 tons, four 4.7-inch guns, six 21-inch torpedoes, 35 knots) a full 5,500 yards behind, and then the two American four pipers about an equal distance behind. The Japanese destroyers opened fire, switched on searchlights, and threw starshells up for illumination. Beginning at 11 P.M. on the 19th, both sides fired in earnest at a range of 2,200 with the Japanese destroyers virtually crossing the "T" of the two cruisers. Only the *Java* received a minor hit at this point in the action.

The *Piet Hein* took part in the Battle of Badung Straits, one of the worst sea battles fought by the allies in World War II.

As the cruisers retired, the *Piet Hein* came into view and firing began again. At least one torpedo ripped open the *Piet Hein* at 11:16 P.M. and she sank almost immediately. The *Pope* and *Ford* came up and exchanged torpedoes and gunfire with the two intrepid Japanese destroyers. Most fire missed, although the *Ford* suffered minor damage. The two Japanese destroyers, however, became confused and fired on each other for a few minutes before deciding that the enemy had departed.

The second phase of the battle witnessed the four American destroyers going in first with the Dutch light cruiser *Tromp* (3,350 tons, six 5.9-inch guns, six 21-inch torpedoes, 34 knots) at the rear of the line as the "heavy" to use her guns after the American destroyers fired their torpedoes. The four destroyers, steaming at 25 knots, launched fifteen torpedoes at the enemy, and missed/malfunctioned with all of them. The two Japanese destroyers came out again to do battle. The *Stewart*, leading, saw the approaching Japanese destroyers at 1:36 A.M., fired additional torpedoes and starshell, and opened gunnery fire at 1:43 A.M. The *Stewart* received a direct hit on the bridge at 1:46. When she swerved due to the hit, a near collision occurred between the *Pillsbury* and the *Parrott*. Enemy fire was so effective, and the formation now confused, that the American destroyers did not, as planned, charge the enemy transport, but withdrew from the action. By now the Japanese destroyers were fully alert and proceeded to pound the *Tromp* which was using a bright blue searchlight, making the *Tromp* an easy target, scoring eleven hits on the *Tromp*. The *Tromp* did hit the bridge of the *Oshio*, killing seven men. *Asashio* received minor damage in the action suffering fifteen killed and wounded. But it was not over. Japanese destroyers *Michishio* and *Arashio* had returned from escort duty.

These two Japanese destroyers raced down the strait going in the opposite direction of the Allies and suddenly found themselves sandwiched between the *Edwards* and *Stewart* on one side, and the *Tromp* and *Pillsbury* on the other side. In deadly action beginning at 2:19 A.M. and lasting but a few moments, "ensued a lightning exchange of shells, oaths, more shells, torpedoes." The *Michishio* was repeatedly hit, went dead in the water, suffering 96 killed and wounded.

Scoreboard: Bali lost, *Piet Hein* lost, *Tromp* to the repair yards with the *Stewart* (which ended up being captured at Surabaya and serving as the *Japanese Patrol Vessel #102* during the remainder of the war), for limited damage to the Japanese. The frustration of faulty American torpedoes held.

The end was near. The original plan was to move the veteran 1st Australian Corp, the 6th and 7th Australian Divisions, made famous in the desert fighting, to Java. The 7th would arrive first late in February and eventually be joined by the 6th. The 6th would fight in Sumatra while the 7th would deploy in Java, sandwiching the Dutch army of four regiments between them.

With a victorious Japan heading south and the fall of Singapore imminent, the Australian chief of staff, Lieutenant General Sir Vernon Sturdee, recommended to the Australian Labor Party prime minister John Curtin that the 1st Australian Corp be returned to Australia. In addition, Curtin and Sturdee wanted the British 7th Armored Brigade originally scheduled for Malaya, then Java (it ended up in Burma in time for the retreat from Rangoon) and the Australian 9th Division to be returned as well. When this was cabled to Winston Churchill, a tempest raged.

Eventually the 7th Australian was returned to Australia and assembled there in April while the 6th was detained in Ceylon for several months before going back to Australia. The 9th remained in the Western Desert, to be replaced by the American 32nd Division which was sent on to Australia.

It is interesting to speculate what might have occurred if the 7th Australian had deployed to Java.

Arriving in Java in late February, it would have run the risk of being attacked by the superior Japanese air and naval forces. Also, the 7th was not shipped "combat loaded," that is, with equipment and troops together in each ship, but in a hodge podge of various ships departing and arriving at different times. It most likely would have been destroyed on Java and would not have been present for the defense of Port Morseby later in 1942, where the

Japanese received a decisive defeat in their struggle for New Guinea. Still, one has to feel compassion for the Dutch who fought loyally, and aided the fight in Malaya with planes and bases well after that position should have been written off. The Allies decided at some point that Java was not worth the fight.

In the final act remaining Allied ships fought the final battles in the defense of Java, first in the Battle of the Java Sea.

The Japanese plan called for two major convoys, one from the east and one from the west. As usual with Japanese strategic plans, there were several forces at sea at the same time. Unfortunately, the Allies also split their limited strength. The Japanese western convoy carried the 2nd Division and 230th Infantry Regiment, while the Japanese eastern convoy carried the 48th Infantry Division (minus one battalion), and the 56th Regimental Group (the 146th Infantry Regiment, a company of armor, and the 1st battalion of the 56th Field Artillery Regiment).

Admiral Helfrich was overall commander in Java at this point. He first ordered the Western Striking Force, consisting of light cruisers *Hobart*, *Dragon*, *Danae*, and destroyers *Tenedos*, *Scout*, and *Evertsen*, formed on February 21 and operating out of Batavia (today the capital of Indonesia-Jakarta), to intercept the eastern prong of the Japanese advance. The force steamed out on the night of February 26, and not finding the enemy, returned in the morning. It was ordered out again on the 28th, to retire through Sunda Strait and fall back to Ceylon if no enemy was found. This was accomplished with the loss of the *Evertsen*, and Admiral Helfrich later regretted not sending the Western Striking Force on to Rear Admiral Doorman on the morning of the 27th. If the Western Striking Force had joined up with Doorman's command for the Battle of the Java Sea, the Japanese western convoy carrying the 48th Division might have been turned back or even debilitated. The only hope for the Allies at this point was to turn back at least one convoy to allow the Allied troops on Java to concentrate against the other Japanese beachhead.

Doorman sortied on the afternoon of February 27. The *de Ruyter* led the column of cruisers, followed by the *Exeter*, the American heavy cruiser *Houston* (9,006 tons, nine 8-inch guns—the afterturret of three guns had been knocked out earlier from a bomb hit—four 5-inch guns, 32 knots), the Australian light cruiser *Perth*, sistership to the *Hobart*, and the *Java*. The British destroyers *Electra*, *Encounter* (1,400 tons, four 4.7-inch guns, eight 21-inch torpedoes, 36 knots), and *Jupiter* (1,760 tons, six 4.7-inch guns, ten 21-inch torpedoes, 36 knots) screened the head of the column, while the American destroyers *John D. Edwards*, *Alden*, *John D. Ford*, and *Paul Jones* covered the rear, and the Dutch destroyers *Witte de With* and *Kortenaer* covered the flank.

The Japanese transport fleet consisting of forty-one ships was disposed in two columns with 650 yards between ships and 2,000 yards between columns. It was sailing in a haphazard formation as was to be expected from merchant ship captains suddenly at war and in an organized convoy. Admiral Takagi was slow in catching up to the convoy with his two heavy cruisers *Nachi* and *Haguro* (13,000 tons, ten 8-inch guns, eight 5-inch dual purpose guns, twelve 24-inch torpedoes with reloads, 33 knots), but he did launch scout planes from the heavy and light cruisers to keep the enemy in sight and spot in the ensuing battle. Meanwhile, the escort moved to the front of the convoy and deployed for battle. Rear Admiral Tanaka, soon to become famous for the Tokyo Express off Guadalcanal, led with his flagship, *Jintsu* (5,900 tons, seven 5.5-inch guns—six could bear on a broadside—eight 24-inch torpedoes, 35 knots), followed by *Yukikaze*, *Tokitsukaze*, *Amatsukaze*, and *Hatsukaze* (2,490 tons, six 5-inch guns, eight 24-inch torpedoes with reloads, 35 knots). The newer Japanese destroyers and most of the Japanese heavy cruisers were capable of reloading torpedo tubes, an operation usually lasting 20 to 25 minutes or less on the larger cruisers—a capability lacking in the Allied navies. Also, most of the Japanese light cruisers, along with the older destroyers, even if carrying 24-inch torpedoes, carried the older style torpedo, not the dreaded Long Lance.

The battle was spread over many hours and had six distinct phases. The first opened with a long range gunnery duel. Coming up in a separate column and opening fire at 3:47 P.M.

JAPANESE INVASION FORCE: THIRD FLEET, DUTCH INDIES FORCE (JAVA INVASION)

DIRECT SUPPORT FORCE (BOTH EAST AND WEST JAVA INVASIONS

Vice-Admiral Takahashi, commanding

Heavy Cruisers
Ashigara, Myoko

Destroyers
Asashio Oshio, Arashio, Kawakaze

WESTERN JAVA INVASION

Rear Admiral Kurita, commanding

Heavy Cruisers
Mikuma, Mogami, Kumano, Suzuya

(Chokai *attached in earlier invasions*)

Destroyers
Amagiri, Asagiri, Yugiri

THIRD ESCORT FORCE

Rear Admiral Hara, commanding

Light Cruisers
Natori, *and* Yura

Destroyers
Asakaze, Harukaze, Hatakaze, Natsukaze, Fubuki, Shirayuki, Hatsuyuki, Satsuki,

Minazuki, Nagatsuki, Shirakumo, Murakumo, Hibiki, Akatsuki, Hatsuharu

FIRST AIR GROUP

Rear Admiral Kakuta, commanding

Light Aircraft Carriers
Ryujo *(22 Claude Fighters, 18 Kate torpedo planes and strength at Start of War*

TRANSPORT FORCE

Fifty-six transports (including two Japanese army airplane transports, one of which was lost in Battle of Sunda Straits)

EASTERN JAVA INVASION FORCE

SUPPORT GROUP

Rear Admiral Takagi, commanding

Heavy Cruisers
Nachi Haguro

Destroyers
Ikazuchi, Akebono

FIRST ESCORT FORCE

Rear Admiral Nishimura, commanding

Light Cruisers
Naka

Destroyers
Murasame, Harusame, Yudachi, Samidare, Asagumo, Natsugumo, Minegumo, Yamakaze

SECOND ESCORT FORCE

Rear Admiral Tanaka, commanding

Light Cruisers
Jintsu

Destroyers
Kuroshio, Okashio, Hayashio, Hatsukaze, Yukikaze, Amatsukaze, Sazanami, Ushio Tokitsukaze

FIRST BASE FORCE

A rear force not employed directly in the final attack on Java

Light Cruisers
Nagara

Destroyers
Hatsuharu, Nenohi, Wakaba

SECOND BASE FORCE

Seaplanes tenders Chitose, Mizuho Sanyo Maru, Sanuki Maru *(latter two are capable of holding eight planes)*

TRANSPORT FORCE

Forty-one transports

ABDA COMBINED STRIKE FORCE FOR THE DEFENSE OF EAST JAVA

Rear Admiral Doorman, commanding

Heavy Cruisers
Houston *(USN)* and Exeter *(RN)*

Light Cruisers
Java *(RNN)*, de Ruyter *(RNN)*, Perth *(RAN)*

Destroyers
John D. Edwards, Paul Jones, John D. Ford, Alden, Pope *(all USN)*
Electra, Jupiter, Encounter *(RN)*; Witt de With, Kortenaer *(RNN)*

ABDA WESTERN STRIKING FORCE

Captain Howden (RAN) commanding

Light Cruisers
Hobart *(RAN)*, Dragon, *and* Danae *(RN)*

Destroyers
Scout, Tenedos *(RN)*, and Evertsen *(RNN)*

JAPANESE 16TH ARMY

2nd Infantry Division	38th Infantry Division after used for capture of Hong Kong	48th Mechanized Division after used with 14th Army in the Philippines	56th Regimental Group (Sakaguchi Detachment)

1st Kure Special Naval Landing Force (3 rifle companies & 1 machine gun company, strength 820 men)	2nd Kure Special Naval Landing Force (3 rifle companies, 1 machine gun company, 1 anti-aircraft battery, strength 1,000)	1st and 2nd Sasebo Special Naval Landing Force (each consisted of 3 rifle companies & 1 machine gun company, 800 men each used as a combined unit)

THE DUTCH ARMY ON JAVA, MARCH OF 1942

WEST JAVA COMMAND

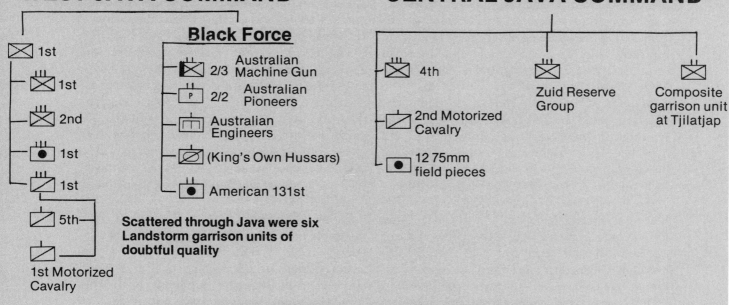

⊠ 1st

▭ 1st

⊠ 2nd

◉ 1st

▱ 1st

▱ 5th

▱ 1st Motorized Cavalry

Black Force

⊠ 2/3 Australian Machine Gun

P 2/2 Australian Pioneers

▭ Australian Engineers

▱ (King's Own Hussars)

◉ American 131st

Scattered through Java were six Landstorm garrison units of doubtful quality

CENTRAL JAVA COMMAND

⊠ 4th

▱ 2nd Motorized Cavalry

◉ 12 75mm field pieces

⊠ Zuid Reserve Group

⊠ Composite garrison unit at Tjilatjap

EASTERN JAVA COMMAND

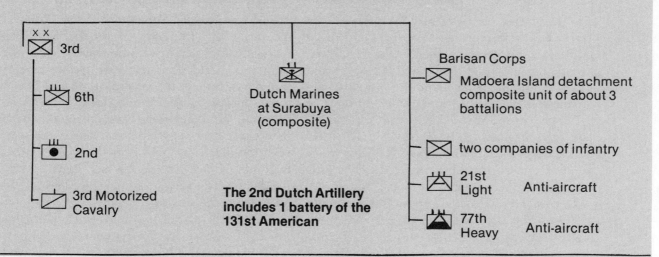

XX
⊠ 3rd

⊠ 6th

◉ 2nd

▱ 3rd Motorized Cavalry

⊠ Dutch Marines at Surabuya (composite)

The 2nd Dutch Artillery includes 1 battery of the 131st American

Barisan Corps

⊠ Madoera Island detachment composite unit of about 3 battalions

⊠ two companies of infantry

◭ 21st Light — Anti-aircraft

◣ 77th Heavy — Anti-aircraft

OR EAST INDIES

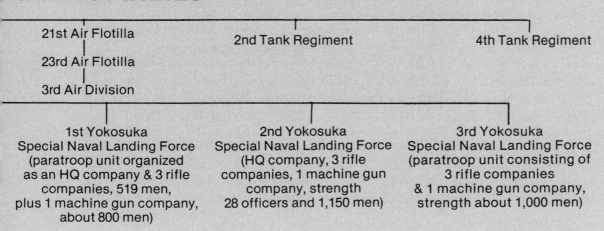

21st Air Flotilla

23rd Air Flotilla

3rd Air Division

2nd Tank Regiment

4th Tank Regiment

1st Yokosuka
Special Naval Landing Force
(paratroop unit organized
as an HQ company & 3 rifle
companies, 519 men,
plus 1 machine gun company,
about 800 men)

2nd Yokosuka
Special Naval Landing Force
(HQ company, 3 rifle
companies, 1 machine gun
company, strength
28 officers and 1,150 men)

3rd Yokosuka
Special Naval Landing Force
(paratroop unit consisting of
3 rifle companies
& 1 machine gun company,
strength about 1,000 men)

were the two heavy cruisers screened by the destroyers *Ushio* (leading) and *Sazanami*, *Yamakaze*, and *Kawakaze*. The scout planes launched earlier were used for spotting gunfire, but not with great effect. Finally, a third column, led by a sistership to the *Jintsu*, came with the light cruiser *Naka* leading the *Asagumo*, *Minegumo*, *Murasame*, *Samidare*, *Harukaze*, and *Yudachi*. The destroyers in the two columns were older ones. Between 3:47 and 4:40 P.M. long range gunfire, with only the heavier ships firing, did little damage. One 8-inch hit the *de Ruyter*, but failed to explode, while at 4:38 P.M. the *Exeter* was hit and set afire. During this time, the Japanese were busily firing torpedoes, torpedoes which the Allies did not know could travel great distances. The *Haguro* fired eight torpedoes at a range of 12.5 miles; the *Naka's* column fired at ranges of 13,000 to 15,000 yards, and only gained one hit. The *Kortenaer* was hit and sank quickly at 4:40 P.M.—the Allies thought a mine was responsible. The *Kortenaer*, as described by someone on *Perth* directly behind her, "capsized and dived under in a few seconds, then broke in halves." During this period of the battle the *Haguro* and *Nachi* fired 1,271 8-inch rounds, while the two Japanese light cruisers fired off 171 rounds of 5.5-inch ammunition. As was typical of daylight action in both the Pacific and Mediterranean in World War II, long range gunnery duels were almost never decisive; little damage could be done at such long ranges.

The second phase lasted about thirty minutes in which the confused Allied fleet, operating with two different languages and four nationalities, tried to get reorganized. Part of the confusion was caused by the *Exeter* which was not in complete control of her movements. The Allied fleet began to retire pursued by the Japanese.

In the third phase the *Haguro* and *Nachi* fired at 19,000 yards on Doorman's cruisers at about 5:20 P.M. It was a long range torpedo salvo which failed to score, and so the Japanese retired. (Admiral Takagi had been less than exploitive of the Allied situation, and later at the Battle of the Coral Sea, he showed a certain lack of aggressiveness.) The *Jintsu* led a charge towards the smoke obscured Allied line, with the *Minegumo* and *Asagumo* closing to 6,500

yards before launching torpedoes. The smoke came from fire on the *Exeter*, numerous Allied smokescreens, and exhaust from many ships in the area.

The *Encounter* and *Electra*, to protect the *Exeter*, considerably slowed, threw a smokescreen to attack the two closing Japanese destroyers. The *Encounter*, at 5:30 P.M. engaged the *Minegumo* in a ten minute fire fight at 3,000 yards, with virtually no damage occuring! The *Electra* hit the *Asagumo*, bringing her to a dead stop for a few minutes. The *Electra*, however, then took two direct hits, slowed, and finally sank at 5:46 P.M.

Doorman did not give up and swung around one more time in hopes of damaging the nearby enemy convoy. The American four pipers searched, but found nothing and at 5:50 all ships, except the two Japanese destroyers *Minegumo* and *Asagumo* were out of sight.

The fourth phase opened with Doorman leading his force north, looking for the convoy. Takagi, meanwhile, knowing that Vice-Admiral Takahashi with the heavy cruisers *Ashigara* and *Myoko*, supported by two destroyers, was near Surabaya, decided his main job was to protect the convoy and retired towards it. At 6:30 P.M. in the gathering gloom both sides spotted the other again. Long range fire at 16,000 yards developed from the Japanese heavy cruisers, with the *Jintsu's* column firing at 17,500 yards, maximum range for the 5.5-inch guns on her. No damage was sustained, and the Allies turned away from the convoy.

The fifth phase opened with another northern thrust by Doorman—but with a reduced force. The *Jupiter* hit a Dutch mine and blew up at 8:25 P.M. The four pipers meanwhile had been ordered to return to Surabaya to refuel and pick up additional torpedoes. The *Encounter* had been detailed to pick up survivors from the *Kortenaer*, and the *Exeter* had retired from the action escorted by the *Witte de With*. So, the final advance was made by the *de Ruyter*, followed by the *Perth*, the *Houston* and the *Java*. At 10:33 P.M. the *Jintsu* and consorts steamed away from the Allies to protect the convoy leaving the *Haguro* (leading) and *Nachi* to deal with the Allies. The Japanese heavy cruisers reversed course to parallel the Allied column so that all were steaming in a northernly direction.

The cruisers exchanged fire for four minutes, beginning at 10:40 P.M., with gunfire reopening at 10:52, and the *Nachi* launching eight and the *Haguro* four torpedoes at a range of 14,000 yards. One hit on the *de Ruyter* caused her magazine to explode and she quickly sank, taking 344 men including Doorman with her. The *Java* was hit four minutes later and this World War I design burst into flames and sank. (Doorman had given verbal instructions to have disabled ships "left to the mercy of the enemy.")

British light cruiser *Exeter* sinks after it was hit in the Battle of Java Sea.

Captain Waller of the *Perth*, who now was the senior officer, decided to withdraw. He later wrote of this decision, "I now had under my orders one undamaged 6-inch cruiser, and one 8-inch cruiser with very little ammunition and no guns aft. I had no destroyers. The force was subjected throughout the day and night operations to the most superbly organised air reconnaissance. . . . (the Japanese) had ample destroyers to interpose between the convoy and my approach—well advertized as I knew it would be. I had therefore no hesitation in withdrawing what remained of the Striking Force. . . ."

The sixth phase took place on March 1. The *Exeter*, after emergency repairs, the *Encounter*, and four-piper *Pope* sortied from Surabaya and fought a three hour and five minute daylight engagement with Takagi's heavy cruisers *Nachi*, *Haguro*, and Takahashi's *Ashigara*, and *Myoko*, with four destroyers. Trapped between the two groups of Japanese ships, the Allied ships were inevitably lost. The Japanese expended 35 torpedoes and 2,650 shells to sink the three Allied ships.

The defeat of the Allies at the Battle of the Java Sea had several causes: Lack of concentration and fatigue from constant operations, air attacks, and enemy advances, as well as a failure to recognize the skill of the Japanese in night combat contributed to the defeat. Many of the Allied warships were older and, of course, did not have the Long Lance torpedoes. Lack of a common language and failure to use the navy codebook were also contributing factors. All in all, a sad day for the Allies, saved only by the bravery of the many sailors who died. It delayed the invasion for

The Dutch destroyer *Kortenaer* sunk within seconds after being hit in the Battle of Java Sea.

twenty-four hours.

The four remaining four-pipers broke through Bali Straits and made it safely to Australia. The *Perth* and the *Houston*, however, decided to break through Sunda Straits, which had an entire invasion fleet present numbering 56 Marus, two heavy cruisers, a light cruiser, and seven destroyers.

The *Perth*, with Waller aboard, led the *Houston* into Sunda Straits, hoping to escape to Australia. The destroyer *Fubuki* first sighted the two Allied ships and alerted the immediate escort fleet. The problem was that the two Allied cruisers were directly opposite Bantam Bay, shaped like a bowl, with fifty-six transports sitting in it busily unloading. Only two destroyers, the *Hatukaze* and *Harukaze* were directly between the Allied cruisers that opened fire at any target, including the transports, that they could see. General Inamura's aide, on the Japanese aircraft transport *Akitsu Maru* (renamed *Ryujo Maru* for the operation as a ruse de guerre; 11,800 tons, twelve 75mm guns—two anti-aircraft—capable of launching, but not landing 20 small planes like Nates and carrying 20 Daihatsu landing craft—for this operation it contained primarily tanks), commented on the start of the attack, "the tremendous sound of the guns. . . . about 16 kilometers NNE of our anchorage there were two battleships continuously firing their large guns. To our left I could clearly see what appeared to be a destroyer (*Harukaze*) which was actively carrying on the fight." All the Japanese warships in the area hurried to the site of the battle while the *Perth* and *Houston* executed a wide loop, still firing at various enemy ships. As Professor Dull has written, "The *Houston* and *Perth* were now doomed to pay the price, as three Japanese cruisers and nine destroyers converged on them." The Japanese fired numerous torpedoes, as did the *Perth*, and sank four of their own transports, although three, including the *Akitsu Maru*, were later raised from the shallow bay and repaired. The *Perth* sank trying to make her way through the straits:

About midnight *Perth's* Gunnery Officer, Lieutenant Hancox, told his captain that very little 6-inch ammunition remained,

Captured Japanese photo shows the *Kortenaer* being hit in the Banka Sea.

and Waller, deciding to try to force a passage through Sunda Strait, ordered full speed and set course direct for Toppers Island. *Perth* had barely steadied on the course, when at five minutes past midnight, a torpedo struck on the starboard side. The report came:

"Forward engine room out . . . speed reduced"; and Waller said, "Very Good." A few minutes later Hancox told Waller that ammunition was almost expended, the turrets were firing practice shells and the 4-inch guns were reduced to star shells. Again Waller said "Very Good." A second torpedo hit under the bridge, also on the starboard side, shortly afterwards; and Waller said, "Christ! That's torn it . . . Abandon ship." Hancox asked: "Prepare to abandon ship?" "No! Abandon ship."

The 368 men who survived the sinking were treated well by the Japanese navy (as were virtually all Allied sailors in the battles around Java in 1942), although later in prison camps treatment was different.

The *Houston* survived for an hour longer,

after being hit repeatedly by shells and three torpedoes. Both captains were lost. In all, 87 torpedoes were launched at the two ships. The aide on the *Akitsu Maru* noted that when shells came their way "the facial expression of the soldiers changed to anxiety." Later, when the *Akitsu Maru* went down the commander in chief of the 16th Army and staff had to swim to shore. Imamura's aide found him "sitting on a pile of bamboos about a hundred meters away. Dispiritedly I limped over to him and congratulated him on the successful landing. I looked around me. Everyone had a black face (with fuel oil) including the commander."

On February 27, the old American aircraft carrier, the *Langely*, rebuilt from a collier in World War I, was heading for Tjilatjap with 32 P-40s. She was caught by land based bombers operated by the Japanese navy. Five hits were scored and she was lost.

Following the Battle of Java Sea, the wounded were taken from ship and put onto waiting hospital train.

Java fell in a few days. There was little more that could be done. The Japanese came ashore at each end of the island and simply overwhelmed the Dutch army, stiffened by some small Allied units, including some American artillery units. One Dutch native regiment of infantry was marching on a road in the open in daylight when it was strafed by Japanese planes. The strafing was sufficient to disperse the entire regiment and make it inoperative. The war was over on March 8 on Java. The Andaman Islands in the Indian Ocean were taken on March 23. All of Sumatra was secured on March 28; Rangoon had already fallen on March 8.

Burma and the Indian Ocean Raid

Burma was viewed by the Japanese as a natural fortress which produced both rice and oil. It also contained the last main land route to Nationalist China, the Burma Road. Japan was determined to seize Burma, although the invasion of that isolated British colony was not easy. The alignment of the mountain valleys made it difficult and Rangoon, on the Indian Ocean, was the main communication route for Burma.

The initial forces defending Burma consisted of the 1st Burma Division made up of the 1st and 2nd Burma Brigades, and the 13th and 16th Indian Brigades. There was a lack of artillery and anti-aircraft equipment and the Indian units had been regularly "milked." Brigadier J.K. Jones, who commanded the 16th Indian Infantry Brigade, noted that in December, "Of the three battalions in the brigade none had been longer in it than six weeks. None of the battalions had carried out higher training of any sort during that year." The start of the campaign saw thirty effective Allied planes stationed in Burma. The price of being unprepared was paid.

The Japanese invaded with the 33rd Division consisting of three regiments, and the 55th Infantry Division consisting of two regiments. These two divisions shared one cavalry recon-naissance regiment (as usual with this designation, it was battalion strength) between them. Total strength was 35,440 men. The Burma Campaign got the leftovers from the main campaigns, and really would not move into high gear until January of 1942 when the 5th Air Division, after Manila had fallen, was transferred to the Burma front.

The Japanese began a series of night bombing attacks on Rangoon, which slowed up unloading by the local longshoremen who were scared to work under bombing attacks. Wavell directed the Burma forces to fight the Japanese as far east as possible, to retain Rangoon for as long as possible. A series of battles took place near the Sittang River in eastern Burma where the Allies suffered severe losses as the Japanese kept slipping around the Allied flanks.

At this point the Nationalist Chinese sent the V and VI Chinese Armies. While they represented some of the better Chinese troops, even including motor transport, some of the Chinese troops were without rifles (a Chinese army was equal to a British division in numbers). Further reinforcements included two Indian brigades and the 7th Armored Brigade Group. The Japanese keep advancing and reinforcing their advantage in the air with additional units available

The *Dorsetshire* was a British armored cruiser of the Devonshire Class.

after the fall of the Dutch East Indies. March and April saw a major advance to take Rangoon. During late March and early April, while Nagumo roared through the Indian Ocean with five fleet carriers, most of the 18th and the 56th Infantry Divisions landed at Rangoon.

At this point it became an impossible situation for the Allies and a steady Japanese advance brought the fall of Mandalay on April 30. By May, Japanese troops were on the border with India, and India was in her most dangerous hour. Some people think that if the Japanese had mounted their major effort then in the Indian Ocean Basin that the British could have been knocked out of the war and the Axis powers could have linked up. Erich Raeder, the commander-in-chief of the German navy hoped for just such a course, but it was not to be.

After the destruction of Force Z, the British were forced to fall back on a sea strategy they seldom used. They had to operate their Eastern Fleet as a "fleet-in-being," that is, they had to maintain some sort of reasonable strength in that theater that would appear to the Japanese as a threat. But that same fleet had to keep from engaging in combat except in the most favorable circumstances, for if it were lost, there would not be adequate force behind it to stop the Japanese advance. Going hand and hand with this was the conviction that Ceylon had to be defended to the utmost.

The new commander was Admiral Somerville, a flyer who regularly went up from the carriers based previously at Gibraltar, now in the Indian Ocean, Having recently seen a well trained air crew on the fleet carrier *Ark Royal*, Somerville was disappointed in the newer *Formidable* and *Indomitable*. They were, in his view, just not adequately worked up and the air crews were trained inadequately. Fortunately, after Churchill's interference with the role of Force Z and its subsequent destruction, Somerville received only limited prodding from Churchill, who was a forceful man who wanted his fleet to be constantly doing something, even when they should have been concentrating on training and staying alive.

So what could Somerville field? He had the battlefield *Warspite*, a modernized World War I ship, that fought at Jutland. Armed with eight 15-inch guns, it could steam at about 24 knots. The other battleships of his force were extremely poor. The *Resolution, Ramillies, Royal Sovereign,* and *Revenge* were World War I specimens, steaming at 20 knots and armed with eight 15-inch guns. The only way Somerville could hope to take the Japanese fleet was in a night action or by launching a surprise air attack. (Somerville did have one ace up his sleeve in the form of a secret naval base at Addu Atoll in the extreme southern portion of the Maldive Islands—the Japanese never discovered it.) Due to the differences in speed between his units, Somerville divided his fleet into two separate units. One was his fast squadron containing the two fleet carriers and the *Warspite*, while the slower squadron contained the old battleships.

The Japanese roared in with two forces. The main strike force, under Vice-Admiral Nagumo, consisted of the four fast battleships of the *Kongo* class protecting five fleet carriers. They were the *Akagi, Hiryu, Soryu, Shokaku,* and *Zuikaku* (the *Kaga* was in Japan). A smaller force made up of the light carrier *Ryujo*, six cruisers, and four destroyers raided the Bengal coast inflicting tremendous damage and even worse panic. Sea movement on this coast came to a standstill for many months, leading indirectly to the starvation of hundreds of thousands in 1943, in what today is Bangladesh.

When intelligence sources alerted Somerville that the Japanese were coming, he deployed his forces to the sea on April 2. Unfortunately, after two days of patrolling, he cancelled the operation, thinking that Nagumo was not coming. Two heavy cruisers, the *Cornwall* and *Dorsetshire* (9,900 tons, eight 8-inch guns, four 4-inch anti-aircraft guns, eight 21-inch torpedoes, 32 knots) were ordered to Ceylon and the old light carrier *Hermes* and some minor craft were milling about Ceylon . . . when the Japanese struck.

Colombo was hit at dawn on April 5 by 315 planes, although radar gave early warning of the attack. The planes concentrated on the port installations, and got into a real dogfight with 36 Hurricanes and six Fulmar fighters. Fifteen Hurricanes and four Fulmars were lost for the loss of one Zero, but six Val divebombers were lost as well. A flight of six Swordfish torpedo planes redeploying from Trimcomalee to Colombo came through during the air raid and were destroyed. The destroyer *Tenedos* finally was sunk in Colombo harbor. But Nagumo did not find the British fleet.

He did find the two heavy cruisers, though, and they were attacked by 53 Val divebombers. With no Combat Air Patrol, on a clear day, the *Cornwall* and *Dorsetshire* were massacred. Diving from 12,000 feet, the Vals scored eight hits on the *Cornwall* and repeated hits on the *Dorsetshire*. The attack began at 1:38 P.M. and both ships were sunk by 2:00 P.M. Records state that 422 died in the attack and no planes were lost.

Nagumo took his force away for two days, still groping for the British fleet, then reversed course and roared in for a raid on Trimcomalee, on the other side of Ceylon. An attack was launched on the port at dawn on April 9, 1942. It was made up of Kates and Zeros, as Nagumo wanted to hold back the Vals in case the British fleet was discovered. The 22 Hurricanes and Fulmars rose, and shot down three Zeros and one Kate, for the loss of eight Hurricanes and three Fulmars. One pilot of a Fulmar commented later on the Zero, "the Fulmar was far too slow for these little bastards, who could turn on a sixpence, pull up into a stall, do a roll off the top, and cock ten thousand devils of a snook at you." The damage was quite deadly, one Kate blowing up the bomb storage dump! One additional Kate was lost here. What is significant is that every raid cost the Japanese planes, and more importantly, valuable air crews. Attrition was slowly taking a toll on the elite Japanese pilots.

After Nagumo's scout planes sighted the light carrier *Hermes* and destroyer *Vampire*, he attacked with 85 Vals. As a British naval officer commented on the attack, it "was carried out perfectly, relentlessly and quite fearlessly, and was exactly like a highly organized deck display. The aircraft peeled off in threes diving straight down on the ship out of the sun." The *Hermes* was hit forty times by British count and sank within twenty minutes. The *Vampire* was also disposed of. The awesome ability of the Japanese pilots was probably never surpassed in the course of the war.

Where was Somerville? He had deployed his slow division back to covering convoys in the Indian Ocean and tried to ambush the Japanese, coming close (or possibly close to his own destruction), but failed to get a blow in. Somerville commented after this action, when things looked so bleak and he did not know that the Japanese were not going to return, that he could

do nothing now to help Ceylon—they have practically no air force left so it looks to me as if the Japs can walk in

any time they like. It really looks as if we might lose India just for the sake of a handful of aircraft and one or two decent ships.

But the Americans were busily bombing Tokyo with the Doolittle Raid and Yamamoto was planning for his decisive battle. India was saved although they faced one final shot from the Japanese in 1944 at Imphal. Japan would get Burma, but no more.

JAPANESE CARRIER STRIKE FORCE

Vice-Admiral Nagumo, commanding

Aircraft Carriers *Kaga, Akagi, Hiryu, Soryu, Shokaku, Zuikaku*
Battleships *Haruna, Kirishima, Hiei, Kongo*

The *Hermes* sunk within twenty minutes after being repeatedly hit.

Heavy Cruisers *Tone, Chikuma*
Light Cruiser *Abukuma*
Destroyers *Tanikaze, Urakaze, Isokaze, Hamakaze, Arare, Shiranuhi, Kazumi, Kagero, Maikaze, Hagikaze, Akigumo*

Vice-Admiral Somerville, commanding

Aircraft Carriers *Indomitable* (12 Fulmar fighters, 9 Sea Hurricane fighters, 24 Albacore torpedo planes) and *Formidable* (12 Martlet fighters, 21 Albacore torpedo planes)
Battleship *Warspite*
Heavy Cruisers *Dorsetshire, Cornwall*
Light Cruisers *Enterprise, Emerald*
Destroyers *Napier, Nestor, Paladin, Panther, Hotspur, Foxhound*

FORCE B (Slow Class)

Vice-Admiral Willis, commanding

Light Aircraft Carrier *Hermes* (12 Swordfish torpedo planes)
Battleships *Resolution, Ramillies, Royal Sovereign, Revenge*
Light Cruisers *Caledon, Dragon, Heemskerk* (RNN)

Destroyers *Griffin, Norman, Arrow, Decoy, Fortune, Scout, Vampire* (RAN), *Isaac Sweers* (RNN)

Ceylon Based Air Units

The Royal Air Force had two squadrons of Hurricanes based at Colombo, and one at Trimcomalee. One additional fighter squadron made up of Fulmars was based at Trimcomalee. One RAF squadron of Blenheim bombers was based at Colombo along with some Catalina flying boats.

The Royal Navy had two squadrons of Fulmars based at Trimcomalee, along with one squadron of torpedo planes there consisting of Swordfish and Albacore.

BRITISH AIRPLANE CHARACTERISTICS

Fulmar (820 mile range, 8 MGs, 253 m.p.h.)
Hurricane MK II (480 mile range without tanks, 12 MGs, 4 cannon, 342 m.p.h.)
Albacore (521 mile range, 2 MGs, 1 torpedo or 1500 lbs., 163 m.p.h.)

THE EARLY CARRIER RAIDS

By early 1942 the Pacific Fleet had seen the fall of Wake Island and the arrival of Admiral Nimitz, with Admiral Kimmel departing for a fate he did not fully deserve. The Southern Resource Area was still battling on against the Japanese onslaught, but the end in Southeast Asia seemed obvious given the strength of the Japanese and the weakness of the Allies in that theater. But the Americans did have a large surface navy, even if it was minus the battleship line,

and she had her fleet carriers. Admiral King, commander of the entire navy summed up the situation nicely in a letter to Secretary of the Navy Frank Knox, dated February 8, "The 'defensive-offensive' may be paraphrased as 'hold what you've got and hit them when you can,' the hitting to be done, not only by seizing opportunities, but making them."

The first decision concerned America's commitment to protect Australia and New Zealand.

It was impractical for Great Britain to shift enough forces to the South Pacific at that time, given her commitments to Europe. This entailed reinforcements from American land, air and sea to various strategic islands in the South Pacific. Such garrisoned bases would protect Australia and New Zealand from the Japanese, without a fight, and would be bases from which the Allies could launch a counterattack later against Japan. The most important contribution at this early stage of the war from the navy of the United States was a carrier task force. It was ordered by Admiral King and carried out by Admiral Nimitz. But before the arrival of this force in the South Pacific, the first successful American carrier raids in the Central Pacific were made.

Vice Admiral Wilson Brown and Vice Admiral William F. Halsey commanded the two carrier task forces that operated in the Pacific at this time. Ideally, both should have had two fleet carriers, although until the *Hornet* arrived from the Atlantic, one task force had only one fleet carrier. Brown tried to lead a raid against occupied Wake Island in January, but a Japanese sub sank an oil tanker key for the refuelling of Brown's task force. So it fell to Halsey to carry out the first successful carrier raid.

The first raid was against the Marshalls on February 1 by Halsey's Task Force 8, which had been covering the *Yorktown*, a major convoy to Samoa loaded with troops and supplies to garrison that key post. Halsey was ordered, with the convoy safe, to raid the Japanese occupied islands in the Central Pacific. Rear Admiral Fletcher, with the *Yorktown*, would attack the Gilberts at the same time.

The Marshall Islands is a series of atolls in the Central Pacific about half way between the Hawaiian Islands and New Guinea. They are atolls, or coral islands that usually have a lagoon and little height—and Japan gained them from Imperial Germany in 1914. Vice Admiral Shigemi Inoue, who commanded the area from Rabaul, was one of the most air minded of Japanese admirals. Inoue often said, "who commands the air commands at sea." Inoue was more familiar with land based air and was about to receive some unique lessons in it. The Japanese had for air defense in the area nine Nell bombers and 33 Claude fighters (648 mile range, drop tanks extend that by 250 miles, 2 MGs, 270 m.p.h.) of the Chitose Air Group and the Yokohama Air Group of the 24th Air Flotilla. Additional reconnaissance planes operated in the area as well. This was a small force for such a large area, but Japan could spare little to a garrison as distant as the Marshalls.

As Halsey approached with the *Enterprise*, the executive officer delivered a little ditty to the pilot waiting room. Commander Jeter's ditty went:

> An eye for an eye
> A tooth for a tooth
> This Sunday it's our turn to shoot.
> —Remember Pearl Harbor

Not only would planes from the *Enterprise* get a crack at these Japanese controlled islands, but two shore bombardment groups were detached for gunnery practice. Rear Admiral Spruance had the heavy cruisers *Northampton* and *Salt Lake City* and one destroyer bombard Wotje, while the heavy cruiser *Chester*, accompanied by two destroyers, hit Taroa Island.

The *Enterprise* allocated thirty-seven Dauntless divebombers and nine Devastator torpedo planes (armed with bombs for horizontal bombing) with no fighter escort for Kwajalein Atoll. Wildcats, armed with 100-pound bombs, bombed and strafed the two minor islands of Wotje and Taroa, combined with shore bombardment groups.

Surprise on Sunday dawn was achieved in most of the attacks, although four Dauntlesses were lost in the Kwajalein attack. The harbor was packed with small crafts and ships. Several Japanese ships were damaged at Kwajalein and Wotje, the principal one being the old light cruiser *Katori*. Spruance's cruisers caught a small auxiliary gunboat (converted from a civilian craft) off Wotje and after spirited resistance, sank it—the only Japanese ship actually sunk that day. After valiantly attacking the *Northampton* and *Salt Lake City* and the escorting destroyer *Dunlop*, and finally sinking after about a thirty minute action with the *Dunlop*, the navigator of the *Salt Lake City* remarked, "Well, if the Japs want to put up a monument to that little guy I'll contribute."

Halsey stayed in the area most of the day,

while the hornet's nest he had disturbed woke up more and more. The Japanese got an air-strike with the Nells going in on the *Chester* in the late morning, and achieved nothing. They wanted to rearm with torpedoes, but the torpedo depot was on Roi and Roi was too damaged. So, finally rearmed with bombs, five Nells, under Lieutenant Nakai, went at the *Enterprise* about 1:30 P.M..

As the Japanese Nells approached their target, they took advantage of cloud cover as well as an unconventional glide-bombing attack to get close to the *Enterprise*. The *Enterprise* had Combat Air Patrol, the term for local fighter protection for the fleet below, both fighters flying high and Dauntless divebombers flying low to defend against attacking torpedo planes. Yet IFF (Identification—Friend or Foe) had not been installed yet, and with such a small strike mixed with returning friendly planes, it was difficult for the air patrol to achieve much against the incoming Japanese strike. Finally, to add to the confusion of Nakai's attack, several Wildcat guns were jamming!

The Nells emerged from the overcast at 6,000 feet at about 285 m.p.h. With the lack of experience that Halsey's force had for real battle, their anti-aircraft fire was consistently behind, and not leading the attacking planes. These big lumbering twin engine bombers released their bombs at 3,000 feet, following through to 1500 feet, but the *Enterprise*, moving at 30 knots speed, neatly maneuvered away from hits. But then, as the Nells flew off in formation, one turned back toward the task force. It was Nakai's plane, apparently too damaged to return to base. He decided to crash his plane into the *Enterprise*. Closer and closer, Nakai chased the running *Yorktown*, firing with everything she had at the approaching flaming bomber. Finally, at the last moment, the *Enterprise* turned as the Nell, now with both the pilot and co-pilot dead or disabled, flew straight. The right wingtip of the Nell, as John Lundstrom tells it, "scraped the port edge of the flight deck opposite the island and tore off the tail of (a Dauntless) whose gun was manned (by the martyr of Midway, Bruno Gaido), parked forward. The wing ripped off at the fuselage and clattered onto the deck, spraying the area with gasoline from its ruptured fuel tank." The remainder of

the plane fell into the sea. Bravery, in this war, was not a monopoly for either side.

At 4:30 in the afternoon two more Nells made an attack on the *Enterprise*, a conventional attack at 14,000 feet moving at 160 m.p.h. The 5-inch anti-aircraft guns from the fleet opened up first, while the air patrol waited for the Nells to complete their attack and move away from the anti-aircraft fire. The Nells dropped their bombs, missing, and as they turned away the waiting air patrol moved in. Commander Wade McClusky was in charge of this flight (he commanded the fighters on the *Enterprise* and was later promoted to command of the Dauntless divebombers on the *Enterprise* at Midway). Lieutenant James G. Daniels III raced up behind one of the silver twin-tailed Nells and opened up on it. The Nell caught fire and as it plunged into the ocean, Daniels yelled into his radio, "Bingo! Bingo! I got one!"

The *Yorktown* attacked the newly occupied Gilberts, location of Tarawa Atoll. The loss of six planes in this operation was primarily due to overcast stormy weather. There were few worthwhile targets in the island group, and the only real damage inflicted was the loss of two Kawanishi H6K4 flying boats known as Mavis (2,981 mile range, 3 MGs and one 20mm cannon, 211 m.p.h.). These four-engine seaplanes had a tremendous range and were incredibly large, comparable to a Catalina or PBY. A third flying boat found the *Yorktown*. It was sighted and chased in view of the entire Yorktown Task Force. Two Wildcats, tiny compared to this monster craft, dived on it and steadily worked it over. Flame erupted along the fuselage, and as the plane headed for the sea, engulfed in flames, the executive officer of the *Yorktown*, Captain J.J. Clark yelled into the microphone, "Burn, you son-of-a-bitch, burn!" One of the pilots who scored the victory countered by saying, "We just shot his ass off!"

So the first successful counterattack occurred. The Japanese immediately responded by a sortie of four fleet carriers from Truk Lagoon, the main fleet base in the Central Pacific for the Japanese in the Caroline Islands. Fleet carriers *Shokaku* and *Zuikaku* were ordered to Japan in case of an attack there. A further twenty-one bombers were dispatched from Formosa to the South Pacific. Yamamoto's chief of staff Rear

Admiral Matome Ugaki said of this attack, "The emphasis on our current Southern Operations (Malay, Philippines, Netherlands East Indies) has left the Marshalls area with insufficient forces, so this was the enemy's opportunity and he seized it. He not only held our forces in check, but was able to obtain some significant results. This attack was 'Heaven's admonition for our shortcomings.'"

The next raid was against Rabaul by the fleet carrier *Lexington* (37,681 tons, twelve old 5-inch guns, 63 planes, 33 knots) under the command of Vice Admiral Brown. The *"Lady Lex"* and her sistership, the *Saratoga*, were converted from battlecruiser designs that had been started but not completed in the early 1920s due to the Washington Treaty. The *Kaga* and *Akagi* began their careers in a similar way. Giant vessels, quite popular in the navy, and the experience with them, laid the foundation for the Yorktown class of fleet carriers. With the *Lexington* were four heavy cruisers and ten destroyers. The plan called for an attack from the northeast of Rabaul and involved bombers from Australia hitting Rabaul and a shore bombardment from cruisers.

The Japanese were on alert for this raid by heavy radio traffic from Pearl, which usually meant that a fleet carrier task force had departed that base. Flying boats spotted Brown's Task Force a full day before it was ready for an attack off Bougainville, the largest island in the Solomon chain and closest of those islands to Rabaul. Brown decided to cancel the attack, but to fool the Japanese, he proceeded on towards Rabaul the rest of the day, into the afternoon. That night he planned to reverse course.

But the Japanese sent in new Betty bombers crewed by veterans who had attacked the *Prince of Wales* and *Repulse* just a few months earlier. Armed with bombs, seventeen attacked the *Lady Lex* in two groups.

The first group of nine went in at 11,500 feet at 195 m.p.h. The air patrol quickly knocked five down. Anti-aircraft fire was terrible, missing the Japanese by so much that it endangered the friendly air patrol. The four bombers missed with their bombs and then split up and dived for the "floor," but none from this group was to get home. Two Wildcats were lost.

Lieutenant Commander John Thach made one kill when he realized that shooting up a Betty's fuselage killed or wounded the crew even if it did not bring the plane down. Later that day he got a second victory by firing at the fuel tanks. Thach's influence on fighter tactics for the fleet carriers was vital in the coming months.

Meanwhile, a legend was born. The second group of bombers came in for attack after all the Wildcats that had attacked and pursued the first group were low on ammo and fuel. Only two unused Wildcats were in position to defend the Task Force and one found that his guns were jammed. Butch O'Hare had the best aim of the fighter pilots on the *Lexington*, and his first dive into the Japanese formation nailed two. O'Hare dived low and then climbed back above the tight formation of Japanese bombers and came back down at them. He damaged a third craft (which later ditched into the sea), and knocked down a fourth. Every Japanese gun in the formation was on his plane, as O'Hare's wingman with the jammed ammo belt, was keeping his distance trying to get it to unjam. By now the Japanese were at their bomb release point and anti-aircraft fire was exploding all around. O'Hare stayed in the thick of it. In the third pass O'Hare went for the lead plane to destroy the Japanese aim in the attack, as all planes in Japanese bomber forces released when the lead plane, which had the most skillful bombardier, dropped its bombs. O'Hare hit it, and the other four released their bombs well, but luckily missing. On a fourth pass, O'Hare ran out of ammo. So, he got three kills, and damaged two planes that went down later. He was credited at the time with six kills and as the first American Ace (five confirmed kills made one an Ace) in World War II—O'Hare became a hero—later to have his name given to Chicago's airport.

The shock felt by the Japanese at the loss of all but two of their new planes (one was shot down on the way back by a Dauntless divebomber on patrol) was substantial. Additional planes were ordered moved to Rabaul and the planned attack on Lae in New Guinea was delayed by almost a week, which allowed Admiral Brown to deliver his first, and only, successful port attack as a commander of a task force. It was sandwiched between Halsey's raids on Wake and Marcus Islands.

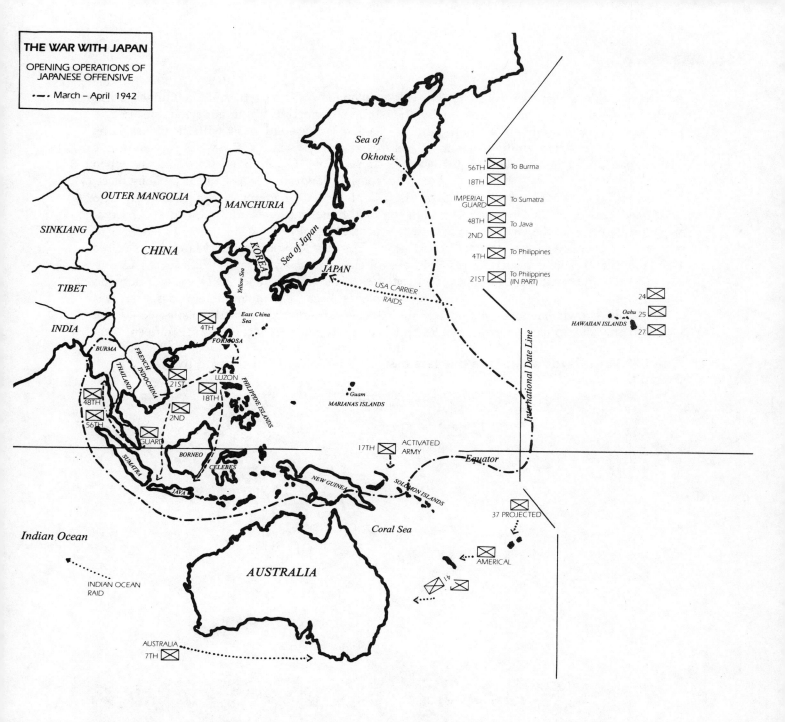

THE WAR WITH JAPAN

OPENING OPERATIONS OF
JAPANESE OFFENSIVE

–·– March – April 1942

The Battle of the Coral Sea

With the Japanese tied down in the Far East, the *Enterprise* raided Wake and Marcus Islands. Both are isolated atolls in the North Central Pacific. Wake was bombed by planes and bombarded by heavy cruisers on February 24, with one plane lost, while Marcus was hit by the same task force on March 4. Both attacks achieved little, except to stir up the Japanese and place Japan on a nationwide alert for several days.

Brown's Task Force, now reinforced by the *Yorktown*, was operating in Australian waters when he learned that the Japanese were landing troops on New Guinea on the north coast of that large island. Fuel considerations would allow for operations with both fleet carriers for only a limited period of time.

Originally Brown intended to raid Rabaul, but with the invasion in progress at Lae and Salamaua on the northern New Guinea coast, Brown decided to try an audacious surprise attack from the south coast with the planes flying overland, crossing a 7,500 foot pass in the 15,000 foot Owen Stanley Mountains, then roaring down on the assembled Japanese fleet. Captain Ted Sherman of the *Lexington*, who later in the war made admiral, was key in organizing the raid.

The attack took place on March 10. The 104 aircraft involved were 18 Wildcats, 61 Dauntless divebombers, and 25 Devastator torpedo planes. Because of the mountain pass, there was some concern that torpedo planes could not carry torpedoes that high, so thirteen were

The USS *Hornet* was one of the carriers assigned to Force 16 operating in the Pacific.

B-25s prepare to launch from the deck of the *Hornet*.

Bomber takes off from the *Hornet* on its way to the historic raid over Tokyo.

armed with torpedoes, and the other twelve with two 500-pound bombs each. The strike departed at dawn, launching about 45 miles from Port Moresby in New Guinea, the key remaining Allied base there.

The Japanese had sixteen ships present of which half were transports, the rest old destroyers except for the *Kiyokawa Maru*, a seaplane tender, and one very small cruiser, the *Yubari*, flagship of Rear Admiral Kajioka, leader of the Wake invasion. There was absolutely no air opposition to the attack and it was a surprise to the Japanese who had been busy loading the previous two days.

Thach led the fighters on strafing runs and dummy runs. The purpose of a dummy run was to race in, but not firing, to draw fire on a Wildcat rather than a slower, more vulnerable dive-bomber or torpedo bomber. Firing 50 caliber slugs into an old destroyer or transport can do serious damage. The other planes ranged up and down in the large bay attacking ships with bombs and torpedoes. With little opposition

Photograph taken from the escort ship *Enterprise* captures a B-25 on its way to Tokyo.

and the element of surprise, they did hurt the Japanese.

The Americans lost one divebomber in the attack. Only one Japanese plane rose, a Dave, and while brave, it was shot down. Two transports and the armed merchant cruiser *Kongo Maru* (8,624 tons, four 5.5-inch guns, 18 knots) were sunk while the *Kiyokawa Maru* and one other transport suffered some damage. Other minor ship damage was inflicted and 375 Japanese were killed or wounded. Admiral Ugaki wrote of this attack that "It is extremely regrettable that again the enemy was able to escape unharmed."

Reports on the fleet carriers for inflicted losses on the Japanese were much higher, claiming nine ships, including two heavy cruisers, sunk. Overestimating damage in attacks to the enemy was a common problem for all navies throughout the war.

The next raid was the most dramatic of the war in the Pacific and put the icing on the cake as far as Yamamoto was concerned. The raid on Tokyo meant to him that Midway and a decisive battle was imperative. The Japanese had to find a way to deal with these raids. Sadly, for the Japanese, their original cure of shifting land-

based air to the area and attacking the enemy naval forces was a failure.

Appropriately on April 1, 1942, a strange sight greeted Captain Mitscher, officers, and men of the *Hornet*. Sixteen B-25s, with seventy officers and 130 enlisted men started loading. Army medium bombers on an American aircraft carrier? The next day, the task force departed Alameda Naval Air Station and proceeded west. Target: Tokyo.

What had happened was that in January of 1942, Admiral King was discussing with Captain Francis S. Low possible divisionary raids to capture the Japanese attention. Such an attack would be the first installment for Pearl harbor. They came up with the idea of launching Army Air Corps B-25s as they had range to carry them to Japan, something that the navy planes lacked. The B-25s could not land on the *Hornet*, but they could fly from it. With the enthusiastic support of "Hap" Arnold, the general of the Army Air Force, an idea was born.

The trip across the Pacific was filled with planning and preparation, including lectures on "how to make friends and influence Japs" if captured. Since the *Hornet* could not fly off her planes (the B-25s had to remain on the flight deck throughout the trip), Vice Admiral Halsey escorted the *Hornet* with the *Enterprise* and others.

After one last refueling on April 17, the carriers and cruisers—the destroyers were left behind because of their limited fuel capacity—pushed towards Tokyo, only 1,000 miles away. Planes were supposed to depart 500 miles from Tokyo and attack at night, but 700 miles away the task force ran into a picket line of small craft. Thus the raid was launched 668 miles from the heart of Tokyo, where most of the planes were bound. Three B-25s were sent to raid Osaka, Nagoya, and Kobe.

The raids hit Japan in the early afternoon, and while targets were military in nature, some civilians were accidently killed. Little real damage was done. Captain Mitsuo Fuchida remarked on this raid that "at 1300, *Akagi* received a report that Tokyo had been bombed". . . . such widespread enemy action came as a distinct shock, and we in the Nagumo force did not know what to make of it." (Later after realizing that these B-25s were carrier launched) "The Americans, with characteristic Yankee boldness and ingenuity, the enemy, had evidently devised a means of launching heavy land-type aircraft from carriers and had employed this new stratagem to penetrate the Japanese defenses."

Two planes failed to arrive at safe airfields or friendly areas of China, while a third landed in

Aerial view shows Yokosuka Naval Base in Tokyo taken from a B-25 participating in Doolittle's Raid.

Nationals inspect wreckage of General Doolittle's plane in China after the raid.

the Soviet Union (and was interned for the war). Eight prisoners were sentenced to die for killing civilians—three were, the other five had their sentences commuted. The others crash landed in China and eventually the crews made it to friendly havens. Colonel Doolittle later went on to command the Army Air Forces in North Africa as his reward for his daring raid.

What made this raid even more interesting, beyond the Allied propaganda value (including FDR's famous comment that the B-25s came from Shangri-la!) is the Japanese reaction to it. While their plans for an attack against Midway (Operation MI) were well along, there were still two other schools of thought advocating further attacks against India and the physical linking up with the other Axis forces in the Indian Ocean, as well as moving down through the southwest Pacific to cut Australia off from her sea links to the West Coast of America. Doolittle's raid finally cemented the go ahead for Operation MI.

Doolittle's raid also created a great deal of embarrassment for the Japanese army and the navy, due to the fact that the fighting services had an almost religious devotion to the Emperor and his safety. An attack on Tokyo brought

danger to his person, and was thus a grave dereliction of duty.

What must be remembered, too, throughout this early period of the war, is that the Japanese maintained strong forces in Japan for her defense. At one point in February the aircraft carriers *Shokaku* and *Zuikaku* were in Japan, as well as the 21st Air Flotilla after her successes in Southeast Asia. The 26th Air Flotilla took over these duties after April 1, 1942, like the U.S.A.'s elaborate plans for defense of the West Coast in 1942, or the panicky reaction of one politician, after Pearl Harbor, who advocated defense preparations in the Rocky Mountains to defend the rest of America after the West Coast fell to the Japanese advance!

Before the decisive battle of Midway burst upon the Pacific, there was the first naval battle in history between two enemy fleets in which no surface ship came in sight of the enemy fleet. The battle was fought entirely with air units from opposing fleet carriers. The Battle of the Coral Sea set the tone for many of the battles in the rest of the war. It was a curtain raiser for the Battle of Midway and directly affected the fortunes of war for the South Pacific.

WAR AT SEA

Japanese fighter and bomber planes bomb Clark Field in the Philippines. The city of Manila is depicted in the distance.

PEARL HARBOR

Below: Panoramic scene painting by Lt. Commander Griffith Coale depicts the attack on Pearl Harbor. From left to right: *Nevada, California, Oglala, Oklahoma, Maryland, Arizona.* At left: B-1 destroyed in the attack. At right: Capsized *Oklahoma.* Far right: Destroyed *Arizona* off Ford Island.

The *Lexington* burns and sinks (above and right), but the sinking of the Japanese carrier *Soho* (top) made the Battle of Coral Sea an American victory.

CORAL
SEA

MIDWAY

During the Battle of Midway, the USS *Yorktown* burned for several days after it was hit by a Japanese torpedo-bomber attack. A Japanese submarine attack finally sank it. At left: *Yorktown* plies the seas. At right: *Yorktown*, hit and burning.

General Wainwright's surrender to General Homma on the front porch of a house on Bataan was photographed by the Japanese press, and later the subject of a painting.

The immediate goal of the Japanese was to secure Port Moresby, thus completing the conquest of all of New Guinea, and moving down the Solomons chain and establishing an airbase in the southern portion of those islands. The importance of Port Moresby lay also in its ability to allow Allied airpower to range to and beyond Rabaul. If held by the Japanese, it would be an airbase from which Australia could be harassed. The seizure of all of the Solomons aided in future advances to isolate New Zealand and especially Australia. Australia was especially feared by the Japanese war planners as a potential base from which the Allies could counterattack the Japanese defensive perimeter.

The Allied goal was primarily to stop the Japanese advance. Secondly, it was to prepare bases for future advance. One of the key areas to be developed was the Tonga Island chain where there was an excellent anchorage capable of holding the entire Allied fleet!

The Japanese plan called for reinforcing the 4th Fleet based at Rabaul with major warships, including at least one fleet carrier and launching amphibious operations against Tulagi and Guadalcanal in the Solomons and Port Moresby, with the main attack force (the ubiquitous South Sea Detachment). It should be noted that the Japanese still were operating with little more than a reinforced Army regiment and several Special Naval Landing Forces units in this part of the world, while the Allies were busily assembling divisions of infantry to hold the Japanese back. The Japanese hoped to seize these key positions and then move the major warships, especially the fleet carriers, back to Japan to prepare for the operation against Midway. The Japanese wanted to start the operation in early May and move their hopefully undamaged units back to Japan to be ready for operations in early June.

JAPANESE FORCES AT THE CORAL SEA

CARRIER STRIKE FORCE

Vice-Admiral Takagi, commanding

Aircraft Carriers
Zuikaku (20 Zero fighters, 22 Val divebombers, 20 Kate torpedo planes) and Shokaku (18 Zero fighters, 21 Val divebombers, 19 Kate torpedo planes)

It should be noted that the Zuikaku had their spare Zero fighters, and the Shokaku five that were without pilots destined for the Rabaul garrison. Takagi would be delayed 24 hours on May 2 due to bad weather by the need to fly these planes to Rabaul, an operation that would not be completed during this battle.

Heavy Cruisers
Haguro and Myoko (flagship)

Destroyers
Ushio, Akebono, Ariake, Yugure, Shigure and Shiratsuyu
Fleet Train: one oiler

PORT MORSEBY INVASION FORCE

Rear Admiral Abe, commanding

Tsugaru
Twelve transports carrying the main portion of the 3rd Kure SNLF and most of the 144th Infantry regiment of the South Seas Detachment (three battalions) auxiliary craft and two oilers

ATTACK FORCE

Rear Admiral Kajioka, commanding

Light Cruisers
Yubari (flagship)

Destroyers
Oite, Asanagi, Mutsuki, Mochizuki, and Yayoi

CLOSE COVER FORCE

Rear Admiral Marumo, commanding

Light Cruisers
Tenryu (flagship) and Tatsuta
Seaplane carrier Kamikawa Maru
Three gunboats

CLOSE SUPPORT FORCE

Rear Admiral Goto, commanding

Light Aircraft Carriers
Shoho (8 Zero fighters, 4 Claude fighters, 6 Kate torpedo planes)

Heavy Cruisers
Aoba (flagship), Kako, Kinugasa, and Furutaka

Destroyers
Sazanami

TULAGI INVASION FORCE

Rear Admiral Shima, commanding

ML
Okinoshima (flagship)

Destroyers
Yuzuki

APD
Kikuzuki
One transport and auxiliary craft carrying part of the 3rd Kure SNLF. There were approximately 6 fighters at Lae, 57 at Rabaul, and 86 bombers at Rabaul

Japanese army strength in the South Pacific did not get a real boost until May of 1942 when the 17th Army was activated under General Hyakutake. It initially consisted of nine infantry battalions, drawn from several formations.

Doolittle's men were required to live in mountainside air raid shelters when Japanese planes retaliated following the attack.

General Doolittle's fliers were shown off to the press as they were moved about China.

Japanese carrier forces had three types of planes on the large fleet carriers: divebombers, torpedo bombers, and fighters. Japanese light carriers (such as the *Shoho*, which was converted from a tanker) carried two types, fighters and either torpedoes or divebombers. The *Shoho* was originally used only for ferrying aircraft, but just before the *Coral Sea* was released for combat duties.

The Val, or Japanese divebomber (915 mile range, 3 MGs, 551-pound bombload, 240 m.p.h.) was similar to the American Dauntless. Normally twenty-one were carried, three as spares, the other eighteen organized into two *chutai's* of nine planes each. Highly maneuverable, the Val was not as rugged as the Dauntless. It also carried a smaller bombload.

The Kate, or Japanese torpedo bomber (1,237 mile range, 1 MG, 1,764-pound torpedo or bombload, 235 m.p.h.), occasionally used as a horizontal high-altitude bomber, was much superior to the American Devastator. The Kate had a three-man crew and was organized into

six-plane chutais. As with the Val, twenty-one were carried on each large carrier except for the *Kaga* which carried a total of thirty. An additional advantage over the Americans was the superior torpedo which allowed for release at a higher air speed (thus making the plane less vulnerable to damage or destruction just before the release point).

The Zero was the standard fighter. The normal complement was twenty-one planes organized into two nine-plane chutais with three spares. When flying from a carrier, the Zero had a radius of about 300 miles, on land 500 miles. The difference was due to slower carrier flight deck operations, as well as over-water operations. A brilliantly designed plane, highly maneuverable, it, along with all of Japan's aircraft, lacked armor and defensive protection. Thus, in May of 1942, American pilots began using incendiary bullets to take advantage of the vulnerable fuel tanks on the Zero and other Japanese aircraft.

The standard Japanese fighter formation for

ALLIED FLEET AT CORAL SEA
Task Force 17 was broken into parts. Overall command was Rear Admiral Frank Jack Fletcher

TASK GROUP 17.2

Rear-Admiral Kinkaid, commanding

Heavy Cruisers

Minneapolis *(flagship),* New Orleans, Astoria, Chester, *and* Portland

Destroyers

Phelps, Dewey, Farragut, Aylwin, *and* Monaghan

TASK GROUP 17.3

Rear-Admiral Crace RN, commanding

Heavy Cruisers

HMAS Australia *and* Chicago

Light Cruisers

HMAS Hobart

Destroyers

Perkins *and* Walke *(the* Farragut *was detached to 17.3 when it operated separately during the battle)*

TASK GROUP 17.5

Rear-Admiral Fitch, commanding

Aircraft Carriers

Lexington *(21 Wildcat fighters, 36*

Dauntless divebombers, and 13 Devastator torpedo planes) and* Yorktown *(17 Wildcat fighters, 35 Dauntless divebombers, and 12 Devastator torpedo planes)*

Planes available at dawn on May 7, 1942

Destroyers

Morris, Anderson, Hammann, *and* Russell

TASK GROUP 17.6

Captain Philips, commanding

Two oilers

Destroyers

Sims *and* Worden

The seaplane tender Tangier *was at Noumea with 12 Catalina flying boats*

ALLIED LAND BASED AIR

There were 19 B-25s, 19 A-24s, and 14 A-20s at Charters Towers, 12 B-25s and 80 B-26s at Townsville, with about 50 P-39 fighters. There were about 50 P-39

fighters in New Guinea at Port Moresby. 48 B-17s were at Cloncurry Darwin had 90 P—40s Sydney had 100 P-39s

Both sides had submarines in the area but neither side achieved much with them. The Americans had 11 subs, the S-37 through the S-47. These were older subs. The Japanese had seven, the I-21, I-22, I-24, I-28, I-29, RO-33, and the RO-34. After the Battle of the Coral Sea, the I-22, I-24 and I-27 took on midget submarines and attacked Sydney Harbor in the so called "Battle of Sydney." The midget subs had a near miss on the heavy cruiser Chicago and sank the barracks ship HMAS Kuttabul. All midgets sunk eventually and the commander of one became the only Japanese in the war to be elevated to "War God" status, an unusual and rare honor in the tradition of Japan.

cruising was three planes arranged as follows:

X

X   X

When combat was imminent they sometimes adopted a formation with 100 to 200 meters between planes looking somewhat like this, right or left echelon, with right echelon shown:

X

X

X

Usual Japanese fighter tactics called for the Japanese fighters to sweep down from above at the rear or side, firing at the target plane, then pulling up and away as the next plane came into the attack.

Japanese pilots were trained much differently than American pilots. Most were non-officers, i.e. enlisted men. In contrast, in the American Naval Air Corps in December of 1941, only about 13% were originally enlisted men. This was due in part to an American law requiring naval aviators to command American carriers. Japanese training lasted about six months; the numbers graduated were quite small, which meant that to replace lost pilots during the war was very difficult. About 400 hours of flying time for officers was normal, while 254 was the minimum for enlisted graduates.

The big Japanese advantage at the start of the war was the actual combat training gained in the war against China. From 1937 on, the pilots received actual training through fighting there. Problems arose when an air unit took heavy losses, and there were no replacements available to move directly on board a carrier. Thus the *Zuikaku*, after the Battle of Coral Sea, had largely rookies straight out of school for replacements and thus could not go to Midway.

The early American successes can be credited to the Dauntless divebomber (1345 mile range, 4 MGs, 1200 pounds of bombs, 250 m.p.h.). Crewed by two men, this rugged plane could take a great deal of damage and was even sometimes used as a Combat Air Patrol unit. Because of its range, it was used for scouting purposes, although usually armed with just one 500-pound bomb. The usual fleet carrier had two

squadrons of Dauntless divebombers. One was a bombing squadron, while the second was designated for scouting. Almost 6,000 were built in the war years and they were given progressively more powerful engines. The SBD-3, introduced in March of 1941, had self-sealing fuel tanks, a great advantage in combat.

The Devastator torpedo plane (716 mile range, 2 MGs, 1 torpedo or 1000 pounds of bombs, 206 m.p.h.), first built in 1937, was hopelessly outclassed by 1942. With a three man crew, only 129 were built.

The Wildcat fighter (770 mile range, 6 MGs, 318 m.p.h.) was not quite the equal, but close to it, for fighting the Zero fighter. With self-sealing tanks, introduced along with armor on the Wildcats shortly after the start of the war, a Wildcat could fly 816 miles at 150 m.p.h. In practical terms, that gave it a radius of action of about 200 miles; if landbased, it would be about 250–300 miles. It should be noted that while the armoring was protection against the machine guns on Japanese aircraft, that same armor could not stop Japanese 20mm cannon fire from the Zero. The Wildcat pilots were well schooled, as was all the navy, in gunnery tactics, and the carrier pilots were particularly adept at firing at an acute angle to the enemy, called deflection shooting. This would be a big advantage in dealing with the nimble Zero, which would allow time only for a fleeting shot before it darted away from the slower and less maneuverable Wildcat.

The Americans used officers primarily for pilots, though Secretary of the Navy Josephus Daniels, under President Woodrow Wilson, did establish a program in 1917 allowing for enlisted men to undertake pilot training, a progressive and successful program. The majority of the fighter pilots on the *Lexington* were products of this program (about 13% of all Navy and Marine pilots were enlisted men in 1941) which gave it a unique esprit d'corp.

American pilots had received a great deal of flying time experience by the outbreak of war, though, like the Japanese, this declined as the war progressed. At the time of the Battle of the Coral Sea, 27% of the fighter pilots on the fleet carriers had more than 1,000 flight hours, while 50% had 300 to 600. Unlike the Japanese, Americans pulled veteran pilots from time to time and rotated them back to training camps in America to impart their unique knowledge to new and upcoming trainees.

Before the development of the Thach Weave, at the time of Midway, the standard American fighter formation involved the six-plane division made up of two-plane sections. It looked something like:

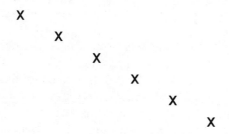

The standard echelon formation was common to both navies at this time. It appeared something like:

The problem faced by the American pilots was devising a tactic that would permit combat with an enemy plane that was faster and more maneuverable than the Wildcat. The Thach Weave eventually solved this problem.

The Japanese began their operation, called Operation MO, by moving seaplane tenders and small craft into the northern and central Solomons. Shortland Islands, off Bougainville witnessed seaplane operations from it early in May. The purpose of this operation was to extend the range of reconnaissance throughout the Coral Sea. As with so many Japanese operations, several different task forces were operating at the same time, and, as was so often, the Allies knew in advance that the Japanese were in the vicinity. Because of this advance warning imparted by ULTRA, the Allies surprised the Japanese with their early reply to the Japanese attacks, and the strength of this Allied resistance.

Action moved into second gear with Rear Admiral Shima landing an invasion force made up of part of the 3rd Kure Special Naval Landing Force at Tulagi Island, just off Guadalcanal, on the morning of May 3. Rear Admiral Goto's warships protected this force by moving to the central Solomons. There was no opposition facing the Japanese on this island, only the growing Coastwatcher Program.

This was sooner than Rear Admiral Fletcher expected, as his refueling operations were not complete. The problem with fuel in this area is twofold. First, it has to be moved there by tanker. Secondly, the larger warships carry plenty, but destroyers use up their fuel quickly in high speed operations. Both Fletcher and Rear Admiral Fitch were slow in performing this refueling operation in the first days of May.

Fletcher decided upon an immediate strike, with the *Yorktown*, as he was unaware of the status of the *Lexington*, detached to the south to refuel though in reality capable of joining the *Yorktown*. This situation could not be clarified as radio communications would alert the enemy of the Allied presence. The *Yorktown* moved into position for a strike on the 4th, while Goto retired, not expecting the Allies to attack since the island had now fallen to the Japanese. The strike was from attack planes, with no fighters, since it was unlikely the Japanese could deploy fighters that quickly to that area. The 28 dive-bombers armed with 1,000-pound bombs and twelve Devastators, armed with torpedoes, went in.

At 8:15 A.M. the *Yorktown's* plane's completed the sweep over Guadalcanal's mountains and attacked in clear weather a surprised, anchored, and unloading Japanese force. The divebombers dived from 10,000 feet and should have hurt the enemy badly, but, at 7,000 feet the planes moved into a warm air layer, which fogged the bombsights! All bombs from the divebombers missed. The flagship, the large minelayer *Okinoshima* (5,000 tons, four 5.5-inch guns, 20 knots) received much of the attention. Only one torpedo hit the fast transport *Kikuzuki* (1,913 tons, two 4.7-inch guns, six 24-inch torpedoes, 37 knots), which sank. A second strike was ordered with twenty-seven divebombers and eleven torpedo planes. One group of divebombers caught three converted minesweepers near

Savo Island (off Guadalcanal, and in the waters soon to be renamed Ironbottom Sound due to the tremendous number of ships sunk there); two ships were sunk. The rest of the second strike scared the Japanese ships well, and even shot down two Dave floatplanes, but missed all ship targets.

Four Wildcat fighters went in afterwards and shot down three Pete floatplanes (460 mile range, 3 MGs, 230 m.p.h.) operating from the Shortlands. They also strafed the third minesweeper, the *Tama Maru*, already shook up from the earlier attack by the divebombers, and forced her to beach. (The .50 caliber machine gun bullets could really damage a ship!) Next they strafed the older destroyer *Yuzuki*, killing the captain, nine others, and wounding twenty, forcing her to retire to Rabaul. A replacement destroyer was used for a later operation on May 15 for taking Nauru and Ocean islands near the Gilberts. Not a bad score! Unfortunately two Wildcats were lost when they ran out of fuel. As they approached Guadalcanal, the pilot of one, Scott McCuskey, radioed his wingmen, "Let's go native!" They were later both retrieved from the island.

A third strike by twenty-one divebombers did little, though, again, scaring the flagship *Okinoshima*. Ironically, after all this, the *Okinoshima* was sunk off Rabaul on May 11 by the submarine S-42. Obviously the strike planes needed some target practice, and Nimitz later said that "The Tulagi operation was certainly disappointing in terms of ammunition expended to results obtained."

Fletcher retired and over the next two days completed refueling and prepared for the enemy advance. The Japanese obliged in part by moving the invasion force south from Rabaul towards the tail of New Guinea. They planned to establish a seaplane base there in the many islands present. Then, turning west, the Japanese planned to continue the advance on Port Moresby, while land based air from Lae pounded that port in preparation for the invasion. The wild card was the fleet carriers under Takagi. They were operating north of the Solomons and looped east coming around near the southern tail of the Solomons and then headed south, with the intention of smashing the American carrier task force.

Action began in earnest on the 7th of May with the detached oiler *Neosho* and escorting destroyer *Sims*, having successfully refueled the task forces, retiring slowly to the south. They were sighted and tracked by Japanese scout planes from the two fleet carriers. Unfortunately for everyone involved, they were reported as a carrier and a cruiser. Rear Admiral Hara, commander of the two fleet carriers, accepted that report without reservation and ordered a total strike. Hara later said "in the end it did not prove to be a fortunate decision." Hara's 5th Carrier Division launched a strike of eighteen fighters, twenty-four torpedo planes, and thirty-six divebombers. It must be understood that the 5th Carrier Division was viewed by the other two Japanese fleet carrier divisions as the worst of the lot. After the battle, in which the Japanese thought they had sunk possibly both the *Lexington* and the *Yorktown*, the joke was that "Son of concubine gained a victory, so sons of legal wives should find no rival in the world." This contributed to a bad case of Victory Disease.

Just as this strike went out, the real American task force was located to the west of the Japanese fleet carriers. But for the *Neosho* and the *Sims*, it was too late. The Japanese quickly found them, but delayed attack while they searched for a nearby more worthwhile target. With fuel running low, they attacked. The attack of such magnitude, even by the "son of a concubine," could only have one result. The Sims took three 500-pound bomb hits, and sank quickly. The *Neosho* took seven hits, including a kamikaze, and eight near misses. Yet this 8,000 ton, 553 foot long ship would, with engines knocked out, drift for four days before being sunk by a friendly destroyer that took off the remaining survivors. Losses were particularly heavy as the lieutenant in charge of radioing the position where the *Sims* sank gave the wrong location. This delayed rescue operations.

The first American act of the day, beyond, like the Japanese, sending out scouting units at daybreak, was detaching Rear Admiral Crace's surface force to attack the invasion fleet. In this day of missed signals, the Americans located a small portion of the invasion fleet moving through the islands near the tail of New Guinea. It was erroneously coded, making Fletcher think that the Carrier Strike Force had been located. So at 9:26 A.M. the *Yorktown* and the *Lexington* began launching a strike. It consisted of 18 Wildcats, 53 Dauntlesses, and 22 Devastators. By 10:13 all planes were aloft. The torpedo planes were initially at wave top but rose to 4,000 feet, escorting fighters at 6,000 feet and divebombers at 18,000 feet with escorting fighters. A textbook co-ordinated strike was going in.

By now the scouting pilot had reported back to the *Yorktown* and the error was corrected as best possible. Fletcher opposed the idea of calling back the strike and the Army Air Corps had found the invasion fleet, so the target was this force. Ironically none of the scouts had actually seen the *Shoho* group (They had spotted other Japanese forces in the area instead.), but the strike from the *Lexington* and the *Yorktown* located it first. Their main target was the converted tanker *Shoho* whose air patrol was one Zero and two Claudes.

The first attack was made by three Dauntlesses, the command group for the strike. All bombs missed, though one near miss literally blew five parked aircraft overboard. Next came ten Dauntlesses of the scouting group armed with 500-pound bombs. They were to "soften" up the target while other divebombers launched a co-ordinated strike with the Devastators. Two Claudes darted in and out of the diving Dauntlesses, pushing over at 12,000 feet to pull out at 2,000 feet, but the rapidly maneuvering *Shoho* avoided all hits. Doctrine called for the divebombers to dive again at the supporting enemy ships and drop 116-pound underwing bombs. This proved impossible due to the persistence of the Japanese fighters.

The *Shoho* took this moment to launch three more fighters, but with the *Yorktown's* planes also arriving, doom was upon her. The *Lexington's* bombing Dauntlesses first scored with two 1,000-pounders hitting the poorly subdivided *Shoho's* vulnerable and unarmored decks. The two hits were scored from 2,500 feet. Lieutenant Commander Weldon Hamilton who scored the first hit and led the group of divebombers remarked later that this was a "spectacular and convincing pageant of destruction." The torpedo planes from the *Lexington* had descended from 4,000 feet to 100 feet, dropping height for

their torpedoes. They launched from both sides of the *Shoho's* bow, and the attack paid off—five torpedo hits! Speed dropped and a list began.

The *Yorktown's* planes went in against a sinking enemy ship. Possibly as many as eleven more bomb hits were scored and at least two more torpedo hits. The *Shoho* was the first of twelve carriers to be sunk by American airpower in the war, and the first of twenty carriers to be lost by the Japanese in the war. Lieutenant Commander Robert (Bob) E. Dixon from the *Lexington* divebomber group gave a prearranged signal to the *Lexington*, "Scratch one flat top! Signed Bob."

Meanwhile Crace's force had been attacked by twenty Nells armed with bombs, twelve Bettys armed with torpedoes, and about eleven Zero fighters from Rabaul, which missed though two sailors died and seven were wounded. Both torpedoes and bombs were used, and apparently four Bettys were splashed. Crace had been attacked by Allied planes as well, of Douglas MacArthur's command (which MacArthur covered up as best he could by ignoring the incident and saying it never happened). Crace remarked on the American Army Air Corps bombing that, "Fortunately their bombing, in comparison with that of the Japanese formation a few moments earlier, was disgraceful." Admiral Crace, after the action, strongly advocated air support for such detached operations in the future. It should be noted that the Japanese were using new crews on the Nells which were not up to the pre-war training standards. This occurring so early in the war with so few losses was ominous for the future of Japan.

Admiral Fletcher was by no stretch of the imagination a brilliant admiral, but he was capable. After the return of the strike, and preparation for a second strike, Fletcher had to decide if a strike against the escorting ships of the *Shoho* were worthwhile. The Japanese escort was not, as long as the Carrier Strike Force and had not been located. Weather conditions were deteriorating, and with early nightfall approaching (it was late fall in that part of the world), Fletcher decided to take a passive role and let land-based air locate the enemy.

Vice Admiral Inoue at Rabaul, learning of the

Navy torpedo planes attacked and sunk the *Soho* in the Battle of Coral Sea.

loss of the *Shoho*, ordered the cruisers and destroyers escorting the transports to form a squadron for a night attack against the American surface fleet. This forced the transports to retire northward, and thus the Japanese invasion plans for Port Moresby further unravelled. To complicate matters, the Carrier Strike Force had to steam away from the American position to recover the straggling planes returning from the *Sims/Neosho* strike. Finally, the only sighting reports were of Crace's ships, and some were inaccurate, reporting the presence of carriers.

The frustrated Japanese decided to gamble and launched a limited strike with their best night pilots. This allowed them to go out, strike the enemy a deadly blow, and return for a night carrier landing. At 6:15 P.M. twelve Vals and fifteen Kates were in the air. They flew towards Crace's task force, but the *Yorktown's* radar picked them up and the *Yorktown's* fighter director Officer Frank F. Gill sent in four Wildcats on a long range interception. Meanwhile, the existing air patrol of eight planes was reinforced so that eventually thirty Wildcats were aloft.

The four Wildcats surprised the Japanese for-

mation (the Japanese did not have radar on ships, let alone on planes at this stage of the war). Diving down, the lead Wildcat opened fire at 700 yards and before pulling out of its dive knocked down two Kates. One Wildcat got another confirmed kill, while another Kate was damaged. Due to the rain, the Kates had closed their canopies and so their 7.7mm machine guns were not even deployed. Over the next thirty minutes, Wildcats came across isolated Japanese strike groups, primarily the Kates, and disrupted the attack. The Japanese strike dispersed in all directions and when it finally returned to the *Zuikaku* and the *Shokaku*, seven Kates and one Val had been lost, for the loss of two Wildcats (one piloted by Leslie Knox, a native of Brisbane, Australia). Ironically, two groups of three Vals each actually slipped over the American Task Force. Confused, the Vals actually signalled the *Yorktown* to land! A Japanese pilot later wrote that, "As the lead plane, with its flaps down and speed lowered, drifted toward the carrier deck to land, the pilot discovered the great ship ahead was an American carrier!" The Vals in question did not attack (they had dropped their bomb earlier when they

Anti-aircraft Formation Adopted by Crace's Detachment

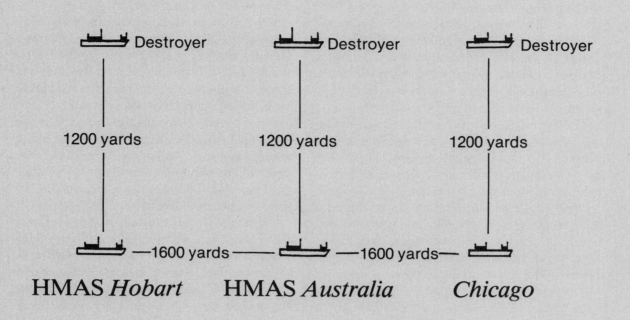

Destroyer   Destroyer   Destroyer

1200 yards   1200 yards   1200 yards

—1600 yards—   —1600 yards—

HMAS *Hobart*   HMAS *Australia*   *Chicago*

SHOHO'S FORMATION BEFORE BEING ATTACKED

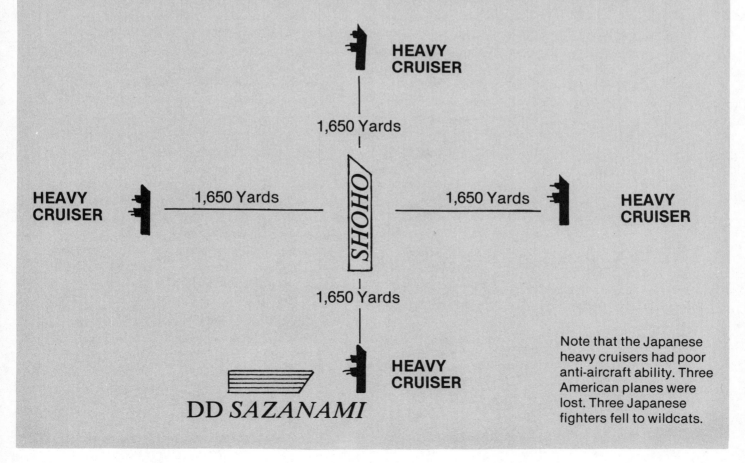

HEAVY CRUISER

1,650 Yards

HEAVY CRUISER   —1,650 Yards—   *SHOHO*   —1,650 Yards—   HEAVY CRUISER

1,650 Yards

DD *SAZANAMI*   HEAVY CRUISER

Note that the Japanese heavy cruisers had poor anti-aircraft ability. Three American planes were lost. Three Japanese fighters fell to wildcats.

thought they were heading home) and returned to their proper home. Another group of Vals at 8:57 P.M. did the same thing with the *Lexington!* Needless to say, by this time the ships in Task Force 17 were nervous and began firing at planes, including friendly returning Wildcats. One additional Wildcat was lost that night when it was unable to find the carriers.

The Japanese, with the returning strike coming back at about 10 P.M., deployed in a unique pattern with support ships close by. Then, with the planes nearby, all ships switched on searchlights aimed into the sky to illuminate the carriers and facilitate safe landings, permitting all but one plane to land safely over the next two hours. At 10 P.M. the two enemy task forces were the closest they had been all day to each other—100 miles separated them.

The morning search pattern for the Task Force 17 was of 360 degrees. Normally a search pattern covered sectors up to 180 degrees. Commanders usually assumed that there would be

no enemies to the rear, but not on the morning of May 8 in the Coral Sea.

Admiral Inoue decided to cancel his night strike, although he did order the heavy cruisers *Furutaka* and *Kinugasa* to reinforce the Carrier Striking Force. They joined up in the night and operated at the rear of the Japanese formation. Inoue definitely delayed the invasion of Port Moresby by two full days to May 12. By now Admirals Takagi and Hara knew from the returning night strike where the American carriers were and could prepare for them in the morning. They, like the American admirals, also decided to scout 360 degrees in the morning.

After the early morning departure of scouting planes (most departing at 6:00 A.M.), the Japanese and American fleet carriers readied early morning strikes. The Japanese made use of their island based planes extensively, although the rain soaked runways on Rabaul tended to reduce the effectiveness of that base.

The big advantage that morning lay with the

Flames across the sky.

The Battle of the Coral Sea / 147

Japanese who were under cloud cover, while Task Force 17 was outside of the front under clear skies. However, the Americans got lucky and a Dauntless scout located the enemy force at 8:20 A.M. At 8:22 A.M. a Kate, piloted by First Class Petty Officer Mamoru Kanno, radioed the Carrier Strike Force, "Have sighted the enemy carriers." It appeared that a straight-up knock-down fight was about to begin.

The Japanese quickly organized a strike, under the command of Lieutenant Commander Kakuichi Takahashi, and at 9:15 A.M. eighteen Zeros, thirty-three Vals and eighteen Kates were on their way. Takagi ordered his Carrier Strike Force to follow his planes in at 30 knots. The decision was an error since the distance between the enemies was about 210 miles at this time, well within the range of the Japanese aircraft but practically out of range for some of the American aircraft, especially the Devastators that had notoriously short legs. The decision to fight at long range with the Japanese aircraft, especially with their superior ability at this used later in the war. Any advantage the Japanese had due to their long range aircraft was further nullified by the American decision to close the Japanese precisely due to the long range of the contact made by the American scouting plane.

Because of the poor atmospheric conditions the American sighting report was not clear on the *Lexington* and the *Yorktown*. But it was certain that the Japanese Kate scouting Task Force 17 had had its radio messages overheard, though not understood, by the American forces, and Fletcher knew he did not want a strike force loaded with weapons and fuel sitting on his decks with an enemy force approaching, so a launch was ordered, even with the incomplete information. Task Force 17 launched fifteen Wildcats, thirty-nine Dauntlesses, and twenty-one Devastators, divided into two groups (the *Yorktown's* strike departed ten minutes earlier than the *Lexington's* strike), and were on their way by 9:25 A.M.

At this point in the war a strike from an American fleet carrier went in by itself as a tactical unit and was not coordinated with that from another carrier—the early departing group from the *Yorktown* went in first against the Japanese fleet.

Japanese air patrol doctrine at this point of the war was based on prewar doctrine, due to the American advantage of radar. The Americans could "see" an approaching strike with radar, while the Japanese had to visually sight the approaching enemy. The Japanese maintained a small high altitude air patrol, and on May 8, 1942, it included six Zeros and one Ace from the war with China. The patrol operated against divebombers, while low altitude patrols operated against torpedo planes. May 8, on the decks with engines warmed up and running and pilots in the cockpits sat reinforcing Zeros. Weather was a help in hiding the Carrier Strike Force unless it was discovered by the enemy, then the advantage switched because reinforc-

Gun crew members of the destroyer *Wasp* wait at battle stations for the Japanese air attack.

ing Zeros on the deck could not rise until the enemy planes were visually sighted. If attacked from high enemy planes (such as divebombers coming in at 17,000 feet), they had a limited climbing ability. Seven more Zeros were launched when the *Yorktown's* group was sighted.

The American attack was aided when the *Shokaku* was sighted in the open with the Japanese Task Force somewhat scattered due to recent landing of air patrol planes needing fuel. The *Zuikaku* was sighted, but ran in under the overcast, which was probably a help as the *Yorktown's* strike was concentrated against only one target (with the poor American aim displayed in these early carrier actions, it was an advantage).

Seven divebombers went in first, and again suffered from a burden of fogged bombsights, the same problem that plagued them during the attack at Tulagi (Nimitz's staff labeled this the "outstanding material defect" of the battle). No

hits were scored, but no planes were lost, although several Dauntlesses were shot up.

The remaining planes now went in with the divebombers leading off while lumbering torpedo planes moved into position. One hit was scored forward on the *Shokaku* by a 1,000-pound bomb. Lieutenant John J. Powers earned a posthumous Medal of Honor for taking his plane down, damaged by anti-aircraft fire, to 200 feet, instead of the usual 2,000 to 1,500 feet, before releasing his 1,000-pounder. He did not survive the blast from the bomb as it tore up the deck of the *Shokaku*, putting her temporarily out of action and afire but still steaming at 34 knots (about 39 m.p.h.). Two divebombers were lost, that of Powers and one other to a Zero.

The torpedo planes were escorted in by four Wildcats. The Wildcats were effective in occupying the Japanese air patrol, and shooting one Zero down in the process, while the torpedo planes deployed in a line abreast and went into

Navy torpedo and divebomber planes attacked the Japanese carrier *Shokako* and sent her back to Japan for repairs after the battle.

A column of water rises high in the air after a bomb explodes alongside the burning Japanese carrier *Soho*.

the attack at about 125 miles an hour. Dropping point was 1,000 to 2,000 yards from the target. The attack failed to score any hits, the Japanese remarking afterwards that the Devastators launched "slow torpedoes [at] long range. We could turn and run away from them."

The *Lexington's* strike suffered from an inability to find the target. Approximately half of the total aircraft (virtually all of the divebombers) of the strike failed to find the target. Four divebombers attacked in the teeth of eleven Zeros on air patrol. Three were lost, but one more hit was scored on the *Shokaku*. The torpedo planes attacked bravely, two launching torpedoes from 600 yards out, but though five hits were claimed, none actually scored. However, the third bomb hit sent the *Shokaku* on her way back to Japan for repairs, where she almost capsized.

Now it was the American turn. As the late Professor Paul S. Dull remarked on the incoming Japanese strike, "Despite their fewer planes (sixty-nine) the Japanese had the advantage, since their air strike force had a good balance of plane types and clear idea of where the American ships were. They also had experience in battle. The American carriers fighter protection

(CAP) was inadequate and poorly placed."

There were several false alarms that morning as returning scout planes triggered excitement in Task Force 17. A giant Mavis flying boat, vectored to the task force from the earlier sighting by the Kate, came, but was quickly shot down. Tension that morning continued to build. Frank F. Gill, the fighter direction officer, made some errors in his dispositions of the air patrol, primarily putting some Wildcats too far out at too low an altitude. Japanese torpedo planes came in at 10,000 feet and dropped down to attack unlike American doctrine, which kept them much lower on the run in towards the target. Further, some overcast was present, and the pilots were probably, naturally, looking down for torpedo planes instead of up.

As the Japanese approached, the Kate that had been on duty watching Task Force 17, was running low on fuel and began to return to the Carrier Strike Force. She sighted the incoming Japanese strike, joined with it and flew along until the strike sighted the American fleet, then with the gratitude of all, headed back to home. That Kate, piloted by the brave Kanno, was shot down during its return by Wildcats in the returning American strike that passed it an op-

Vice Admiral Frederick Sherman was the *Lexington's* skipper during the Battle of the Coral Sea.

posing course.

The torpedo planes went in first, dropping down from 10,000 feet to 4,000 feet. A Wildcat got one. Two more were shot down by Dauntlesses deployed on the bow of the *Lexington* as an anti-torpedo patrol—however, two Dauntlesses also went down. The Japanese came in closer, and could fly faster because of their superior torpedoes, and launched torpedoes at 500 to 1400 yards out from their target ship. The attack on the *Lexington* was further complicated by the fact that she required 1500 to 2000 yards to turn a circle, while the *Yorktown*, a full 100 feet shorter and a newer and lighter design, required much less room, a vital consideration when several torpedoes, from different angles and directions, are approaching. Finally the Japanese Kates launched a proper anvil attack, calling for torpedoes

A Japanese torpedo plane flies low over an escort destroyer as it prepares to launch a final torpedo at the crippled *Lexington*.

Several huge explosions ripped through the *Lexington* after she was hit. This photo captures an explosion that occurred when many men were still on board.

When the *Lexington* was first hit only her topside caught fire.

coming towards the bow, on both sides. If the target ship turns one way to show its bow towards the torpedoes, it exposes its long vulnerable side to the other incoming torpedoes. Thus the *Lexington* took two torpedo hits at 11:20 A.M. The *Yorktown* was luckier, and avoided hits. The speed of the two ships during the actual attack was 32–33 knots.

The first torpedo hit was thought to have been the least damaging. However, one of the rooms evacuated due to gas fumes and malfunctioning ventilation had electric motors powering the internal communications network, an extensive system on a large ship—these engines were left running.

The divebombers came in the last moments of the torpedo plane attack and the escorting Zeros kept the Wildcats away from them. The rapidly maneuvering *Lexington* took only two hits, and several damaging near misses. Even the vaunted Japanese accuracy had its off days, or possibly the "sons of concubines" were not as good as the pilots on the other four fleet carriers. It is possible that the Japanese also suffered from fogged bombsights. These two hits killed and wounded many men in the anti-aircraft batteries (which got one of the attackers), but did little vital damage.

The *Yorktown* only took one hit, a 551-pound bomb that went down through four decks before exploding, so much of the damage was internal. About seven near misses shook her up, but she survived. The Japanese reported both the *Yorktown* and the *Lexington* as being crippled and sinking. Although the Japanese flight leader, Takahashi, stayed in the area to watch the *Lexington* sink, she did not oblige him yet. Takahashi sent a new report in, "Cancel sinking report on *Saratoga*." (The *Lexington* was of the *Saratoga* class.) He, too, died on his return to the Japanese fleet carriers.

The withdrawing forces from each strike suffered losses on the way home to their respective carriers. Planes engaged in dogfights at different altitudes on the way back. The Japanese lost nineteen planes directly, and twelve so heavily damaged that they were jettisoned into the sea. American losses were equally heavy.

Things looked good for Task Force 17 when disaster struck at 12:47 P.M. on the *Lexington*. Gas fumes from leaking fuel tanks had built up around the electric motors still running in the Internal Communication Center causing a massive explosion that ripped through the bowels of the *Lexington*, igniting fires, and sending up a cloud of smoke that almost engulfed the entire ship. The *Lexington* was doomed. The order to abandon ship was given and performed sadly, but smartly. She continued to burn furiously and was sunk by torpedoes that evening, with her captain, Frederick C. Sherman, being the last to leave the "Lady Lex."

The problem for Task Force 17 was twofold at this point. First, the *Yorktown*, with some orphans from the *Lexington*, many of which were damaged, had only seven torpedoes left in the magazine for the Devastators, and had only thirty-one planes total by afternoon of May 8 capable of forming a strike. Secondly, Fletcher had intelligence that the *Kaga* was in the enemy's lineup, and a land based scout reported another fleet carrier present, perhaps the rumored *Kaga*. Finally, Nimitz ordered a retirement to conserve his fleet carrier strength fearing that the attack on Port Moresby had been turned back, which it had. As Nimitz said later, "inflicting damage on your enemy is no compensation for being sunk yourself."

The Carrier Strike Force had only thirty-nine planes immediately available, mostly Zeros, and Admiral Takagi, who was not one to press home a success as shown at the Battle of the Java Sea, agreed with his orders from Inoue to retire to Truk. It should be noted that Japanese naval officers tended to be physically overweight as a rule and out of shape. This physical state may have translated into affecting their work, as several times during the war many higher Japanese officers tended not to perform their duties with vigor. Inoue issued these orders because he felt he needed more than one partially equipped fleet carrier to support the invasion fleet off Port Moresby due to Allied land based air in the area. Admiral Yamamoto, when he learned of this retirement, was furious. The failure to not pursue a hurt enemy force to complete its destruction is a cardinal error in warfare. Yamamoto ordered the Carrier Striking Force to pursue the enemy, but May 9 was spent in refueling and by the tenth it was too late. Task Force 17 was gone, ending the first sea battle in history in which enemy ships did not

Before abandoning the ship, seamen look over the damage done to the *Lexington's* #2 gun gallery.

Men scramble down the lifelines as the fire begins to spread.

see each other during the battle.

The Americans lost more ships than the Japanese in this battle, but they halted the invasion of Port Moresby. The Americans learned more from the battle than the Japanese did. The Americans improved their air doctrine and started the process by which more fighters would be included in the future on board fleet carriers. The Americans also worked on damage control so nothing like what happened to the *Lexington* could occur again. It gave that vital element in warfare: experience. Samual Eliot Morison, chronicler of the exploits of the American navy in World War II wrote of the Battle of the Coral Sea,

There is no greater teacher of combat that can even remotely approach the value of combat itself; call Coral Sea what you will, it was an indispensable

preliminary to the great victory of Midway.

The morale value of the battle to all Allied nations, coming as it did immediately after the surrender of Corregidor, was immeasurable. Captain Sherman's statement (during the Court Martial always done when a ship is lost), articles by shipboard correspondents and numerous interviews with survivors printed in their home-town papers, told a story of cool efficiency, relentless action, superb heroism and determination. That story of the last fight of "Lady Lex," her calm abandonment, the devotion of her crew to their ship and their captain, transcended mere history; the American people took it to their hearts and store it up in the treasury of folk memory.

★★★ Midway, The Turning Point ★★★

At the time of the Battle of Coral Sea, Admiral Nimitz wanted most of his firstline fleet carriers in the South Pacific, maintaining communication to Australia—his intelligence service indicated that the Japanese did not intend any actions against the allies in the Central Pacific. This was, however, shortly, to change.

ULTRA revealed that Japan wanted to launch a major assault against the island of Midway (called Operation MI by the Japanese). Nimitz reasoned that if Midway were reinforced and prepared to defend against such an assault that it could be repulsed. Nimitz also decided that if he could ambush the approaching Japanese

forces, when they did not expect to encounter U.S. fleet carriers, that he could gain a favorable result, a victory that could halt the continuing Japanese advances. Nimitz ended up gaining a victory beyond his hopes and dreams! (American intelligence in Washington and Hawaii were not altogether convinced that Midway was the Japanese target. Some felt Hawaii or even the West Coast, where black out precautions were in effect during the Midway operation, would be attacked.)

Yamamoto was faced with three possible courses of action. One was to continue attacks in the Indian Ocean with the seizure of Ceylon

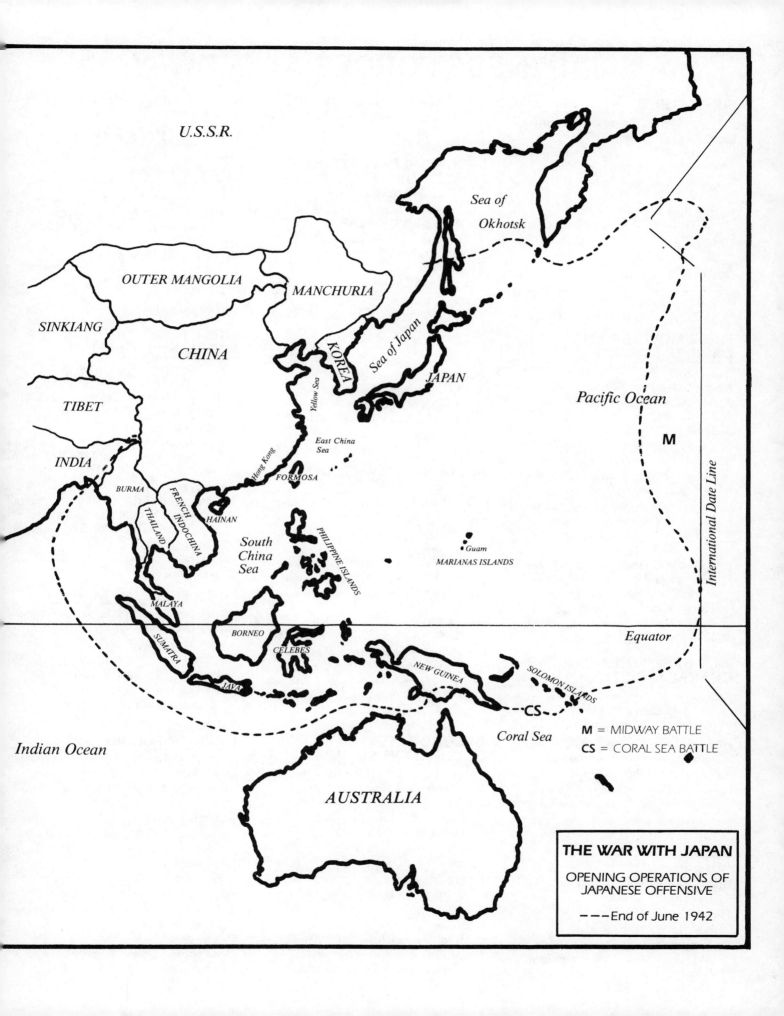

U.S.S.R.

Sea of Okhotsk

OUTER MANGOLIA

MANCHURIA

SINKIANG

CHINA

KOREA

Sea of Japan

JAPAN

Pacific Ocean

M

Yellow Sea

TIBET

East China Sea

INDIA

Hong Kong

FORMOSA

BURMA

FRENCH INDOCHINA

THAILAND

HAINAN

South China Sea

PHILIPPINE ISLANDS

International Date Line

•Guam

MARIANAS ISLANDS

MALAYA

BORNEO

SUMATRA

CELEBES

JAVA

NEW GUINEA

SOLOMON ISLANDS

Equator

CS

Coral Sea

M = MIDWAY BATTLE

CS = CORAL SEA BATTLE

Indian Ocean

AUSTRALIA

THE WAR WITH JAPAN

OPENING OPERATIONS OF
JAPANESE OFFENSIVE

— — — End of June 1942

JAPANESE FORCES AT MIDWAY

FIRST FLEET

Admiral Yamamoto, commanding

Light Aircraft Carriers

Hosho *(9 Claude fighters, 6 Jean B4Y torpedo planes) (978 mile range, 1 MG, 173 m.p.h., 1 torpedo or 1,102 pounds of bombs)*

Battleships

Yamato *(flagship)*, Nagato *and* Mutsu

Light Cruiser

Sendai

Destroyers

Fubuki, Shirayuki, Murakumo, Hatsuyuki, Isonami, Uranami, Shikinami, Ayanami *and* Yukaze

FIRST MOBILE FORCE, CARRIER STRIKE FORCE

Vice-Admiral Nagumo, commanding

Aircraft Carriers

Akagi *(flagship) (18 Zero fighters, 18 Val bombers, and 27 Kate torpedo planes)*

Kaga *(18 Zero fighters, 18 Val bombers, and 27 Kate torpedo planes)*

Hiruu *(18 Zero fighters, 18 Val bombers, and 18 Kate torpedo planes)*

Soruy *(18 Zero fighters, 18 Val bombers, and 18 Kate torpedo planes and 2 experimental Judys used for scouting)*

It should be noted that in actual numbers at Midway, these four CVs carried 73 fighters, 74 Vals, and 81 Kates, as well as 21 Zero fighters of the 6th Air Group intended to garrison Midway.

JAPANESE FLEET CARRIER CHARACTERISTICS

Akagi, *41,300 tons, six 8-inch guns, twelve 4.7 inch anti-aircraft guns, 91 aircraft, 31 knots)*

Kaga, *42,541 tons, ten 8-inch guns, sixteen 5-inch dual purpose guns, 90 aircraft, 28 knots)*

Hiryu, *20,250 tons, twelve 5-inch dual purpose guns, 73 aircraft, 34 knots)*

Soryu, *18,800 tons, twelve 5-inch dual purpose guns, 71 aircraft, 34.5 knots)*

Battleships

Haruna *and* Kirishima

Heavy Cruisers

Tone *and* Chikuma

Light Cruisers

Nagara

Destroyers

Akigumo, Makigumo, Yugumo, Isokaze, Hamakaze, Arashi,
Kazegumo, Urakaze, Tanikaze, Nowaki, Hagikaze, *and* Maikaze

Fleet Train:

eight tankers

SECOND FLEET, STRIKE FORCE, SUPPORT FORCE, MAIN BODY

Vice-Admiral Kondo, commanding

Light Aircraft Carriers

Zuiho *(12 Claude fighters, 12 Jean torpedo planes)*

Battleships

Hiei *and* Kongo

Heavy Cruisers

Atago *(flagship)*, Chokai, Myoko, *and* Haquro

Light Cruisers

Yura

Destroyers

Murasame, Yudachi, Harusame, Samidare, Asagumo, Minegumo, Natsugumo, *and* Mikazuki

Fleet Train:

four tankers

SECOND FLEET ESCORT FORCE

Rear-Admiral Tanaka, commanding

Light Cruiser

Jintsu *(flagship)*

Destroyers

Kuroshio, Oyashio, Hatsukaze, Yukikaze, Amatsukaze, Tokisukaze, Kasumi, Kagero, Arare, *and* Shiranuhi

Patrol Boats

No. 1, 2, and 34 carrying troops, three subchasers, and four minesweepers. Fifteen transports with 5,000 troops (Ichiki Detachment, Kure & Yokosuka 5th Special Naval Landing Force) and one tanker

SECOND FLEET, OCCUPATION SUPPORT FORCE

Rear-Admiral Kurita, commanding

Seaplane Tenders:

Chitose *(16 Jake fighters — 460 mile range, 230 m.p.h., 3 MGs, two 132 pound bombs)*

Kamikawa Maru *(8 Jake fighters, 4 Pete scout planes)*

Heavy Cruisers

Kumano *(flag)*, Mogami, Mikuma, Suzuya

Destroyers

Arashio, Asashio, *and* Hayashio

Patrol Boat #35 with 550 troops. This force was detailed for the occupation of Kure Island and setting up of a seaplane base.

SPECIAL DUTY FORCE

Captain Harada

Seaplane Carriers

Chiyoda *and* Nisshin *(Modified to carry midget submarines, about twelve each. To be deployed around Midway after its capture to attack Allied ships)*

FIRST SUPPLY FORCE

Destroyer

Ariake

Two freighters

FIRST FLEET, 2ND BATTLESHIP DIVISION

Vice-Admiral Takasu, commanding

Battleships

Hyuga *(flagship)*, Ise, Fuso, *and* Yamashiro

Light Cruisers

Kitakami *and* Oi *(special ships armed with 40 Long Lance 24-inch torpedoes each)*

Destroyers

Asagiri, Yugiri, Shirakumo, Amagiri, Umikaze, Yamakaze, Kawakaze, Suzukaze, Ariake, Yugure, Shigure *and* Shiratsuyu

Fleet Train:

Two Tankers

FIFTH FLEET, MAIN BODY

Vice-Admiral Hosogawa, commanding

Heavy Cruisers

Nachi *(flagship)*

Destroyers

Inazuma, Ikazuchi

Fleet Train

two oilers and three transports

SECOND STRIKE FORCE, CARRIER FORCE

Rear-Admiral Kakuta, commanding

Light Aircraft Carrier

Ryuio *(flagship) (16 Zero fighters, 21 Kate torpedo bombers)*

Aircraft Carriers

Junyo *(24 Zero fighters, 21 Val dive bombers)*

Heavy Cruisers

Maya *and* Takao

Seaplane Tender

Kimikawa Maru *(6 Pete scout planes, though capable of 12)*

Destroyers

Akebono, Ushio, Sazanami, *and* Shiokaze

Fleet Train
1 oiler

ATTU OCCUPATION FORCE
Rear-Admiral Omori, commanding
Light Cruisers
Abukuma *(flagship)*
Destroyers
Hatsuharu, Hatshshimo, Wakaba, *and* Nenohi

1 minelayer
1 transport with 1200 men of the Army North Sea Detachment under Major Hozumi

KISKA OCCUPATION FORCE
Captain Ono, commanding
Light Cruisers
Tama

Destroyers
Akatsuki, Hibiki, *and* Hokaze
3 minelayers
2 transports with 550 troops of the Maizuru 3rd Special Naval Landing Force under Lieutenant Commander Mukai.

AMERICAN FORCES AT MIDWAY

TASK FORCE 16
Rear-Admiral Spruance, commanding
Aircraft Carriers
Enterprise *(flagship) (27 Wildcat fighters, 33 Dauntless divebombers, 14 Devastator torpedo planes) and* Hornet *(27 Wildcat fighters, 34 Dauntless divebombers, 15 Devastator torpedo planes)*

Heavy Cruisers
New Orleans, Minneapolis, Vincennes, Northampton, Pensacola
Light Cruisers
Atlanta *(a new class of anti-aircraft cruiser armed with sixteen 5-inch guns)*
Destroyers
Balch, Conungham, Benham, Ellet, Maury, Phelps, Worden, Monaghan, Aylwin, Dewey, *and* Monssen

TASK FORCE 17
Rear-Admiral Fletcher, commanding
Aircraft Carriers
Yorktown *(flagship))25 Wildcat fighters, 34 Dauntless divebombers, 12 Devastator torpedo planes)*

Heavy Cruisers
Astoria *and* Portland
Destroyers
Hammann, Hughes, Morris, Anderson, Russell, *and* Gwin
NOTE: *Plane totals are for operational planes available. Thirteen planes were under repair or inoperable.*

FLEET TRAIN
Destroyers
Blue, Ralph Talbot
One oiler

FRENCH FRIGATE SHOALS GUARD
Destroyers
Clark
One tanker, two tenders, some minor craft

TASK FORCE 1
Vice-Admiral Pye, commanding
Aircraft Carrier & Scout
Long Island *(12 Wildcat fighters, 8 fixed wheel SOC Seagull Recon planes)*

The SOC-3 was used primarily as a cruiser-launched seaplane, 679 mile range, 2 MGs, 165 m.p.h., 650 pounds of bombs)
Battleships
Maryland, Pennsylvania, Tennessee, Colorado, New Mexico, Mississippi, *and* Idaho
Eight Destroyers

MIDWAY ISLAND DEFENSES
Captain Simard, commanding
6th Marine Defense Battalion, 2 companies of the 2nd Battalion of Marine Raiders.
8 PT boats, 4 small patrol craft.
2 PT boats at Kure Island.
SHORE BASED AIR: *USN contingent 32 PBY long range scout planes, 6 Avenger torpedo planes,*
Marine contingent - 20 Buffalo fighters, 7 Wildcat fighters, 11 Vindicatior divebombers, 16 Dauntless divebombers
Army Air Corps contingent - 4 Marauder B-26 medium bombers, 19 B-17 bombers

USA FORCES IN THE ALEUTIAN ACTION

TASK FORCE 8
Rear-Admiral Theobald, commanding
Heavy Cruisers
Indianapolis *and* Louisville
Light Cruisers
Nashville *(flagship),* St. Louis, *and* Honolulu
Destroyers
Gridley, Gilmer, McCall, *and* Humphreys

TASK FORCE 8.1
Captain Gehres, commanding
Seaplane tenders
Williamson, Gillis, *and* Caco *servicing 20 PBYs and one B17.*

TASK FORCE 8.2
Captain Parker, commanding

Gunboat Charleston
Fourteen patrol craft
Five Coast Guard cutters
One tanker
These ships were placed in an offshore line for search purposes, but did not sight the Japanese ships during the action.

TASK GROUP 8.3
Brigadier General Butler, commanding
Cold Bay: *21 P-40 fighters, 12 B-26 bombers, 2 B-18 bombers*
Point Otter on Umnak: *12 P-40 fighters*
Kodiak: *15 P-39 fighters, 17 P-40 fighters, 5 B-17 bombers, 2 LB-30 bombers*
Anchorage: *25 P-38 fighters, 15 P-39 fighters, 4 P-36 fighters, 7 B-17 bombers, 5 B-18 bombers, 12 B-26 bombers, and 2 LB-30 bombers.*

TASK FORCE 8.4
Captain Craig, commanding
Destroyers
Case, Reid, Brooks, Sands, Kane, Dent, Talbot, King, *and* Waters
Named Destroyer Striking Force

TASK FORCE 8.5
Six submarines (s type) present and ineffective

TASK FORCE 8.9–FLEET TRAIN
Two tankers
One freighter

(now Sri Lanka) and a possible linking up with the European Axis forces. This option, surprisingly, had the least support within Japan's military, in part due to the view that the U.S.A. was the main enemy. Furthermore, the Japanese army wanted to commit troops to Burma, and not to Ceylon. Exercising this option could have forced Great Britain out of the war, or at minimum turned the Indian Ocean Basin into an Axis lake. After the fall of Singapore, Great Britain might have suffered the fall of Ceylon leading to intense turmoil in India. The effect on the British 8th Army (facing Rommel) in Egypt could have been catastrophic.

A second course, strongly supported by the Japanese chief of staff, was to advance through New Caledonia, Fiji, and Samoa, with the idea of cutting off Australia from the U.S.A. Yamamoto did not discount this approach, but decided to wait until after the Midway operation to pursue this advance. The big advantage of this approach would be that the Japanese and the U.S. would both be operating far from home bases; an operation against Midway was close to Hawaii but far from Japan. Further, the Japanese would have been within range of their own land-based aircraft, something that did not exist in regards to an attack on Midway. In passing it should be noted that a discussion for invading Australia was broached in early 1942. The Japanese army did not want to undertake such an operation against the Australian mainland, due to a perceived lack of troops.

The third option, the one Yamamoto wanted to adopt, was advance against Midway. It was an operation that would include a diversionary action against Alaska and occupation of two islands in the Aleutian Island Chain. It was an operation that would use more fuel than the Japanese fleet used in an entire year during peace time. Yamamoto perceived that by advancing against Midway, he would force the American fleet to react, as it was a post threatening Pearl Harbor, and would represent the first base on the other side of the International Date Line. Yamamoto assumed that a surprise attack against Midway would bring the American fleet onto the scene within one to three days. By then the invasion would have occurred and a mighty Japanese fleet would be assembled in the area for a decisive battle. The destruction of the

American carrier force would bring America closer to the negotiating table. The point that must be made is that Yamamoto did not expect to see any American fleet carrier force until the Japanese had reduced Midway and captured it. They certainly did not expect to see the U.S. Navy in force before the landing on Midway. Still, Yamamoto told Nagumo, the commander of the Japanese fleet carriers, that half of the air units on board the fleet carriers were armed with anti-ship armaments (torpedoes and armor piercing bombs) and not ground attack weapons (high-explosive bombs). The violation of this directive was one of the key failures of the Japanese at Midway.

As with too many Japanese strategic plans, the plan called for complex and involved maneuvering of several fleets and their arrival on a rather tight schedule in several areas of the central and northern Pacific. Finally, at the appointed hour, the much reduced American fleet, probably with but two fleet carriers, was to show up for impending destruction.

The first move was a submarine reconnaissance of Alaska while long-range seaplanes refueled in French Frigate Shoals (an uninhabited lagoon in the Central Pacific) from submarines and then proceed to fly over Pearl Harbor to assess the situation. (A similar air operation by Japan had been performed on March 3–4 and March 10 of 1942 and had achieved little). Additional scouting operations were to be undertaken from Paramushiro (in the Kuriles), Wake, and Marcus Islands. The second move called for the 2nd Carrier Striking Force to launch an air raid on Dutch Harbor, on the island of Unalaska, on June 3. This diversion was to cover a landing of 1550 troops on Attu and Kiska. It would also throw off the American response to the main Japanese offensive. Just after that attack, the 1st Carrier Striking Force would bomb Midway on June 4 and stand ready to attack any American naval forces that appeared, while the 2nd Fleet Strike Force, covering the invasion fleet, approached Midway. Next, 1st Fleet, Battleship Division 1, would hurry to the area to help complete the destruction of the weakened American fleet. The older battleships in Battleship Division 2 sailed with the *Yamato*, eventually turning to the northeast to support the 2nd Carrier Strike Force in its attack against Alaska.

The USS *Yorktown* sits in dry dock at Pearl Harbor.

On the 5th of June the Japanese invaded Midway with the 2nd Fleet Strike Force, captured it, and established an air and seaplane base.

Japan was using all but two fleet carriers, five heavy cruisers, and ten light cruisers of their major combatants. She was using 113 warships and sixteen submarines for this operation.

How would Nimitz respond?

First, he placed both Alaska and Midway on alert and rushed as many reinforcements to each area as possible. Midway received between May and early June: radar, over twenty additional anti-aircraft guns, eventually a hodge-podge of 121 aircraft from the Army, Navy, and Marines, P.T. boats, five Stuart tanks, as well two rifle companies of the Second Marine Raider Battal-

ion. This augmented the original prewar garrison of 834 men of the Sixth Marine Defense Battalion. The problem with this force was that it was thrown together from several sources, especially the air units, and so could not be properly coordinated and, in the case of some of the pilots, included new recruits. Secondly, Midway was an extremely small island and there were, in effect, no fallback positions. It was a tiny atoll and all of it would have to be occupied.

The twenty-six submarines were deployed by Nimitz although in the course of the operation they proved largely ineffective. The *Nautilus* fired three torpedoes at a sinking and stationary *Kaga*, but only one hit, . . . and it was a dud.

Nimitz next organized his fleet carrier task

force. Built around the *Enterprise* and *Hornet*, it would normally be commanded by Vice-Admiral Bill Halsey, but he was ill with a skin disease and unable to leave the hospital. Halsey suggested his cruiser commander, a man from the gun school and not a flyer, Rear-Admiral Raymond Spruance, to replace him. Nimitz accepted this recommendation and so to the fore came America's most thoughtful and brilliant fighting admiral of World War II.

Spruance kept Halsey's staff together, and took orders from the commander of the other task force built around the damaged *Yorktown*, Vice-Admiral Jack Fletcher, who was hurrying north after the Battle of Coral Sea. The *Yorktown* needed a full month of repairs to reach 100% efficiency from the damage suffered at Coral Sea—as she limped into Pearl on May 27, she was trailing an oil slick. Over the period of three days, emergency repairs, involving 1400 workmen, were performed to put her back in the line.

Fletcher planned to use his flagship, the *Yorktown*, as both the reserve fleet carrier and the fleet carrier offering scouting duties to the other task force. The *Hornet* and the *Enterprise* were then free to launch all their planes in air strikes. Ideally, they would be in position to the northeast of Midway to launch an airstrike against the Japanese main carrier force when least expected.

Rear-Admiral Robert A. Theobald was given a small surface fleet and was rushed northward to be available for possible attacks against the Japanese diversionary operations in the Aleutians.

America's battleship fleet did not participate in the Midway Operation due to the Japanese battleship fleet being concentrated in the same harbor in Japan with the fleet flagship, the *Yamata*. No radio communications to transmit plans from the flagship *Yamato* were necessary. Thus, Nimitz did not know that the Japanese were employing all their battleship strength. Nimitz, through his intelligence, thought that only two or four of the Kongo class fast battleships were being used by the Japanese in the operation. Further, since the American battleships used an incredible amount of fuel oil, Nimitz stationed the American battleship fleet in San Francisco. It did sortie during the opera-

tion, but was too distant to offer real support.

Finally, the *Salt Lake City* and seaplane tender *Tangier* were planted in the South Pacific to simulate radio traffic of an aircraft carrier task force. Surprisingly, the Japanese on the *Yamato* did not fall for this trick—but did note unusually heavy radio traffic from Pearl Harbor, including much in a high priority code. There was suspicion on board the *Yamato* that an American carrier force was operating from Pearl Harbor before the Japanese struck at Midway. However, they could not alert Nagumo in the 1st Carrier Strike Force because the *Yamato* had already gone to sea and was maintaining radio silence.

Rear-Admiral Kakuta, under the cover of fog, took his 2nd Carrier Strike Force under the American air-reconnaissance and through a line of picket ships without being sighted. He was able to launch an air attack from 165 miles away towards Dutch Harbor, believed to be the only airbase that the Americans had in the area. Due to bad weather, only the *Ryujo's* small strike of twelve planes got through. Fine weather over Dutch Harbor did not help much as no ships were damaged and while some fuel tanks were hit, only twenty-five soldiers and sailors died in the attack. One Japanese plane was lost.

A second strike was launched against Commander Craig's destroyer strike force stationed near Dutch Harbor when it was sighted by a returning airplane. This force, normally nine destroyers, but only six destroyers at the time of the airstrike, was to provide direct defense of the area around Dutch Harbor. Ideally, they would attack an invasion fleet at night. Fortunately, though, the second airstrike failed to find them and lost two planes shot down, and two others heavily damaged when P-40s from a base unknown to the Japanese (Otter Point), ripped into the flight.

The Japanese carriers were only 130 miles south of Dutch Harbor and they still had not been firmly sighted. That night Kakuta moved towards Adak Island, which he was to "soften up," but bad weather precluded this, so once again he moved in toward Dutch Harbor. Another strike against Dutch Harbor yielded a few more dead and a few more buildings damaged and destroyed. Meanwhile, an army airstrike finally went in against the Japanese carriers, scoring no hits, although a B-26 and a B-17 were lost. A few other planes were lost by both sides in this desultory battle, altogether a very minor operation for all involved, due in part to the bad weather.

In the course of the next few days Kakuta was called south after the disaster at Midway. Then he was ordered north, again by Yamamoto, to proceed with the capture of Kiska and Attu. Kakuta and Admiral Hosogaya (the overall commander in the north) were even given additional reinforcements, the principal ones being the fleet carrier *Zuikaku*, the light carrier *Zuiho*, battleships *Kongo* and *Hiei*, as well as heavy cruisers *Myoko*, *Haguro*, *Tone*, and *Chikuma*. The campaign ended with the withdrawal of naval units after the bloodless capture of Attu and Kiska.

An important footnote to the action in the Aleutians tells of Petty Officer Tadayoshi Koga from the *Ryujo* who had his Zero hit by one bullet, causing the oil pressure gauge to drop, though no actual fuel was being lost. Koga brought his plane down on Akutan Island, a designated emergency landing island, but Koga,

Ensign Jack Reid and the crew of the first patrol plane to sight the Japanese off Midway on the morning of June 3, 1942.

breaking his neck during the rough landing on marshy ground, did very little damage to his plane. Five weeks later his Zero was sighted from the air. Shipped to San Diego by October of 1942, a full report on the Zero aided in devising tactics against the Zero and pointed the way for the eclipse of Zero as the supreme fighter in the War in the Pacific.

Every morning from Midway departed lumbering PBYs (also known as Catalinas) and occasional B-17s on patrol for approaching enemy forces. In the last few days PBYs tangled with Mavis flying boats from the Japanese islands. While none were lost, several PBYs were shot up. Surprisingly, the Japanese did not seem suspicious of the increased radio traffic from Pearl and Midway, nor of the extra-long range patrols (as well as Japanese submarine reports of extensive activity both day . . . and night on Midway). Overconfidence, brought on by the fever of victory, was taking its toll.

Ensign Jack Reid, piloting a PBY on June 3, 1942, 700 miles from Midway, turned to his co-pilot Ensign Hardeman at 9:25 A.M. and asked, "Do you see what I see?" Hardeman looked over and said, "You are damned right I do." Commander Toyama on the light cruiser *Jintsu* later

recalled that on that day he was pleased that the lumbering transports were keeping station when suddenly a destroyer on the port side hoisted a signal and fired a smokeshell. There, in the distance, out of range of guns, hovered a PBY. Reid saw twenty-seven ships and reported, erroneously, "Main Body." This led to some confusion, but Nimitz, radioed his fleet that these were obviously not enemy fleet carriers, which were to the north, while this sighting was from the southwest, where the invasion fleet was coming, originally lifting anchor from Saipan.

The Second Fleet was attacked twice that day, once by a flight of B-17s dropping bombs from great altitude—all missing—and the second from an unusual source, three PBYs out of Pearl, and a fourth that was also unique; they all were equipped with radar. They were armed with torpedoes and with the radar to guide them home at night. They took off for a night attack on the approaching transports. Three managed to find the transports and launched an attack at 1 A.M. on June 4. Pushing these lumbering birds at full throttle into the midst of an enemy fleet only 50 feet off the water was quite a feat. One PBY almost broadsided an enemy

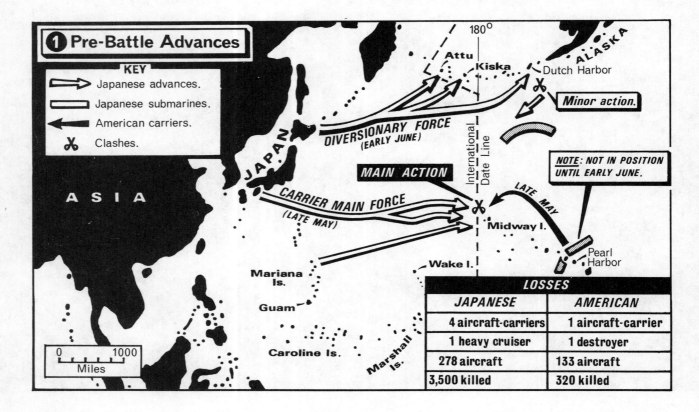

① Pre-Battle Advances

KEY
⇨ Japanese advances.
▭ Japanese submarines.
⬅ American carriers.
✂ Clashes.

180°

ASIA

JAPAN

ALASKA
Attu   Kiska   Dutch Harbor

Minor action.

DIVERSIONARY FORCE (EARLY JUNE)

International Date Line

NOTE: NOT IN POSITION UNTIL EARLY JUNE.

MAIN ACTION

CARRIER MAIN FORCE (LATE MAY)

LATE MAY

Midway I.

Wake I.

Pearl Harbor

Mariana Is.

Guam

Caroline Is.

Marshall Is.

0   1000
Miles

LOSSES	
JAPANESE	AMERICAN
4 aircraft-carriers	1 aircraft-carrier
1 heavy cruiser	1 destroyer
278 aircraft	133 aircraft
3,500 killed	320 killed

destroyer! The PBYs achieved surprise and each of the three launched torpedoes at about 1,000 yards from a sea of targets. Lieutenant Hibberd remembers one crewmen yelling at him, "Drop that damn thing and let's get the hell out of here!" But he held on a bit closer, released the torpedo, and heard an explosion as he roared towards home with tracer bullets peppering his plane. On board the tanker *Akebono Marua* a torpedo hit the forward section, killing thirteen and wounding eleven. Surprisingly, the tanker was not hurt badly and could still maintain 12 to 14 knots, so she kept station and the invasion fleet plodded on.

Meantime Nagumo with the 1st Carrier Strike Force was approaching Midway Island. He was moving in under a heavy cloud cover and it was unlikely he would be sighted. Yamamoto decided that he should not report the attacks on the invasion fleet to Nagumo, so to not give positions away.

On Midway, the pilots all know that the enemy was approaching and the 4th would see a lot of action.

Normally Commander Mitsuo Fuchida would have been leading the first raid against Midway on the morning of June 4th, but he was recovering from an appendicitis operation. Lieutenant Joichi Tomonaga of the *Hiryu* was for leading instead the first wave and this quiet hard-drinking officer looked forward to the operation. The first strike consisted of 108 planes, thirty-six Vals from the *Akagi* and *Kaga*, thirty-six Kates from the *Hiryu* and the *Soryu*, and nine fighters from each of the four carriers. The Kates were carrying 1,770-pound type 80 general purpose bombs, while the divebombers were armed with 532-pound type 25 general purpose bombs. By 4:45 A.M. The planes had moved to launching stations, started their engines, launched, formed up, and the first wave was on its way to Midway.

Nagumo also launched at 4:30 A.M. seven scout planes from the various cruisers and battleships to search out the east, for possible enemy ships, out to a range of 300 miles. The 300 miles was plenty of distance because, as a rule, American planes could not have the range of the Japanese planes, especially the American torpedo planes. The heavy cruiser *Tone* had trouble launching one of her planes and it was not until 5 A.M. that the last one from her went out. Nagumo also ordered the second strike to be brought up from below on all four fleet carriers and to be armed and readied with anti-ship weapons so to be ready for possible contacts in the early morning, no matter how unlikely, with American ships. Some twenty-four fighters were placed on combat air patrol over the fleet. Nagumo would have liked more fighters, but with space on his carriers taken by fighting for the future land garrison on Midway, with the *Zuikaku* and *Shokaku* missing, and the expectation that the USN was not present in strength . . . .

Lieutenant Ady on a PBY saw a small seaplane whip by on an opposing course at 5:10 A.M.; it was one of the scout planes sent out from the Japanese support warships. He radioed that contact when he saw at 5:30, through a break in the clouds, two Japanese fleet carriers. Jackpot! He had to be careful to not be jumped by enemy fighters that could easily bring him down, so he played in the clouds as he reported "5:34, enemy carriers" . . . "5:40, ED 180, sight 320 degrees" . . . "5:52, two carriers and main body of ships, carriers in front, course 135, sped 25." On the American carriers there was some confusion as other reports were arriving. Also, the message mentioned only two carriers, and Fletcher knew that there were more than two out there. Where were those others?

Lieutenant William Chase in his PBY had just seen at 5:40 a huge formation of fighters and bombers. Chase did not bother with encoding this message and sent *en clair*. "Many planes heading Midway bearing 320, distance 150 miles."

The message did not get things moving as quickly as it should have, even though the commander of Midway, Captain Simard U.S.N., did not want his planes caught on the ground as they were at both Pearl and the Philippines. It was not until radar picked the planes up 93 miles from the island at abut 5:55 that orders to get the planes airborne were finally given. B-17s, sent to attack the enemy force sighted the previous day, had already been armed and launched. They were ordered to change course and attack this new enemy force. PBYs had already been launched on search missions that morning, but, still, on the island there were over sixty aircraft needing to be launched. It required time for fighters to reach altitudes high enough for proper attacks against enemy planes.

As the Japanese approached the island, an interesting footnote to history was getting prepared. Film director John Ford had arrived a few days previously from Pearl Harbor. He had been flown by Admiral Nimitz to Midway with camera equipment to film the approaching attack! He picked up some shrapnel in his shoulder in the course of the day, but got great action shots.

The action opened with American fighters knocking down two Kates in an attack from above. Most of the Marine fighters got in one pass before the escorting Zeros roared into them. Unfortunately for the Marines that day, they learned that the Wildcat might be an equal, but the lumbering overweight Buffalo was an all too easy target. Lieutenant Charles Hughes said of the Buffalo fighters that it "looked like they were tied to a string while the Zeros made passes at them." Of the twenty-five fighters that rose that morning, six struggled back due to America's inability to be prepared for war or to avoid it. The Japanese lost eleven aircraft to all causes in the airstrike against Midway.

At 6:31 the guns on the island opened up on the attackers. Anti-aircraft accounted for a few planes, but hangers, buildings, fuel tanks were all hit. Zeros came down to strafe after that, wreaking havoc everywhere. On the ground eleven died and eighteen were wounded.

The Japanese felt that with such stiff resistance another strike was warranted to "soften" the target. Lieutenant Tomonaga radioed the First Carrier Strike Force that, "There is need for a second attack."

Nagumo was faced with a difficult decision. If he launched a second strike at Midway, he had to rearm planes currently on deck for land based targets, that is, until the first strike returned to the carriers and refueled and rearmed, he had no effective force to confront any naval force that the Americans might have in the area. As Professor H.P. Willmott put it, "The problem, dodged by Yamamoto . . . (with his splitting up of Japan's aircraft carriers to various forces, instead of a massive concentration) was how the First Carrier Strike Force in the absence of a reserve, was to operate against one target while safeguarding against the possibility of encountering an enemy task force at sea."

Nagumo decided that, since most of the scouts had been out for sometime, the American navy was probably not around. Also, the first American planes from Midway were about to attack, a trigger for Nagumo to attack Midway with a second strike.

Six Avenger torpedo planes and the four Army B-26 bombers sighted the Japanese fleet and launched an immediate, uncoordinated attack. The Avengers were immediately jumped by Zeros and all but one were lost. While the Avenger was brand new and would shortly replace the Devastators from all the aircraft carriers, both planes shared one fatal weakness: speed at which a torpedo had to be dropped was quite slow.

Characteristics of American, Japanese, and British Torpedoes in 1942.

	SIZE	EXPLOSIVE CHARGE	DROPPING SPEED
U.S.A.	22.4-inch	600 pounds of Torpex	110 knots
Japan	17.7-inch	331 pounds of Type 97	260 knots
Britain	17.7-inch	388 pounds of TNT	145 knots

Captain Collins lead in the four B-26s at 200 feet, as they were armed with torpedoes. He remembers, after racing through a curtain of anti-aircraft fire to get a good position for the final attack run on the *Akagi*, one of the planes broadcasting by radio, "Boy, if mother could see me now!" Of the four bombers, the last two were lost and the second one actually had Lieutenant Russ Johnson bombardier strafing the carrier deck with the nose gun! The *Akagi* lost two men, had No. 3 anti-aircrafted gun placed out of action, and the transmitting antenna cut from the strafing.

At 7:15 A.M. this first strike American attack was over and the order to rearm planes went out to the carriers. Midway would be attacked a second time. Planes were sent below where plane crews scurried to remove torpedoes and armor-piercing bombs while additional general purpose bombs came up from the magazines below.

At 7:28 the late departing scout plane from the *Tone* reported, "Sight what appears to be ten enemy surface ships in position bearing 10 degrees distance, 240 miles from Midway. Course 150 degrees, speed over 20 knots." They were within striking range. And Nagumo's fleet was dispersed due to rapid maneuvering during the last air attacks. Yamamoto felt that the presence of the American fleet was a surprise, but was not concerned. It would mean a victory that much earlier. Admiral Yamamoto, back on the

Yamato, had not yet become suspicious of the fact that the Americans were not reacting to the Japanese, but were acting on their own plan.

Again, when every minute counted, Nagumo discussed what to do with his staff, and at 7:48 ordered, "Prepare to carry out attacks on enemy fleet units. Leave torpedoes on those attack planes which have not as yet changed to bombs."

Starting at 7:55 A.M. sixteen Dauntless dive-bombers under Major Loften R. Henderson from Midway "glidebombed" (the pilots were too inexperienced for proper divebombing) the

Crewmen battle fires aboard the *Yorktown* after it was first hit.

The base on Midway Island was also hit during the Japanese attack. Planes, such as the bullet-riddled TBF shown here, and hangars (opposite page) were damaged.

Hiryu and *Soryu*. The Japanese received a good scare, but all bombs missed. (Henderson died in the attack, but lived in immortality by having an airfield on Guadalcanal named after him.) Eight Dauntless failed to return. It was all over for them by 8:12.

The *Tone's* searchplane was still reporting, but was a very poor scout. It did not send in many messages, and they were not too accurate. After the *Akagi* pointly radioed at 8 A.M. concerning the type of ships the scout had, it reported at 8:09, "Enemy is composed of five cruisers and dive destroyers." No carriers.

At 8:14 the next attack came in from the B-17s that had been diverted from their early morning run against the invasion fleet. Instead of 8,000 feet, as the day before, they came in at 20,000 feet. By 8:20 the *Soryu* and *Hiryu* had been bombed again, but missed again. Some Zeros made a few half-hearted passes at the B-17s, but out of respect, they did not press home their attacks. The B-17 was a difficult and big target to bring down. By now things were getting even more complicated for the Japanese as their strike against Midway had returned and was trying to land. With the B-17 attack in pro-

gress, they milled around waiting for a break in the action to land. At 8:20 the *Tone's* scout plane sent a message to the commanders standing on the *Akagi's* bridge: "The enemy is accompanied by what appears to be a carrier." At 8:30 the scout plane reported two enemy cruisers on the horizon, implying the presence of a second task force.

Next up were the eleven old and slow Vindicator divebombers that had been unable to keep up with the Dauntlesses. Only two were lost because they did not attack the carriers, but opted for the battleship *Haruna*, which they missed. This was the last attack from Midway.

Nagumo now had a difficult decision. The first wave was running out of fuel and needed to land. The combat air patrol was low on fuel

and some of the fighters were out of ammunition. The torpedo planes were still below decks and many planes still were armed with ground attack armaments. At 8:30 Rear Admiral Yamaguchi signaled from the *Hiryu*, "Consider it advisable to launch attack force immediately."— for any Japanese to signal a superiority their impatience was highly unusual.

Nagumo decided that the best course of action was to recover the first strike and air patrol fighters that needed to land. Decks needed to be cleared, and by now, with the constant changing of armaments, bombs and torpedoes were literally lying around, many had not been returned to the magazines because of the need for speed and the element of command confusion that had manifested itself. All they needed was time, but as Commander Fuchida later said, "Victory in battle does not always go to the stronger; it often goes to the side which is quicker to react boldly and decisively to unforeseen developments, and to grasp fleeting opportunities."

Nagumo was still trying to decide what was best for optimizing Japan's chances, not realizing that the U.S. knew where he was and quite possibly had a strike already on its way. Nagumo knew at 8:30 that his position had been known to the enemy for at least two hours, plenty of time to put together and launch an attack. Considering the superior range of Japan's planes, following Yamaguchi's suggestion made the best sense. There were bound to be enemy incoming planes at this point. To clear the decks of the planes already on the decks, with their weapons, forming up over the First Carrier Strike Force and lashing out at the American carriers made sense. Some of the congestion on the decks would have been relieved and enough damage might have been done to the Americans to force a retreat or disrupt further attacks. Nagumo was about to be attacked with virtually everything on his fleet carrier decks, littered with weapons and lines filled with aviation gas.

Spruance, with the two carriers that were to make the main strike, wanted to close the enemy to within 100 miles, but that would mean delaying an attack until 9 A.M. The only report Spruance had was from 6:02 and by delaying an attack, he might learn more and better intelligence (It would not be until 8:38 that further data locating the enemy would arrive. Part of the problem was that Midway's radio traffic was on another frequency and could not be heard on board the Enterprise or Yorktown.) His chief of staff, the difficult Captain Miles Browning from Halsey's staff, urged that the attack be launched quickly at 7 A.M., although that meant the planes would be flying 155 miles and would have little fuel for a margin of error. Browning was obsessed with the element of surprise, and rightfully so. Spruance went with his man, and made a second important decision: he launched everything he could when only two Japanese carriers had been sighted.

First off were sixteen fighters for the combat air patrol, being launched one every twenty to thirty seconds. High patrols operated with eight of the sixteen at 18,000 feet for the Hornet and Enterprise; the others would operate as lower. The Hornet next launched ten fighters for escort, and thirty-four Dauntless divebombers, half armed with a single 500-pound bombs, and the rest with 1000-pounds bombs. Then fifteen Devastator torpedo planes rose from the Hornet. The divebombers steadily climbed to 18,000 feet, with their escort about 2–3,000 feet above that. The Hornet's strike went out separately from the Enterprise's strike, due to delays getting the planes off the deck.

The Enterprise began launching thirty-three divebombers at 7:06 A.M., fifteen armed with 1,000-pounds, six with 500-pounds, and nine with 500-pound bombs and two 100-pounds bombs each, three unknown. After a delay until 8:06 A.M., the Enterprise launched ten fighters, and fifteen torpedo planes. The delay on the deck of the Enterprise caused Lieutenant Commander Wade McClusky to take his divebombers off separately. (McClusky had started the war as a flight leader for Wildcats but had been transferred to the Dauntless just before this battle.) He took his planes up and without fighter escort, headed out.

The formation adopted by the divebombers was, as described by Lieutenant Clarence E. Dickinson, "six wedge-shaped sections, inverted Vs, three planes in a section . . . " somewhat like:

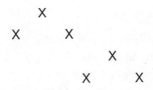

The planes in the sections flew at various altitudes as they were "stepped down" in their six wedge-shaped sections.

Uncoordinated with Spruance's strike, the Yorktown began launching at 8:30 A.M. Twelve Dauntlesses went up first, and cruising at 100 knots, headed off towards the enemy. Following them, at 130 knots, went seventeen Dauntlesses armed with 1,000-pounders. The divebombers from the Yorktown had some quick surprises after launch. There was a new device on them that allowed them to electronically arm their bombs when in flight. It was used by several of the pilots and instead of just arming the bombs (which apparently it did quite well), it released them! The commander of *Yorktown's* flight broke radio silence to warn all his other pilots not to use the new device. Six fighters went last as an escort as they were fast enough to catch up to the two departed forces. Fletcher was a little more deliberate in his attack and did not commit all his forces, due to the lesson learned at the Battle of Coral Sea where he attacked on the first sighting, and missed the main enemy force.

America was still new to carrier warfare, and,

frankly, this attack was uncoordinated, the various plane types ending up going off separately and largely unescorted. Commander Waldron of the *Hornet* was first to sight the enemy. He had deployed his planes in a long line—part of the line sighted the outer ring of the Japanese carrier force. He sent a sighting report, but it was not picked up by the *Hornet*.

At 9:18 Nagumo recovered his planes, but in the course of the morning lost three planes overhead, along with eleven at Midway. He was getting ready for his planned 10:30 strike against the enemy carriers when the heavy cruiser *Chikuma* reported enemy torpedo

Black smoke billows from oil storage tanks hit during Midway Island bombing attack.

planes approaching.

Waldron thought about attacking from two directions, but the Zeros were so thick and deadly that he decided to concentrate his force in a spearhead aimed at the enemy carriers. None of the torpedo planes survived. One man survived in the water, Ensign George Gay, who launched his torpedo at 800 yards at the *Soryu*. Gay later recounted that he had been hit by a bullet in his upper left arm just before launching his torpedo. "He shifted the stick to his left hand, ripped his sleeve, pressed a machine gun slug from the wound with his thumb. It seemed like something worth saving, so he sought to put it in the pocket of his jacket. When he found his pocket openings held shut by his safety belt and parachute straps and life jacket, he popped it into his mouth." Shot down just after launching his torpedo, and with his rear gunner dead, Gay watched the middle innings of this battle unfold, as the power hitters came up for a swing.

The torpedo planes from the *Enterprise* went in next. Ten were shot down while the other four managed to return home. No hits were scored on their targets, the *Kaga* and *Akagi*. No fighter escort helped them although the *Enterprise's* escort had been present at 22,000 feet, reporting the total absence of Japanese air patrol at that altitude. These fighters had not heard over the radio the call for them to come down and help the torpedo planes, who naturally felt betrayed.

Where were the divebombers that had left first and were faster, but had not attacked? *Hornet's* divebombers never found the enemy, and with fuel dwindling quickly, were forced to abort. They had proceeded to an area where earlier reports placed the Japanese fleet, to the south. When they failed to find them, several planes ditched, but most landed safely on Midway, refueled, and returned to the *Yorktown* later in the day. McClusky's group from the *Enterprise* was also running low on fuel—he took a guess and headed north. Up ahead, he sighted the wake of a speeding destroyer. It was the detached *Arashi* that had attacked the submarine *Nautilus*. Earlier, the *Nautilus* had been sighted lurking near the First Carrier Strike Force had been attacked by the *Arashi*. McClusky pointed the divebombers in the direc-

tion the *Arashi* was steaming. At 10:02, twenty-eight minutes before the Japanese strike was to take off, McClusky sighted the enemy and made a report. McClusky was at about 20,000 feet, while Lieutenant Dickerson, leading a division (two sections of three each), was at about 15–16,000 feet so he did not see the Japanese carriers until about five minutes after McClusky first sighted them. The *Enterprise* immediately had Captain Browning shouting back in the microphone, "McClusky, attack, attack immediately!"

The divebombers from the *Yorktown* had been droning alone at 15,000 feet with their 1000-pound bombs. On their first leg out (they had stated later than the *Enterprise's* planes) they sighted the Japanese at 10:03. Incredible accidental timing?

The first phase of the action saw the fighter escort for the torpedo planes from the *Yorktown*, four Wildcats, take on about twenty Zeros. All but two came in a string formation, to make a firing pass. It appeared something like:

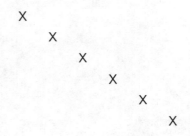

The group was commanded by the legendary Lieutenant Commander John Thach, inventor of the "Thach Weave" to defeat the Zero. The Weave demanded teamwork. Planes literally weave in and out in opposite directions, somewhat like passing a ball in football. The plane coming in would take out the Zero chasing the first American plane. The key difference was that planes did not fly all in formation, but interacted. It received its debut in this action. Unfortunately the rearmost plane was lost by two rogue Zeros surprising Thach's formation from the rear. Thach shot one fighter down, and tried his weave and came head on from below on the Zero. Thach said later that, "I was so mad that I was determined that I was going to run into this bastard because he jumped my

Navy SBD fighter planes made the attack on the *Mogami* and *Mikuma*.

poor, little inexperienced wingman." Thach got three that day, while one Zero, or two, were shot down by the remaining two wingmen.

Two other escorts, operating closer to the torpedo planes, became involved in a fierce battle with the Zeros; eventually the torpedo planes were attacked, but ended up getting the *Hiryu*, the only planes to do so during this part of the action. Only two torpedo planes from the *Yorktown* survived to return, but this action had sucked down all the Japanese air patrol, which ended up numbering, with fighters landing and taking off during the entire morning, 41 Zeros, eleven which were shot down in the course of this attack by the Americans.

Poised overhead were the divebombers of the *Enterprise* and the *Yorktown*. The moment of truth had arrived when McClusky's group of divebombers sighted all four fleet carriers. He felt that he could handle two of them. McClusky's squadron pushed over towards the *Kaga* and *Akagi*. Lieutenant Dickerson describes a divebomber attack:

Right after the skipper and his division had started I kicked my rudders back and forth to cause a ducklike twitching of my tail. This was the signal for my division to attack. In my turn I pulled up my nose and in a stalled position opened my flaps. We always do this, throw the plane up and to the side on which we are going to dive, put out the

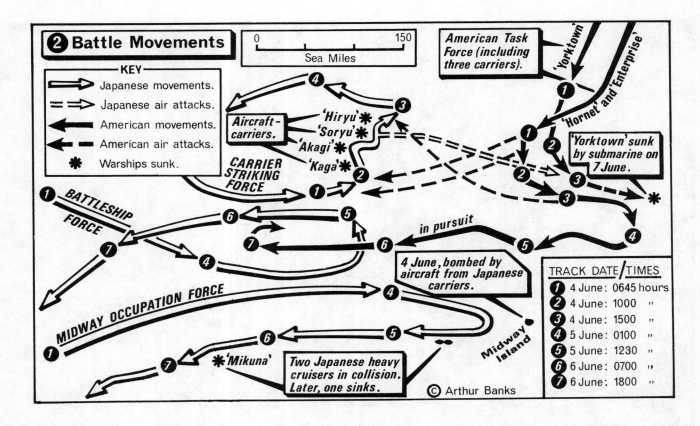

② Battle Movements

0 — 150
Sea Miles

—KEY—
⇨ Japanese movements.
⇢ Japanese air attacks.
← American movements.
⇠ American air attacks.
✳ Warships sunk.

Aircraft-carriers.

'Hiryu' ✳
'Soryu' ✳
'Akagi' ✳
'Kaga' ✳

CARRIER STRIKING FORCE

American Task Force (including three carriers).

'Yorktown'

'Hornet' and Enterprise'

'Yorktown' sunk by submarine on 7 June.

BATTLESHIP FORCE

in pursuit

MIDWAY OCCUPATION FORCE

4 June, bombed by aircraft from Japanese carriers.

Midway Island

✳ 'Mikuna'
Two Japanese heavy cruisers in collision. Later, one sinks.

© Arthur Banks

TRACK DATE / TIMES
① 4 June: 0645 hours
② 4 June: 1000 "
③ 4 June: 1500 "
④ 5 June: 0100 "
⑤ 5 June: 1230 "
⑥ 6 June: 0700 "
⑦ 6 June: 1800 "

flaps as brakes and then peel-off . . . as I put my nose down I picked up our carrier target below in front of me . . . .

The carrier was racing along at thirty knots, right into the wind. She made no attempt to change course. I was coming at her a little bit astern, on the left-hand side. By the time I was at 12,000 feet I could see all planes ahead of me in the dive . . . the target was utterly satisfying . . . near the dropping point I began to watch through my sight. As I was almost at the dropping point I saw a bomb hit just behind where I was aiming, that white circle with its blood red center (on the *Kaga's* deck) . . . I saw the deck rippling and curling back in all directions exposing a great section of the hanger below. That bomb had a fuse set to make it explode about four feet below the deck.

Four bombs slammed onto the crowded decks of the *Kaga* immediately igniting a furnace of death and destruction. At 10:25, just as the *Akagi* was in the act of launching Zeros, two 1,000-pound bombs hit the deck. Both carriers were mortally wounded.

A total of eighteen of the divebombers failed to return to the *Enterprise*. Most were lost to a casual attitude and lack of planning towards the return flight to the carrier after action. Most ditched into the sea due to a lack of fuel.

The divebombers from the *Yorktown* began pushing over towards the *Soryu*. Three 1,000-pound bombs of the thirteen dropped ripped open the vitals of this fleet carrier and twenty-seven bombers and torpedo planes, fueled and ready for launching, added to the inferno on board the *Soryu* that morning. Damage was so obvious that several of the final divebombers went after a battleship and a destroyer, but missed. Three fleet carriers down and one to go!

The *Akagi* would not sink until June 5, the *coup de grace* being delivered by Japanese destroyers. She lost only 221 men killed. The *Kaga* sank at 9:25 A.M. after two violent internal explosions. She lost about 800 killed, many from the engine rooms. The *Soryu*, totally on fire, sank at 9:15 P.M., and at 9:20 was rent by a tremendous internal explosion underwater. At least 718 died. All three lost their captains, the *Kaga* by a bomb blast during the attack, the other two in death when their ships sank. The Japanese carriers had been designed for quick handling of aircraft and not for defensive qualities. With the added disadvantage of having "readied" aircraft parked on deck and in the hangers, nothing probably could have saved the Japanese carriers.

On board the *Hiryu* need for an airstrike seemed obvious to Rear Admiral Yamaguchi. If he delayed attack, he could mount a full strike, and he reasoned another attack from the U.S. could be some hours away. But Yamaguchi launched eighteen Vals and six Zeros by 10:40 A.M. Twelve of the Vals had 551-pound semi-armor piercing bombs, while the other six had general purpose bombs that would normally be used against Midway. The attack was led by Lieutenant Michio Kobayashi.

Kobayashi followed home a flight of *Yorktown's* planes at 13,000 feet. However, as he neared the American Task Force, the

Crewmen walk along the sloping deck of the sinking *Yorktown*.

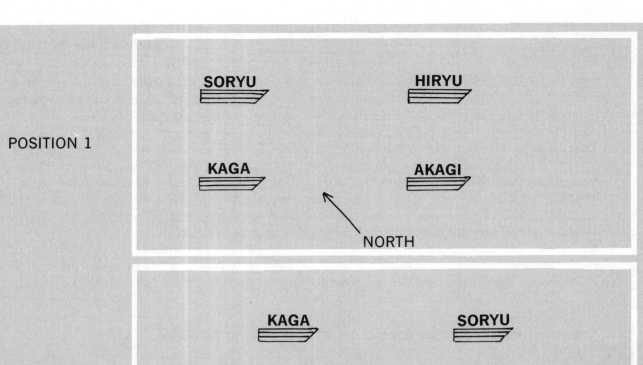

POSITION 1

SORYU   HIRYU

KAGA   AKAGI

NORTH

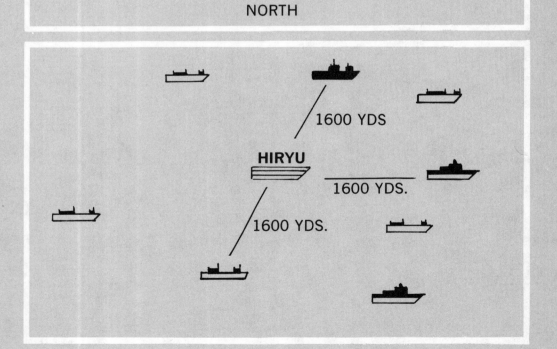

POSITION 2

KAGA   SORYU

AKAGI   HIRYU

NORTH

FINAL DISPOSITION
TO PROTECT
THE *Hiryu*

1600 YDS

HIRYU

1600 YDS.

1600 YDS.

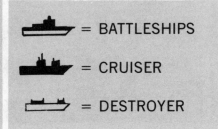

= BATTLESHIPS

= CRUISER

= DESTROYER

Yorktown directed in by radar twelve Wildcats that tore through Kobayashi's formation, immediately knocking down six Vals. The *Yorktown's* returning flight had not been aware that it was being followed. However, the American radar had an IFF capability which identified to the *Yorktown's* operators at 65 miles distance that an enemy formation was present with the *Yorktown's* planes.

Meanwhile, the *Yorktown* had launched additional scouting planes at 11:50 A.M., as Fletcher was still concerned about other enemy carriers. Eventually it was this scouting group that located the *Hiryu*. With the knowledge of an incoming strike, the *Yorktown* took defensive measures in securing the deck and hanger space. About 800 gallons of aviation fuel was thrown overboard. Speed was worked up to 30 knots. Returning divebombers were waved off, and most flew onto the *Enterprise* for a safe landing, although some even tried to join up with the friendly air patrol. Eventually a staff officer came to Admiral Fletcher and reported, "The attack is coming in, sir." Fletcher replied, "Well, I've got on my tin hat. I can't do anything else now."

The escorting Zeros were poorly handled that day and gave little assistance to Kobayashi's Vals. Still, Kobayashi bored in on his target (he would die in the attack), determined to hurt the

Escort vessels take up positions around the sinking *Yorktown*.

Yorktown, as he must to try to regain the balance needed for any sort of a Japanese victory. Only seven Vals made it through the fighters and the flak. Bombs were released at 1,000 feet beginning at 12:10 P.M. But of these seven—only one bomb clearly missed—three were near misses and three scored hits on the *Yorktown*. Two hits caused little real damage, although the first hit exploded on the deck killing many men. The third bomb penetrated to the second deck where it exploded near the boiler uptake. For some reason, Lieutenant Charles Cundiff had a premonition down in emergency boiler control and shouted, "Hit the deck," just before the explosion. His men obeyed and none were hurt! The bomb blast literally blew out most of the fires in the boiler room and brought the *Yorktown* to a dead stop. The loss of power was serious, but damage control parties went to work immediately. Thirteen Vals and three Zeros failed to return.

Yamaguchi, on the *Hiryu*, now launched a second attack. He had six Zeros and ten Kate torpedo planes ready for launching at 3:10 P.M. Tomonaga led this attack. Yamaguchi knew

The *Yorktown* lists heavily before sinking the day after the attack.

that there were three enemy carriers, as a scout plane (the new experimental Judy divebomber of which there were two on the *Soryu* at the start of the day) had reported all three. Also, a pilot from the *Enterprise's* torpedo squadron had been captured earlier that day and had revealed that there were three American fleet carriers. This unfortunate pilot would later be executed while still on board a destroyer; his crime, apparently, being victory.

Tomonaga led his planes out at 13,500 feet at 3:30 P.M. He sighted the *Yorktown* at 4:30 P.M., but thought it was a different carrier than the one Kobayashi had attacked as it looked in fine condition, proof of how efficient America's damage control worked. Spruance was just over the horizon and he had reinforced Fletcher's task force with two cruisers and two destroyers. Tomonaga decided to execute a standard split attack which involved five planes coming in from two directions (90 degrees) on the *Yorktown*. Two torpedoes scored on the *Yorktown*, jamming her rudder, causing a list to the port, and further explosions and fires.

The *Yorktown* eventually was abandoned. The following day there was discussion and

The destroyer *Hammann* picked up survivors from the *Yorktown's* crew.

attempts to bring her into port with a small salvage party. Progress was being made when the I-168 fired four torpedoes. One missed, two went under the destroyer *Hammann* lying alongside and hit the *Yorktown*. The last one hit the *Hammann*, which sank within three minutes. The hero that day was Seaman Berlyn M. Kimbrell who set all the depth charges on the *Hammann* to "safe" (this would keep them from exploding at pre-set depths when the *Hammann* sank), put life jackets on all the men gathered on the fantail, pushed them into the water, and left last. Kimbrell died in the underwater explosion that occurred when the *Hammann* finally sank. The *Yorktown* lingered on until 6 A.M. on June 7 when she rolled over and sank. Earlier, Fletcher had decided he could no longer command the carriers with the *Yorktown* disabled and handed over command to Spruance.

The Japanese First Carrier Strike Force had several important events occur in the late morning and early afternoon of the 4th. Nagumo had been transferred off the *Akagi* and handed over command to Rear Admiral Abe on the *Tone*. Abe informed Yamamoto of the losses. The shock was only dimly felt on the *Yamato* that morning. The invincible Japanese fleet had been defeated, and losses had obviously been terrible.

Yamamoto, after some discussion, ordered all his units to move to assist the First Carrier Strike Force. The transports were given light protection and moved to an area about 500 miles form Midway so they could either go in for the invasion later or else retreat, but they would not be in danger. Kondo was ordered to take most of the powerful surface ships from this group and hurry to help Nagumo. Kondo had already acted on his own and was moving

Japanese survivors of the Battle of Midway became prisoners of war.

with twenty-three ships toward Nagumo. Kondo was ordered to detach a force to attack Midway with gunfire. He thought about detaching his battleships, but their limited speed would cause them to arrive not at night, but in the morning off of Midway. So Kondo sent in the escorting ships of the Second Fleet, Occupation Support Force, the heavy cruisers *Kumano, Mogami, Mikuma,* and *Suzuya,* with two escorting destroyers. The *Yamato* itself and the entire First Fleet under Yamamoto were also moving to aid Nagumo. Finally, Yamamoto ordered the carriers of The Second Carrier Strike Force to move south from the Aleutians. Since this force needed to refuel and could not be in the area until June 7, too late to influence events, the order was shortly countermanded.

Nagumo's force was informed that the American fleet was only 90 miles away in the late morning so he, now with his flag (and back in command) transferred to the light cruiser *Nagara,* ordered surface combat ships to form line of battle with destroyers in the van. Nagumo feared that the American fleet would finish off the cripples with gunfire. Based on prewar doctrine, this was a logical concern, and if the Americans possessed a more powerful surface force, a real danger. Later reports showed the American task forces moved away, recovering and launching aircraft) Nagumo formed a formation around the *Hiryu* for her last stand.

After the *Hiryu's* two strikes against the *Yorktown,* she had hardly anything left. Six fighters, five divebombers, and four torpedo planes were all that remained for a third strike, with some additional Zeros deployed for air patrol, and one Judy as scout. The crews were exhausted, but the planes could have been launched at 6:30 P.M. Instead the men were given dinner and told that the strike would be at 8 P.M. An excellent example of the way the Japanese command structure thought in terms of what they wanted the enemy to do, instead of what the Americans were capable of doing.

At 7:03 P.M. the *Hiryu's* watch shouted "Enemy divebombers directly overhead." Twenty divebombers dropped down out of the sun against the *Hiryu* while four others dived down on the escorting ships. The attack came as a surprise although the Japanese air patrol did

engage the divebombers in their dives. The first thirteen divebombers missed. Then the first hit landed squarely on the forward elevator platform, hurling it back against the ship's island, and breaking every window on the bridge. Three more bombs ripped through the *Hiryu* with the rest missing. Once again intense flames roared through the ship, although her speed was virtually unaffected. Eventually flames reached the engine room and virtually everyone there died on the *Hiryu* that day. The Japanese, a people who considered death in battle an honor, called the engine gangs performing their duty with the deck literally melting above them and death all around them, heroic.

Air units on Midway made additional attacks during the afternoon, which accomplished little except disrupting futile attempts to save the *Hiryu.*

Rear Admiral Yamaguchi went down with the *Hiryu,* sending a message to Nagumo just before his death, "I have no words to apologize for what has happened. I only wish for a stronger Japanese Navy—and revenge." Four hundred sixteen men died on the *Hiryu.*

The greatest error made after the loss of the first three Japanese fleet carriers was not withdrawing the *Hiryu* to the west. This would not have ended the action, but would have lengthened the distance between the two enemies. The Japanese, with greater range in their aircraft, might have been able to hit the American force and prevented damage to themselves. If the Americans pursued, then they would have been closer to the other converging Japanese surface forces who were attempting to force a night surface engagement with superior forces.

In pursuing this strategy, the forces under Kondo deployed in a long line. Rear Admiral Tanaka, who made his reputation with the Tokyo Express off Guadalcanal later in the year, deployed his destroyers to the right, while the other destroyers and light cruisers deployed to the left. There was a ship spaced every four miles. The battleships *Kongo* and the *Hiei* were six miles astern of the flagship *Atago* which was deployed to the right of the center of the line. Nagumo's surface forces were to sweep down from the north towards the south east.

However, Admiral Spruance had not obliged

the Japanese. He ordered a withdrawal to the east until morning air units could locate and identify the enemy forces still facing him. Early on the morning of the 5th Yamamoto realized the game was up and ordered the Japanese navy to retire.

One final act remained. Kurita's bombardment force was on its way to Midway, less than 90 miles from it when ordered to retire. The I-168 was earlier ordered to surface and fire on Midway, which it did, all eight rounds into the lagoon. Shore batteries forced it to dive and it managed to get away, later torpedoing the *Yorktown*.

American submarine *Tambor* was near Kurita's force and running on the surface. She sighted Kurita's cruisers, but at such a distance, it was not possible to be certain what ships they were; the captain of the *Tambor* made a sighting report stating, "many unidentified ships" (which was a poor report in that neither speed nor heading (direction) was mentioned). The *Tambor* followed on the surface, finally closing the range to identify the distinctive *Mogami*. The Kurita force saw the *Tambor* at the same instant. Flagship *Kumano*, leading the line, immediately turned 45 degrees away and flashed a warning down the line of the following ships. The cruisers were arranged in a line with the *Kumano* leading, then the *Suzuya*, the *Mikuma*, and the *Mogami*. Unfortunately for the Japanese, the navigating officer on the last ship, the *Mogami*, mistook the *Suzuya* for the *Mikuma* and turned too soon. At 26 knots speed, the *Mogami* rammed the rear of the *Mikuma*, crumpling the bow of the *Mogami* and slowing her to 12 knots. The *Mikuma*, with fuel tanks damaged, began trailing an oil slick. Kurita decided to split off his two undamaged cruisers and leave his two escorting destroyers with the two cripples. Both forces, at best speed, headed back towards Nippon.

The *Tambor* failed in her attack, but on the 5th the Midway air units finally did get their first blood, in a dramatic way that pointed to the future in an ironic twist. Spruance and the carriers were on a false scent to the north looking for Nagumo's carriers, now all sunk. Midway directed a strike of six Dauntlesses and six Vindicators towards the two crippled heavy cruisers steaming west. They literally followed

The Japanese cruiser *Mikuma* was bombed and sunk in the last part of the Battle of Midway.

the trailing oil slick to the targets, and once again the Dauntlesses dived, while the Vindicators glide-bombed the heavy cruisers which were putting up a tremendous volume of anti-aircraft fire. All bombs missed, but Captain Richard E. Fleming of the lead Vindicator, when hit with anti-aircraft at the drop point for his bomb, deliberately crashed his plane into the *Mikuma*, a forerunner of the kamikaze attacks to occur late in the war. Commander Fuchida's account of that crash states, the pilot "attempted a daring suicide crash into *Mikuma's* bridge. He missed the bridge but crashed into the afterturret, spreading fire over the air intake of the starboard engine room. This caused an explosion of gas fumes below, killing all hands working in the engine room."

Spruance found an empty ocean, except for the destroyer *Tanikaze* retreating from the now sunk *Hiryu*. In the course of the afternoon the destroyer had 56 bombs from B-17s dropped on her. All missed! Returning Dauntlesses, unable to find a suitable target, also attacked, and failed to hit, though a near miss killed six crewmen and damaged a turret. Another flight of B-17s attacked, and missed again. In the course of this skirmish, a divebomber and two B-17s were lost.

Finally, on the 6th of June, with the Japanese navy all but withdrawn, Spruance got his last lick in by attacking the two retiring crippled enemy heavy cruisers. Spruance's carriers scored six bomb hits on the *Mogami*, and at least five on the *Mikuma*, plus one bomb each on both destroyers. Only the *Mikuma* sunk, largely due to the fact that most of the bombs dropped were not armor piercing—they lacked delayed action fuses and exploded immediately. Thus, no underwater damage could be inflicted by near misses, and the bombs tended to pound and smash the superstructure, but not do severe damage in the bowels of the ships hit. The main blow against the *Mikuma* was caused when her torpedoes were hit by a bomb hit setting off a tremendous explosion. The *Mikuma* lost 648 men dead, while the *Mogami* lost about 300 dead and would be under repair until July of 1943.

So ended the battle. As Admiral Spruance said after the action, "Towards sundown on June 4th I decided to retire to the eastward to avoid the possibility of night action with superior forces. . . . the Japanese did order a night attack. When the day's action on June 6th was over . . . we were short of fuel, and I had a feeling, an intuition perhaps, that we had pushed our luck as far to the westward as it was good for us. . . ." It is interesting to note that

Yamamoto had some ships proceed to Wake to try to decoy, by radio traffic, the Americans into range of the landbased planes present there.

Finally, the *Saratoga* was pulling in from the West Coast and joined the *Enterprise* and *Hornet*. All three considered heading north to engage the Aleutian diversionary force, but it was decided that it was too late to do so. Thus ended the decisive battle, the turning point, of Midway.

Japan's loss of four fleet carriers could never be fully compensated, but more importantly, her valuable pilots, the best in the world for fighting at sea, were devastated. This first major defeat at sea for Japan in World War II was the end of the first phase of the war at sea.

USS *Fulton* was used to transport survivors of the ships damaged in Midway.

BIBLIOGRAPHY with Commentary

Below is a select list of major sources used in the writing of *War at Sea*. Please note that it is not a complete list, but should lead to further reading on the topic.

Cohen, Stan. *East Wind Rain, A Pictorial History of the Pearl Harbor Attack.* Pictorial Histories Publishing Co.—Homespun style with some nice pictures.

Deacon, Richard. *Kempei Tai*, Berkeley—History of the Japanese Secret Service.

Dull, Paul S. *The Battle History of the Imperial Japanese Navy (1941-1945)*, USNI—Unexciting, but excellent for Order of Battle.

Firkins, Peter. *The Australians in Nine Wars*, Pan—General history of the Australian Army.

Francillon, Rene J. *Japanese Aircraft of the Pacific War*, USNI—Excellent.

Gill, Hermon G. *Royal Australian Navy 1939-1945*—Two-volume, Australian war memorial, solid, though with some errors in Japanese.

Hara, Tameichi. *Japanese Destroyer Captain.* Ballantine—Good for Japanese point of view, but has many battle errors.

Jentschura, Jung, and Mickel. *Warships of the Imperial Japanese Navy, 1869-1945*—Standard work on the subject.

Lord, Walter. *Day of Infamy.* Holt—Based on a series of interviews with a multitude of individuals at Pearl Harbor on December 7th. Extremely entertaining.

Lord, Walter. *Incredible Victory.* Harper Row—More scholarly than the above, but not as entertaining. Very good for Japanese point of view.

Lundstrom, John B. *The First South Pacific Campaign.* USNI Press—Dry but excellent history of December of 1941 to June of 1942 in the South Pacific.

Lundstrom, John B. *The First Team: Pacific Naval Air Combat From Pearl Harbor to Midway.* USNI Press—Simply brilliant. Lundstrom goes beyond the easily available sources for the best view of naval air combat, from the American perspective.

Marder, Arthur. *Old Friends, New Enemies: The Royal Navy and the Imperial Japanese Navy.* Oxford Press—Simply the best.

Morrison, S.E. *History of the United States Naval Operations in World War II.* Atlantic Little Brown—Very readable and good.

Morton, Louis. *The Fall of The Philippines.* Government Printing Office—An excellent study. The Army Green Series (named for the color of this multi-volume series) has a warranted reputation as one of the most honest of the various official histories.

Muir, Malcolm Jr. *The Capital Ship Program in the United States Navy, 1934-1945.* University Microfilms International (300 N. Zeeb Rd., Ann Arbor, MI, 48106)—Good thesis.

Muir, Malcolm Jr. *The Iowa Class Battleships.* Blandford Press—Best operational history of these ships.

Prange, Gordon W. *At Dawn We Slept.* McGraw Hill—Very good study on Pearl Harbor, but should be read in conjunction with Admiral Layton's *I Was There.*

Rohwer, J. and Hummelchen, G. *Chronology of the War at Sea, 1939-1945.* Arco—Excellent.

Smith, S.E. *The United States Navy in World War II.* Ballantine—Very good first person history of the naval war from the U.S. point of view.

Stillwell, Paul Ed. *Air Raid: Pearl Harbor Recollections of a Day of Infamy.* USNI—Solid first person stories to add to Walter Lord's book.

Wilmott, H.P. *Empires in the Balance.* USNI—Very good for a synthesis that is well written, but some technical errors creep in and suffers from a lack of Japanese source material.

Wilmott, H.P. *The Barrier and the Javelin.* USNI—Volume II in the series takes one through Coral Sea and Midway. Considers Admiral Yamamoto to have been a poor strategist at Midway.